MW00475345

Sage Advice

To Zeke
a great doctor
and a great Jew.

[with thanks for Felicia!! and David]

in friendship
Yitz Greenberg

SAGE ADVICE

PIRKEI AVOT

WITH TRANSLATION
AND COMMENTARY BY

IRVING (YITZ) GREENBERG

Maggid Books

Sage Advice
Pirkei Avot with Translation and Commentary by
Irving (Yitz) Greenberg

First Edition, 2016

Maggid Books
An imprint of Koren Publishers Jerusalem Ltd.

POB 8531, New Milford, CT 06776-8531, USA
& POB 4044, Jerusalem 9104001, Israel
www.korenpub.com

The publication of this book was made possible
through the generous support of *Torah Education in Israel.*

ISBN 978-1-59264-444-5, *hardcover*

A CIP catalogue record for this title is
available from the British Library

Printed and bound in the United States

Dedicated to

Diane Troderman

communal leader, treasured friend,
a philanthropist with vision, passion, and generosity of spirit

"She speaks with wisdom,
a Torah of loving-kindness is on her tongue."
(Proverbs 31:26)

Contents

Preface

Ethics of the Fathers, or *Pirkei Avot* as it is known in Hebrew, has long been a personal favorite of mine. Beth Joseph Rabbinical Seminary, the yeshiva where I was ordained, was a *musar* yeshiva. *Musar* was the nineteenth-century revival movement which stressed that the Torah's main goal was to create a *mentsch*. The Musarniks viewed Torah culture as an ecology, designed to mold a human being of good character, who would establish ethical relationships and take caring responsibility for fellow human beings. With its focus on character traits and moral formation, Ethics of the Fathers fits this model; therefore, the book was regarded with esteem in the movement. Under the influence of the Musarniks, I also became caught up in the challenge of connecting people to Jewish tradition and making it a force shaping their lives. This too brought Ethics of the Fathers close to my heart. I appreciated the accessibility of the text and admired its implicit goal of popular education. Over the years, these wisdom teachings evoked my enduring fascination and endearment as a paradigm for educators and as a model worthy of emulation.

We live in a time when Judaism continues to struggle with the challenges of modernity and post-modernity, their influence and attractions. One outcome of this struggle is a polarization of camps. One camp favors massive change in the religion to make it intellectually and morally credible. The other insists that the Torah's authority is eternal and therefore, in principle, unchanging and unchangeable.

I have long loved the rabbinic sages[1] – not only for their great teachings and their role in transmitting Judaism, but also because they break the model of either/or. Thus, they simultaneously transformed the tradition and brought it along *in its entirety*. They avoided the arrogance of the modernists who dismiss many elements of the past as obsolete or primitive. The sages understood that the whole of Jewish tradition is sacred. All of it is the record of the encounter between God and Israel. Each of its elements has played a vital role in sustaining the life and mission of the People of Israel down through the centuries.

Through their interpretations, the sages assured that parts of that tradition would be modified (for example, the death penalty[2]) and other parts not practiced (for example, the law of the wayward son[3]). Yet they taught that even those parts should be studied for spiritual insight and as guidelines for living.[4] Once a text, then a practice, and ultimately an institution, a mitzva has become the direct channel of revelation between the Divine and the human; it can never be cast aside. It continues to speak to us, even if only as a paradigm of behavior along the way. It can also offer a model of how to deal with an issue in one context which can shed light on how to deal with the same issue in another context, even in a different civilization. Revelation is not a one-time event; it is continuous. Each encounter with tradition, text, or a mitzva offers new revelations in response to new questions or new settings.

Of all the rabbinic insights, the one that has most influenced my own thinking is that the core process of Judaism – the covenant

1. In the context of this book, the sages are defined as the Jewish leaders who followed the era of prophecy and priests. They came to the fore after the Destruction of the Second Temple. They are often referred to as *Ḥazal*, an acronym for "our sages of blessed memory."
2. See Tractate Sanhedrin, especially ch. 3.
3. See Deuteronomy 21:18–21. See Sanhedrin 71a: "Rabbi Shimon says: '[The wayward son]...never was and never will be.'"
4. "So why was this law [of the wayward son] written [in the Torah]? So that you should study it and receive reward" (ibid.).

of redemption between God and Israel – is an eternal, permanent, *but not fixed* structure. The Torah taught that God restrained Himself, as it were, in order to create a stable, natural world,[5] and self-limited again in order to enter into a relationship with humanity.[6] The sages believed that in their age, too, the Infinite One was acting again in this way. God was now limiting the visible divine activity in history – becoming *less manifest but more present* – in order to summon human beings to a higher level of responsibility in realizing the goals of the covenant. Henceforth, human activity, not overt divine intervention, would account in greater measure for the outcomes of historical events. Likewise, human understanding and analysis – not a new heavenly revelation – would make clear God's instructions for ongoing life along the covenantal way. This understanding is the ultimate source of the sages' authority.

I believe that once again we are living in such a time of divine self-limitation (*tzimtzum*). In our time, God has become even less manifest and even more present – to those who refocus their eyes to see and ears to listen. Thus, human beings have become even more responsible for bringing God's love and care to all creatures. They are now the supreme agents for divine liberation and redemptive activity. Human behavior and teaching – whether openly religious or presented as secular – have become the primary source of making God's presence visible in the world. Human actions make God beloved in people's eyes and provide sanctification of His name.

Yet paradoxically, human beings have also become the primary source of desecration of God's name, of obscuring God's presence and causing God's actions (or human actions done in His name) to be hateful in people's eyes, a source of moral revulsion. At such a time, the wisdom in a work such as Ethics of the Fathers is not only valuable in its own right, it can also serve as a paradigm and guide, teaching us by analogy what we must do to represent God's actions in the world. Thus, it gives us more than its wisdom; it offers the sages as role models, showing us how they responded to God's call to play a leading role in the covenant.

---

5. See Genesis chs. 8–9. In Kabbala, Genesis, i.e., Creation, is interpreted as the outcome of a similar self-restraint by God.
6. Genesis chs. 15, 17, 18:12–19; Exodus chs. 6, 19, 20.

We must study the sages and walk in their traditional yet innovative ways if we are to respond adequately to God's summons to humans to play an even more decisive role in this eternal partnership. This is why, despite the existence of hundreds of commentaries and editions, I dare to offer yet one more edition of Ethics of the Fathers with my own personal commentary.

This edition is distinguished by the following features: (1) A historical-theological introduction portraying the synthesis between continuation and transformation of the Torah's way which the sages achieved. I believe that *Pirkei Avot* was specifically collected and edited to exemplify this synthesis. (2) Thumbnail sketches of the lives of the sixty-six sages whose teachings are gathered here. These are not critical biographies; they are drawn from talmudic sources. However, these sages' lives were narrated by the Talmud to serve as paradigms of the good life. They are offered as models of character traits and virtues, as examples of the kind of human beings who are the intended outcomes of this way of life. (3) A commentary that seeks to understand the life wisdom transmitted in this tractate from the contemporary perspective, with the goal of relating it to the challenges of life in today's world.

The Hebrew text has been newly translated into English for this volume.

This book is offered as a tribute to its editor, R. Yehuda the Prince (and his circle), to the sages quoted in its pages, and to all the sages, in gratitude for their remarkable example and teachings. Ethics of the Fathers is a classic collection of wisdom, its aphorisms selected by some of the greatest rabbinic leaders to represent the era and the values of rabbinic Judaism. It is an invitation to the wise men and women of this era that is unfolding. Ethics of the Fathers should also serve as an inspiration and challenge to our generation to follow in the footsteps of the sages – to offer new wisdom, to uncover new revelation, to unite past, present, and future, and to help the Jewish people and all of humanity find their way through the next phase of the covenantal journey toward a perfected world.

I want to thank Harold Grinspoon and the members of the board of the Harold Grinspoon Foundation for a grant which has underwritten secretarial, research, and administrative costs in the preparation of this and other volumes in my project to develop a Jewish narrative theology for our time. I am grateful to the leaders of the foundation's board, Jeremy Pava and Winnie Sandler, as well as to members Dan Backer, Anne Bloom, Michael Bohnen, Ed Greenbaum, Eric Levine, Arnie Winshall, Bruce Wintman, and Henry Zach; and to Joanna Ballantine, then-executive director of the foundation, for their faith in me and support for the project.

I also express my gratitude to Matthew Miller of Koren Publishers and Gila Fine, editor in chief of Maggid Books, for their judgement and guidance in making this manuscript publication worthy. In addition, thanks are due to Tomi Mager, Deena Nataf, Tali Simon, Josia Klein, Renee Schwartz, and Ellen Davis for their editorial work.

I have dedicated this volume to a dear, devoted friend, Diane Troderman. For decades, Diane has been a remarkable arbiter in Jewish philanthropic matters and a leader in critical educational organizations. She has been the philanthropic eyes and ears for her husband, Harold Grinspoon. In the course of this work she brought me into their circle, to my immeasurable benefit. She and Harold have become cherished, beloved friends, trusted confidants, and supportive coworkers – even as they have brought my wife, Blu, and me into their extraordinary philanthropic initiative in Jewish education to assure the future of the Jewish people. This dedication is a small token of the deep gratitude and love that I feel for Diane and Harold.

Irving (Yitz) Greenberg
Winter 2016/5776

Introduction

Divine Revelation and Human Wisdom in *Pirkei Avot*

A. BIBLICAL VISION AND THE COVENANTAL JOURNEY

Judaism starts with the Bible. The biblical tradition concerning the Jewish people starts with the lives of the patriarchs, the Israelite founding family, which are shrouded in the mists of history and may stretch back as far as 1800–1600 BCE. Early Jewish traditions developed within a Middle Eastern culture of polytheism and mythology. The God of Israel emerged as the one and only Creator of the universe, who sustains the natural order for all creatures and creation. This God is intensely engaged with the world, intervening in nature on moral grounds, and holding human beings to a standard of virtue and mutual responsibility. He enters into covenant with humanity in general, and the Jewish people in particular, leading the latter from slavery and statelessness to freedom and homeland.

The Bible tells us that the world was created by God and, though currently deeply flawed and full of natural and human evil, will ultimately develop and become perfect, a paradise.[1] The Torah predicts that in time, the earth will be reconstructed to uphold life, especially human life, in all its dignity and with all its needs met.[2] With the advent of humanity, God invites humans to join in the divine mission to complete the world. In this invitation, God includes instructions for correcting human society where it fails to sustain (or actively degrades) the dignities of life.

As a first step toward this aim, the Torah teaches that the universal, divine force limited Itself vis-à-vis nature, leaving room for natural laws and autonomous human activity to operate.[3] Proceeding further, God entered into partnership, a binding covenant – *brit* in Hebrew – with all of humanity to fill the world with life and complete the process of perfection. The covenant represents a divine pledge that the intended outcome of history, i.e., the earth redeemed, will not be imposed by divine decree. God thus commits to respecting human freedom; humanity can choose not to accept the *brit*, thereby working on the side of death and against the goals of Creation. But by entering into covenant, God and humanity elect to work together, at human pace and capacity, for as long as it takes to achieve perfection. Since the human act of change is deliberate, sometimes halting, and often set back by willfully evil choices, the final goal will be attained only in many, many generations.

1. Genesis 1:1–2:3. The Creation account itself describes a perfect world. The prophets teach that in the Messianic Age all the flaws that mar the earth will be corrected. There will be no oppression or inequity (Is. 11:4, 9), no war (Is. 2:3–4; Micah 4:2–4), no hunger (Is. 49:8–10; Ezek. 34:25–29). There will be prosperity instead of poverty (Is. 54:11ff., 60:6ff., 66:12). Sickness will be cured (ibid., 29:18, 35:5–6). Life will be extended (ibid., 65:20) and death will be overcome (ibid., 25:8). In *Halakhic Man*, Rabbi Joseph B. Soloveitchik writes that the Creation narrative is not about cosmology (the actual creation of the world), but rather its purpose is to teach us values and halakhic principles. Most important, it teaches that the Creator, "as it were, impaired reality in order that mortal man could repair its flaws and perfect it," and that the central idea in the halakhic consciousness is "the importance of man as a partner of the Almighty in the act of creation" (Rabbi Joseph B. Soloveitchik, *Halakhic Man* [Philadelphia: The Jewish Publication Society, 1984], 101, 99). See also ibid., 105ff.
2. See Genesis 1:20–21, 28. Compare ibid., 8:17, 9:1, 9:7; Isaiah 45:18.
3. Genesis chs. 6–9, especially 8:21–22, 9:1–7.

As the Torah tells it, the family of Abraham, i.e., the People of Israel, came to understand this fundamental truth regarding the purpose of human existence. The People of Israel entered into their particular covenant, teaching and modeling this purpose to all the nations. The divine plan, after all, is hidden, the Deity invisible and unrevealed. In the biblical world, marked by belief in many gods and conflicting natural forces, Israel taught the unity of the Creator and of creation. In a civilization which understood the gods to be arbitrary, angry, and jealous, seeking obedience and bribery, the Torah taught that the Omnipotent One loves humanity and all life.

By their history, the People of Israel modeled how to live and work toward the perfection of the world. The Bible narrates the Israelite experience to illustrate how human beings can live in partnership with God, yet struggle to fill this role; how they can use freedom for good, although they frequently fail to do so; and how the revelations of God are eternal, but also specific to time and place and human understanding. The chronicles of the People of Israel, in this sense, provide instruction for the rest of humanity.

The Exodus of the Israelites from Egypt – their liberation from slavery, entrance into covenant, and journey to freedom and the dignity of a homeland – is the core event of the Bible, a harbinger of universal redemption, and a signpost along the road of history for all humanity. Through rituals of memory, Jews relive the liberation each year, confirming their sustaining partnership with God and drawing from it the strength to persist toward the final goal. The biblical account shows the Israelites' struggle to create a just society reflective of the covenant. Throughout the generations, this task was made even more difficult by the various empires that surrounded, invaded, and influenced Israel. Each generation carried on as far as it could go, then passed on the mission to the next covenantal cohort. Despite powerful cultural pulls on the People of Israel, despite frequent invasion, despite even Destruction and exile, the fundamental model of covenant and the mission toward perfection was never forsaken.

In the Jewish view, humanity is moving from an original Garden of Eden, through a real world of harmony and strife, plenty and privation, justice and discrimination, toward final perfection once more. Whatever the setbacks and whatever the failures along the way, the Bible proclaims that the longed-for Redemption of the world will one day come. In the Messianic Age, life will win out, with all its dignities upheld and all its capacities fulfilled. Judaism, in this respect, is the avant-garde, showing the rest of humanity how to realize its goals.

Judaism believes that by connecting to God, living as He would want us to live, we can progress along the path to earthly perfection. Since the God of Israel, as the Bible tells us, is on the side of the widow and the orphan, the stranger and the oppressed, the needy and the downtrodden, one of the primary ways of serving Him is to practice justice and righteousness toward all His creatures – but especially toward those in need of help.

In biblical times, the local community stood at the center of religious life, exercising mutual responsibility (*tzedaka*), establishing courts and justice systems, celebrating holidays and going on pilgrimages, and, most of all, being held accountable by God for one another's behavior. The national center of religious life, however, was the shrine, where Jews connected to God not through social justice, but through ritual. In the Temple era, setting aside from God's bounty to share it with the poor, with the Temple (in the form of gifts to support its maintenance), and with God's service corps (the priests and levites) was one way of connecting. Observing the yearly cycle of Sabbaths and festivals was another, as was bringing sacrifices of animals and offerings derived from grain. Offerings were brought in gratitude, as various types of expiation for sins, or for ritual purifications, births, and festivals. In Jerusalem, a hereditary priesthood performed the daily service – including twice-daily collective sacrifices for the people – and maintained the eternal flame inside the Sanctuary. God was not visible, but His presence was so manifest that it evoked awe and trembling from pilgrims and worshipers alike. Home rituals such as hospitality and *kashrut* promoted the same values, enabling distinctive connections to God and encouraging mutual responsibility in the private sphere.

The Destruction of the First Temple by the Babylonian Empire in 586 BCE brought with it the loss of Judean national independence as well as a massive transfer of the Judean population from the Land of Israel to Babylonia. It also generated a major crisis of faith. Coming only a century after the collapse of the northern Kingdom of Israel, the transfer of its population by the Assyrians, and the complete loss of ten of the twelve tribes to Jewish history, the Destruction sent the Judeans into bouts of existential doubt: What if God had ended the covenant? Had they been rejected because of their sinfulness and betrayal, serving other gods such as their neighbors' Baal, chthonic deities, or other magic forces? The classical prophets (Isaiah, Jeremiah, Ezekiel, the twelve "minor" seers) assured the people that the Destruction and exile were a means of punishment, not rejection. God would never rescind His love for the People of Israel, nor annul the divine covenant with humankind. God might have exiled them, but He would return them as well. There would be a second exodus.

From the third century BCE onward, the Judeans encountered a remarkable new set of challenges. First among them was exposure to the rising influence of Hellenism. The conquering culture brought with it an emphasis on the body, a tendency toward religious skepticism, and a new set of sophisticated intellectual categories including literary analysis, rhetoric, philosophy, science, and medicine. Hellenism also raised the banner of a universal culture, insisting on the superiority of such inclusiveness and denigrating Jewish particularity as narrow-minded, provincial, unsophisticated, unjustified, and inferior. While the Hellenists persecuted the Jews both physically and spiritually, they also exerted considerable pull on many Jews, especially those involved in commerce and governmental relations.

Jewish responses to Hellenization varied. Some Jews, especially those living in the hinterlands, chose rejection and cultural segregation, and in certain cases even opted for martyrdom as the highest form of serving God. In the urban centers, conversely, many chose outright assimilation, sometimes aggressively collaborating with the Greeks to suppress the Jewish tradition and its practitioners. Slowly, a third possibility developed, whereby certain groups integrated Hellenistic methods into traditional Jewish practices. The Pharisees, and later the rabbinic sages, adopted literary analysis as a means of enhancing the study of classical texts. The successful Maccabean revolt in the second century BCE gave the Jewish community the freedom for intellectual pursuits and the development of the scribal[4] (later, rabbinic) exploration of the sacred texts.

B. RABBINIC ACHIEVEMENT AND THE COVENANTAL JOURNEY

From the latter days of the Second Temple (built around 300 BCE) until the redaction of the Mishna (ca. 200–220 CE), the Jewish religion underwent one of its greatest transformations – a shift from the biblical to the rabbinic age. The core of this great metamorphosis took place in the centuries just before and just after the Destruction of the Second Temple by the Romans in the year 70 CE. In the wake of a century of checkered, often stormy rule by the Maccabeans, shadowed by the turmoil of the Roman takeover of the land, many varieties of Jewish religious thinking flowered. The Jewish revolts against Rome in 66–70 CE – which led to the Destruction of the Temple – and in 132–135 CE comprised a vain attempt to regain independence and bring about the coming of the Messiah. Tragically, both efforts failed.

The aftermath of this tumultuous period of history included huge demographic losses, increased expulsions and exile, and a decline in the standards of living and educational levels of the Jewish community in Israel. However, the most shocking outcome was the abrupt loss of the Temple and its rituals, and the discontinuation of prophetic activity, in the first century CE. Once again, the Jewish people faced a serious crisis of faith. Although the revolts had been undertaken for the sake of God and the Temple, they had failed. Did this mean that the biblical model of the ultimate triumph of Judaism and redemption of the world was false?

In the centuries that followed, the rabbinic sages, hitherto a small, marginalized group, rose to leadership. They provided the people with an answer to their existential question: The Jewish religion, they claimed, is as true as it has ever been, its promise of redemption remains unchanged. The Jewish community must continue living out its covenantal role, through new institutions and channels.

Furthermore, the redaction of the Mishna, the classic rabbinic work, mitigated the spiritual damage wrought by the Destruction by

4. E.g., Ezra, Nehemiah, and the Men of the Great Assembly.

recreating in text a semblance of the world that was lost. Completed around 200 CE, the Mishna became the core of the Talmud – the great rabbinic compendium. In the face of historic catastrophe, the sages' vision remained fixed on eternity, expressed in the timeless words of the Torah. The Temple was in ruins? The Altar gone? Then the full panoply of Temple structure, sacrifices, and priestly rituals was summoned up in the Mishna's tractates of Zevaḥim (sacrifices), Menaḥot (offerings), Me'ila (sacrilege), Tamid (daily sacrifices), Middot (Temple measurements), and Bekhorot (firstborn animals). Jerusalem was seized and closed off to Jews? The yearly cycle of sacred life went on in the tractates of Shabbat, Pesaḥim (Passover), Rosh HaShana, Yoma (Yom Kippur), Sukka, and Mo'ed Katan ("Lesser Festival").

While the Mishna defied historical reality (tacitly proclaiming that present conditions would one day be overcome), the infrastructure of Jewish life could not escape the ongoing oppression by the Romans. As the Land of Israel declined, the center of Jewish life and scholarship gradually moved to Babylon. The Jewish community there resided on the shifting border between the Roman imperium and the Persian Empire. Thus, the Babylonian Talmud, which emerged as the chronicle of rabbinic activity in the area of Mesopotamia, was influenced by both Persian and Hellenistic culture.

Among the influences adopted, the concepts of a World to Come and resurrection (also found in Zoroastrian teachings) led to a heightened focus on this previously ignored theme in Jewish tradition. The Pharisees – and later the sages – rejected the restriction of Judaism to just this world, as subscribed to by the rival sect of the Sadducees. The notion of divine retribution in this world, so dominant in the biblical tradition, was extended to include the World to Come. In time, eternal life – rather than earthly rewards – became a prime motivation for living a good life in this world. In addition, the sages insisted on the resurrection of the dead as a principal doctrine of Judaism, one that granted (or by its rejection, forfeited) admission into the World to Come.

The sages also taught that, just as God had limited Himself at the time of Creation to allow for a partnership with humankind, God was now once again becoming more immanent, less manifestly dominant in the partnership – in order to summon humanity to a higher level of agency. By not stepping in to assure Jewish victory over the Romans, God had demonstrated restraint, continuing the process, begun during the biblical era, of becoming less and less visible in human history.[5] Thus, the sages taught that while the First Temple was destroyed by God because of the sins of the Israelites, the Second Temple's end was the outcome of an unwise war set in motion by the Jews' internal conflicts, stubborn refusal to sue for peace, and reckless fanaticism in waging war against a world empire.[6]

Following this post-Destruction self-limitation of God, the sages related to the Divine Presence – the *Shekhina* – as being closer and more present. God was suffering, even if not visibly, alongside the defeated Jews. The *Shekhina* sorrowed and mourned in the ruins of Jerusalem, wept and haunted the Temple Mount, went into exile with the Children of Israel. However, since God was less manifest, and the Temple was gone, the Jewish people had to develop spiritual antennae to detect the Divine Presence everywhere. As the sages saw it, one advantage emerged from the catastrophe: contact with the *Shekhina* need not be circumscribed. In the Temple era, connection to God could be attained only in tightly restricted circumstances, through the highly sacred framework of the Temple, and by a hereditarily designated and purified few (priests). The public, participating mostly as onlookers, also had to undergo a demanding ritual purification before entering the Temple's outer precincts.

After the Destruction, by contrast, everybody could encounter the *Shekhina* daily. The sages taught that in this new, post-Temple reality, the *Shekhina* could be found in every life situation, even – or perhaps, especially – in moments of sickness, weakness, and need. When people visited the sick, God's presence hovered over the patient.[7] When people comforted mourners, they evoked God's hidden Being to console them.

---

5. See Richard Elliott Friedman, *The Disappearance of God: A Divine Mystery* (Boston: Little, Brown and Company, 1995).
6. This is the portrait drawn by the sages in Gittin 55b–57b. See Jeffrey L. Rubenstein, *Talmudic Stories: Narrative Art, Composition, and Culture* (Baltimore: Johns Hopkins University Press, 1999), 139–175.
7. Shabbat 12b.

When people spoke words of Torah or meditated upon them together, the *Shekhina* was present.[8]

To instill this awareness of the Divine Presence, the sages developed a wide range of blessings, recited, for instance, when eating food, when encountering natural phenomena, upon seeing beautiful people, or while performing mitzvot. Furthermore, they emphasized the study of Torah as the central command of the tradition[9] and a daily requirement. They detected within every word of Torah many levels of meaning, their continuous study uncovering ever more layers of wisdom. They also extended the activity from the intellectual elite to lay people. For the sages, teaching Torah was not a hereditary entitlement[10] and scholarship not a genetic gift. It was essential that everyone should know how to learn Torah, and study was open to anyone willing to make the effort. To that end, the sages instituted a public school system that would include all children, especially the poor and orphaned.[11] In place of the illiterate citizenry of the biblical period, awed by the spectacle of the Temple service and overwhelmed by God's Presence there, the Jewish people were now empowered *en masse*. They too could encounter the Divine Presence and personally participate in the religious life of prayer and home ritual. And so the sages turned the Jewish people into the People of the Book.

This theological breakthrough based on the idea of divine self-limitation had further religious consequences for Judaism. A less manifest God would no longer address the nation through chosen, prophetic messengers. The age of prophecy thus came to an end. Replacing the prophet was the sage – the *talmid ḥakham* who would impart to the people what God wanted from them in the present. The Talmud states:

8. See below, mishnas 3:3–4, 7.
9. *Talmud Torah keneged kulam* – The study of Torah is equivalent to all the mitzvot (Shabbat 127a).
10. See *Pirkei Avot* 2:9, 17, 19, 21.
11. Yehoshua b. Gamla, a High Priest who served in the Temple in the first century CE, is credited in the Talmud as the one who legislated that teachers be funded in every area and city to teach all children Torah (Bava Batra 21a). See also the talmudic instruction: "Be especially careful about educating the children of the poor, for from them will emanate the Torah [in the future]" (Nedarim 81a).

"From the day that the Holy Temple was destroyed, prophecy was taken from the prophets and given to the wise [sages].... Ameimar says: And a wise man [sage] is superior to a prophet."[12] It was in this environment that *Pirkei Avot*, an anthology of wisdom by the important sages of their time, was redacted.

To hear God's voice ("Every single day, a heavenly voice goes forth from Sinai"[13]), the sages exercised their human understanding. They studied the past record of divine instruction – the Written Torah and holy Scriptures – using literary tools to derive instruction from the text. (The most important of these techniques was a system of thirteen conceptual categories by which Torah is to be analyzed and which are generally accorded the status of having been revealed to Moses at Mount Sinai.[14]) Manifold levels of meaning were thus discovered in texts that had for many centuries been understood as having only one interpretation. Moreover, the sages underscored those commandments or situations that cast light on their current reality, established appropriate analogies between present cases and past sources, and applied their rulings accordingly. God's eternal instructions were revealed through the exercise of human judgment.

The sages thus continued the process of divine revelation after the manifest channels of prophecy had closed down. They established a model of a tradition based on an ongoing conversation between sacred texts and the community. Just as the covenantal mission was passed down from one generation to the next, so was the continuing dialogue, the process of learning and living the texts.

The sages' capability proved to be particularly vital due to the dramatic geographic, economic, social, and political changes that swept the Jewish community. Their capacity to elucidate new insights from the classical sources meant that the Torah could contend with changing circumstances and be applied to unfamiliar situations. Through the Talmud,

12. Bava Batra 12a.
13. *Pirkei Avot* 6:2.
14. Sifra, Introduction. The list of these interpretive categories, compiled by R. Yishmael, was placed in the prayer book, to be recited daily at the end of the introductory prayers, just before *Pesukei DeZimra* (verses of song, psalms, and prayers). Thus, the Jewish masses would be educated daily to the significance of these methods.

the sages demonstrated that their literature – the Oral Torah – had been revealed to Moses at Mount Sinai side by side with the Written Torah. In some cases, it was the actual words that were revealed at Sinai; in others, it was the methods and models of application (with the resultant rulings still carrying the authority of the Oral Torah from Sinai).

The sages underscored that the words of the Torah had always contained their new meanings, but that they were communicated on wavelengths that had not been heard in earlier centuries. With their central insight of God's summons of humanity to a higher, more active role, and their use of rabbinic methods of textual analysis, the sages were able to uncover those messages which had been revealed at Mount Sinai but had been "hidden" until now. Their conclusion was: "Everything that a veteran student of Torah will teach before his rabbi in the future [as an innovation, as his own discovery] was [already] told to Moses at Sinai."[15] Thus, the sages dismissed the simplistic view of the contradiction between tradition and innovation. They established a profound continuity between past and present, the former being constantly renewed in the latter by an unbroken chain of transmission.[16]

There was a second, even more radical consequence to the greater role of human understanding in elucidating the word of God. During the biblical era, when God sent direct revelation to the people through the prophet, no two prophets could disagree. If two prophets contradicted each other, one of the two was perforce a liar, a false prophet – claiming to bear a divine message which he had not been given. However, when God assigned humans the task of ascertaining His will by the use of their judgment, two honest, intelligent people could analyze the same text and come up with contradictory conclusions (not unlike two jewelers

15. Y. Pe'ah 2:6.

16. The sages were fully aware of the paradox in this view. The Talmud tells of Moses, the ultimate prophet of the biblical era, visiting the yeshiva of R. Akiva together with the Divine Presence. Moses was shocked, for he could not understand the Torah that was being taught there. He became ill at ease, weak to the point where he felt faint. Then a student asked R. Akiva from where he derived his Torah. The latter answered: "It is a halakha [given] to Moses from Sinai." Moses then grasped the profound continuity in the learning. His strength and joy were restored: "His mind was set at ease" (Menaḥot 29a).

looking at the same diamond from different angles and seeing very different facets and colors).

The Talmud says that at first the significance of disagreements between sages was not grasped because such arguments were rare. They were put down to the fact that the students had not adequately learned from the masters, and were garbling the teachings.[17] Then the students of Hillel and Shammai disagreed on tens – then hundreds – of cases, leading to a crisis: Were the teachings of the two schools becoming two different Torahs? Was one true and one false? The students of both houses finally turned to a divine voice for help and were told that the views "of these [Beit Hillel] and those [Beit Shammai] were both the words of the living God."[18]

Human judgments can legitimately differ; both the house of Hillel and of Shammai may convey true, divine instructions. For purposes of community policy, however, only one view can be followed. Thus the guiding principle became "follow the majority."[19] In the Talmud, the house of Hillel was the majority in the overwhelming number of cases. Moreover, the fact that Beit Hillel welcomed and studied all views, including those of Beit Shammai, made their conclusions more persuasive and more likely closer to the truth.

The sages of the Talmud believed that multiple views provided clearer and deeper insights, so that *maḥloket* (scholarly debate) became the Talmud's standard operating procedure and the prevalent method of seeking the truth.[20] The resolution achieved by clarification through argument provided a greater validation of the truth. The more differing human insights were invoked and the more alternative views were weighed, the more likely that the truth would ultimately emerge.

Thus rabbinic culture provided an expanded way of life that could sustain the Jewish people outside of their land, as a minority in a sea of

17. Sanhedrin 88b.
18. Eruvin 13b.
19. Ibid., quoting Exodus 23:2.
20. Eruvin 13b. Compare Bava Metzia 84a, where R. Yoḥanan complains that he cannot establish the law clearly anymore because of the death of his learning partner, Resh Lakish, who always challenged and contradicted his teachings – leading to clarification of the truth.

hostile religions. Rabbinic understanding enabled closeness to God in a world where the Divine was not manifestly present. If God did not speak anymore in overt revelation, then a covenantal dialogue could be pursued by people turning to Him in prayer.[21] If the sacrifices were no longer available, then deeds of loving-kindness would be the new direct channel to the Divine – as would Torah study; had the prophet Hosea not promised that "I [God] prefer loving-kindness to sacrifice and [find] knowledge of God [superior] to totally burnt offerings"?[22] If the Yom Kippur scapegoat bearing the sins of all Israel could no longer be sent away, if God would no longer intervene to erase the people's sins, then the sages would teach the process of individual repentance (acknowledgement of sin, resolution not to repeat the offense, turning from the wrong path, being spiritually renewed before God and human beings).

The sages filled the home with participatory rituals and celebrations to make it a fortress of spirituality. The Paschal sacrifice could no longer be brought at the Temple, nor could the following meal be eaten by the family together in Jerusalem, so the sages introduced a Seder – a ritual of story, meal, song, and prayer that the family could experience together. The Seder involved the children, inculcating the Passover story with unprecedented power for the next generation. The Book of Esther was incorporated into the Bible, and Jews were instructed to read it in community gatherings. The laws of *kashrut* were expanded, and the use of blessings before and after eating – not to mention exchanging words of Torah during a meal – turned the table into an altar before God. Eating together brought family members into encounter with each other – and with the *Shekhina*,[23] turning the daily meals into covenantal events.

Even as they upheld the eternity of the Torah's rulings, the sages expanded them. Special *ḥesed* (loving-kindness) funds were set up in every community to assist the needy. The poor would receive interest-free loans, in accordance with the Torah's prohibition against charging interest. Laws regulating speech – i.e., prohibiting gossip and slander – were extended,

---

21. See the words of Rabbi Joseph B. Soloveitchik, "The Lonely Man of Faith," *Tradition* 7:2 (Summer 1965): 37.
22. Hosea 6:6.
23. See *Pirkei Avot* 3:4. See also 3:3, 7.

and special economic protection was created for the wife in the case of a divorce. Laws concerning the proper treatment of laborers were developed, extending the Torah's regulations against, *inter alia*, exploiting the laborer and holding back his wages unjustly, even for a day.

Step by step, law by law, ritual by ritual, rabbinic Judaism emerged as more individual-oriented, internalized, home-centered, and universal, seeing all of life as an opportunity for divine encounter. In this new era, leadership evolved from the ministrations of priests and prophets to instruction of sages and teachers. Religious life became more intellectual and theological, but also more participatory; any educated person could be active in it. Yet in spite of these overarching changes, a profound sense of continuity with the biblical tradition was maintained; this was Judaism of two Torahs, Written and Oral.

Of course, the most profound unity of biblical and rabbinic Judaism lay in their common vision of the Jewish journey as the vanguard of humanity's pilgrimage toward its goals. Both biblical and rabbinic Judaism were focused on carrying out the intergenerational covenantal mission, in which Jewry served as teachers and role models on the road to the redemption of the world. This is the primary cord of unity between the biblical articulation and the rabbinic elaboration of Judaism.

When the catastrophe of Destruction and exile struck, the older leadership – the Sadducees, with their overwhelming commitment to and dependency on the Temple – could only posit that religious life must go on as before. But to do so, Jewry would have to recover Jerusalem, the Temple, and direct revelation; this was impossible. The repeated failures to regain independence and rebuild the Temple finally destroyed the older Sadduceean and other alternative leaderships.

By contrast, the sages offered a way of life that moved on. They unveiled a new level of revelation, an intimacy deeper than the ancient partnership. Believing that political revolts and messianic activities led to destruction, they turned messianism into a far-off vision, to be realized only by the Divine. They taught the Jewish people how to step outside of history – at least in ritual and in study – and live in perfect harmony with God. This enabled the Jewish people to carry on the covenantal mission.

The sages went on to develop the teaching system, new institutions, and individualized religious guidance which sustained Jewry for the following millennia. Rabbinic Judaism carried on the biblical tradition and its vision of *tikkun olam*, repairing the world. Despite Christianity's rise to become the dominant religion in the Roman Empire, the sages kept the Jewish sense of chosenness and covenantal mission alive. Ultimately, rabbinic Judaism was both profoundly continuous and fundamentally transformative.

For almost two thousand years, rabbinic culture succeeded brilliantly in giving a powerless Jewish people an ethic and a dignity. The sages enabled a people with neither land nor governmental institutions to perpetuate their culture, to keep their faith alive, and to pass on their traditions. The sages strengthened the biblical faith that the world would be improved, and in time made perfect, by the ongoing partnership between God and humanity. They made this hope so vital that it remained unbroken by persecution, expulsion, and massacre. Rabbinic institutions were so effective and the learning so compelling that they sustained the centrality of the tradition as it moved from one civilization to another: from ancient, to medieval, to modern.

After a century or so, rabbinic culture internalized the policy of waiting for God to send a redeemer to end the exile. Much of the Jewish religious focus was turned inward, and the implications of the Torah for the nations were pushed to the background (or redirected into mystical and, later, kabbalistic channels). The tactical decision of the sages to steer away from messianic activism ultimately generated a culture of passivity and political quietism. (These values hamstrung religious Jews' participation in the bold initiative of Zionism, which returned Jewry to its homeland and generated an extraordinary new renaissance of the people.)

This book is about the accomplishments of the sages. It places before the reader the values and spirit of rabbinic Judaism – in one of the finest distillations of its collective wisdom. *Pirkei Avot* reflects the sages' focus on education as well as their pedagogical genius. I believe that R. Yehuda the Prince, who together with his scholarly circle edited the Mishna, grasped the nature of the miracle of continuity and transformation which the sages had achieved. He realized that the new incarnation of Torah incorporated a more personal set of connections with a closer *Shekhina*. He grasped that the new Jew had to be more learned, his values more internalized, in order to be active in carrying on the tradition. This was to be the religion of the whole community, not just of the rabbinic elite. Seeing that the average person might be baffled by the elaborate legal literature of the Mishna or uninterested in its rhetoric, R. Yehuda determined to produce a work that would speak to the masses. From the great sages of the various generations, he distilled wisdom that would help people live better. He collected words that developed a refined personality, advice that molded character traits, and ideas that shaped religious understanding. All were phrased in short, pithy statements that were easy to take. He put his book, unique in style in the Mishna, before the People of Israel to study and make their own.

Let this remarkable result be added to the list of what God, and the sages, have wrought. As the people were educated and their religious participation heightened, they internalized the values of Judaism and its teachings as they never had before. The sages achieved what the charismatic, divinely deputized prophets never could: the elimination of idolatry and the creation of a faithful, consistently observant community. The people showed extraordinary loyalty to God and the covenant through centuries, nay millennia, of exile and minority status. They outlasted pyramids, hanging gardens, and colosseums erected to proclaim the enduring power of their conquerors. They bore witness to God amid changing civilizations, and realized the human image of God in ever-greater degree. As this book shall try to show, the sages guided not only Jewry but all of humanity on the road to its final Redemption.

C. THE PLACE OF *PIRKEI AVOT* IN THE RABBINIC CANON

This book seeks to make a talmudic pearl of wisdom – *Pirkei Avot* – available to the broader public as well as to those who have grown up with a rabbinic Judaic heritage. I believe *Pirkei Avot* was put together to distill the rabbinic wisdom for the broader public to absorb. This edition is undertaken in the belief that the rabbinic view of life, the biblical tradition, and history can offer spiritual guidance to a world seeking its way amid rapid cultural change and widespread moral confusion. The sages showed that a religion driven by a mission to redeem the world can function beyond any one cultural embodiment. Through their religious creativity and educational talents, they enabled Judaism to transcend its ancient, Middle Eastern host culture and emerge into a new world intact, bringing its heritage fully along. All religions could use such guidance in our era of radical change.

The first phase of this remarkable transition from the biblical world to rabbinic culture was carried out by the sages and teachers (eventually called rabbis) whose work makes up the Mishna – the repository of the Oral Law. The Mishna is the core of the Talmud, the great compendium of rabbinic Judaism and the second pillar of the dual Torah. The Mishna presents to us a virtual world of halakha undiminished by Destruction, unaffected by the ravages of time.

What makes the sages' achievement all the more remarkable, and the undisturbed tone of the sacred lifecycle portrayed in the Mishna all the more stunning, is that this creation took place against a background of frequent war, relentless occupation, political decline, rebellion, repression, expulsion, and destruction. Lest the crushing historical events shatter the paradigm of redemption and of hope, the sages made the heroic decision to articulate an unmarred halakhic world where the Jewish way of life was still whole and unbroken.

Over three centuries passed from the time of the *zugot* (pairs made up of the *nasi* and *av beit din*, i.e., the patriarch and head of the Sanhedrin), in the middle of the second century BCE, to the final redaction of the Mishna by R. Yehuda the Prince in the third century CE. During this time, incessant civil war in the Land of Israel led to a Roman takeover, enforced by a series of extortionate and harsh procurators. Toward the end of the first century CE, the Jews launched a full-scale revolt against the empire, which resulted in the death of over one million Jews and the exile and enslavement of hundreds of thousands. Fifty years later, Jews staged uprisings throughout the Roman Empire, culminating (after another twenty years) in another full-scale revolt under the leadership of Shimon Bar Kokhba. Although each time the Jews in the Land of Israel managed to drive the Romans back for a brief period of time, the revolts were ultimately crushed, leading to another savage repression by Rome in the wake of the defeat. Torah study and Jewish religious observance were outlawed and thousands of sages were executed.

Echoes of the fighting and suffering can be discerned in the biographies of many sages whose teachings are recorded in *Pirkei Avot*, yet the tractate's overall tone reveals little about these historical events. Instead, like the Mishna itself, *Pirkei Avot* depicts a very different reality, characterized by an ancient and sacrosanct way of life, a spirit of hope still strong, an expectation of justice in this life and of reward in the next world, and faith in the future Redemption.

At the end of the second century CE, from about 190 until 220, the great R. Yehuda the Prince, also known simply as "Rabbi" (pronounced *Rabee*, with the accent on the second syllable), took advantage of a period of respite from persecution and better relations with the Romans to edit and publish the Mishna. He recognized that it was vital to write down the oral teachings of the sages so that they would become more readily accessible to the community and be preserved in the face of looming historical changes.

The Mishna is full of thousands of laws and practices, requiring a lifetime of study to grasp. R. Yehuda was keenly aware that most of the people were not scholars. They needed a tradition that they could live by. Jewish life was now practiced in more varied settings and Jews were exposed to more diverse cultures. These challenges drove the sages to reshape the tradition to be more oriented toward the individual; more internalized, participatory, and spiritual. Thus R. Yehuda and his editors created a special volume within the Mishna to distill the life wisdom of its rabbinic creators for the benefit of the individual. Learning *Pirkei Avot* – literally, Chapters of the Fathers, but commonly known as Ethics of the Fathers – would bring the spirit of the Mishna into the everyday lives and thoughts of the people.

D. THE CONTENTS OF *PIRKEI AVOT*

As stated above, Ethics of the Fathers was conceived as a book of wisdom for life: a guide to principles of good living, lessons of personal experience, models of desirable character traits, incentives to learning and mutual responsibility. Initially, the editors selected core teachings, maxims, and sayings articulated by the leading sages of each generation. Although this structure is somewhat modified in later chapters, it remains the dominant editorial selection method. Ethics incorporates teachings by this representative selection of sages, each of whom contributed to the Mishna and to rabbinic culture. There are sixty-six sages whose teachings are included in the five chapters edited by R. Yehuda the Prince. It is written in such a way that the average person can read, enjoy, and apply to his or her own life. *Pirkei Avot* also delineates the kind of person and character that will emerge as a result of keeping the laws, studying the texts, and internalizing the beliefs contained in the Mishna. The book is a masterpiece of popular education. It dramatizes how rabbinic Judaism was intended to serve and engage all people, not just the academic elite.

Pirkei Avot serves one other important purpose. Its opening chapter articulates the continuity of the Oral Torah and Written Torah by specifying the chain of transmission from Moses to the present generation of rabbinic leaders. In part this was a justification of rabbinic authority; the Torah of the sages was derived directly from the Torah given to Moses at Mount Sinai. The laws and practices that guide this stage of the covenantal journey are truly continuous with the Written Torah, which had directed the earlier stage. In making public this transmission, the sages trumped the claims of other sects – the Qumran sect, the Jewish Christians, and the Sadduceean movement – who sought to undermine their authority, discredit their teachings, and cast doubt on the continuity of their tradition.

The sages taught that, contrary to the claims of competing sects, the original Torah had never been hidden away or fabricated, but rather had been entrusted to the true guardians of the Mosaic tradition in each generation. Each cadre delved into the Torah's layers of meaning, bringing forth God's instruction for that time and those circumstances. The sages' "extended" Torah was the true heir of biblical Judaism. Thus they explained that all the rabbinic interpretations of Torah, were not simply the inventions of the rabbinic mind, but stemmed from the Revelation at Sinai. An unbroken chain of transmission stretched from the Giving of the Torah through successive generations of Jewish leaders. Priests, prophets, judges, and sages all presided over legitimate Jewish communities, who lived by the Torah. Each era handed over its augmented tradition to the next; the process continued from country to country and from civilization to civilization. The sages who spoke through the voice of the Mishna were correctly interpreting the Torah, enabling it to guide Jewry on its covenantal way.

While the various sects claimed direct access to prophecy and divine revelation, the sages, more modestly, insisted that God – as a covenantal partner – no longer spoke directly from heaven. They maintained that through their interpretive techniques they were able to divine God's instructions for their era within the sacred texts transmitted over the generations. Ethics of the Fathers, by its indirect polemic against competing theologies and its presentation of living wisdom, upheld rabbinic Judaism as the authentic continuation of biblical Judaism.

E. STUDYING *PIRKEI AVOT*

Over the past millennium, Ethics of the Fathers became a staple of popular adult Jewish learning. It was typically studied on Shabbat, when people have more leisure. Although its redaction was completed by the middle of the third century CE, the practice of studying it on Shabbat is not referred to in the Talmud. The *Geonim* ("Great Scholars"), who led Babylonian Jewry after the closure of the Talmud, are the ones who cultivated the widespread practice of Shabbat study of *Pirkei Avot*. This practice had an important contemporary polemic function, because in geonic times the Karaite movement rose to challenge rabbinic Judaism, insisting that only the Written Torah was valid and rejecting the Oral Law, the Mishna and Talmud, as not reflecting the plain meaning of the biblical text. They also impugned the rabbinic leadership as upstarts who had seized control of the community and falsified the Torah in accordance with their own group's interests.

Pirkei Avot offered a powerful refutation of the Karaites' claims, by proclaiming the legitimacy of the sages as the true disciples of Moses, by presenting interpretations which linked the Oral and the Written Torah, by its sympathetic portrait of the sages, and by its generous sharing of their wisdom.[24] Because Ethics of the Fathers was so easy to understand and had such popular appeal, the whole collection became an ideal text to study in order to inculcate the wisdom of rabbinic Judaism.

---

24. See Jacob Gortner, "Why Did the *Geonim* Establish the Custom of Saying Avot on Shabbat?" [in Hebrew], *Sidra* 4:17–32.

Although I have stressed the polemic purpose of *Pirkei Avot*, it should be pointed out that its statement of the chain of transmission also stands in its own right. This opening statement reflects the sages' awareness that the Torah had been handed down from leadership to leadership, from era to era, and that the baton had been passed to them. They now were responsible for steering the ship of Jewry's fate through the next stage of the Jewish journey. Thus Ethics expresses the focus of the rabbinic mission – the covenantal journey toward Redemption.

Initially, R. Yehuda and his circle put together five chapters of wisdom. Afterward, a sixth chapter was collected from *baraitot* (rabbinic teachings not included in the final edition of the Mishna). This added chapter was called *Kinyan Torah* – literally, the acquisition of Torah – because it was full of praise for Torah study and enumerated the many benefits bestowed on the individual who engaged in it.

The sixth chapter was added as an outgrowth of the widely established custom to read Ethics of the Fathers during the six Shabbat afternoons between the festivals of Passover and Shavuot. The book could then be read at the rate of one chapter a week, making it easier and more user-friendly. Since the sixth Shabbat occurs just before Shavuot, the holiday of the Revelation at Sinai, the chapter of *Kinyan Torah* was most appropriate. It also expresses an implicit equivalence of Written and Oral Torah in its praise of the value of Torah and its study, thereby strengthening the authority of the latter.

Each chapter could be reviewed in a short time, leaving time for commentary and exchange of views if so desired. Over the centuries, more and more communities adopted the custom of studying the book specifically on Shabbat afternoon. Eventually, studying it around Minḥa time, particularly during the summer Shabbat afternoons which are so long, became almost universal. And since those long afternoons run until the fall, studying *Pirkei Avot* was extended until Rosh HaShana, which occurs at the onset of the autumn season. Evidence of its popularity is also found in the hundreds of commentaries written on the book and the countless editions printed.

Let it be said that this edition of *Pirkei Avot* is not offered as simply an exercise in traditional study. The text is a classic because the wisdom in this book is timeless: "Who is wise? One who learns from everyone....

Who is rich? One who is happy with his portion in life" (4:1). It contains a wealth of guiding principles, something for which countless people in modern society are searching. Moreover, it is a repository of heroes and role models for our lives. It is full of unique characters: men of wisdom and brilliance (sometimes in excess), of faith and courage (sometimes at a frightful cost), of searching reflection, of searing pessimism. Here is a gallery of Jewish scholars: authentic, rooted, and living a fully engaged life. Studying their lives is worthwhile, and connecting their teachings to their experiences is fascinating.

Finally, this tractate offers the most accessible entry point into the vast sea of divine instruction, Jewish knowledge, and folk traditions that is the Talmud. We are living in an era where Jews seek in ever greater numbers to reconnect to their heritage. Interest in Jewish wisdom is at an all-time high among non-Jews. The Hebrew Bible is widely known in general culture, thanks in no small measure to Christian dissemination of its texts and teachings, as well as the growth of multiculturalism in American society and education. But the Talmud is still a sealed book to most people: almost unknown, and often the subject of stereotyping and dismissal. Admittedly, the bulk of the Talmud is more complex, more saturated with legal models and language, more filled with rhetorical analysis, and more difficult for most people to understand. However, *Pirkei Avot* offers a delicious taste of Talmud; hopefully, the appetite will grow with the eating.

Those who go even deeper into Ethics of the Fathers will find that it offers many models of how to bridge Jewish wisdom and general culture, how to apply traditional concepts to new circumstances. In chapter 6, the rewards for studying Torah are listed, including becoming a friend and a beloved person, developing the ability to give counsel and understanding, being imbued with humility and reverence, being distanced from sin and drawn closer to virtue, learning the qualities of modesty and patience, and being forgiving of insults – not a bad description of the rewards of learning the wisdom of the Ethics of the Fathers.

Pirkei Avot

כָּל יִשְׂרָאֵל יֵשׁ לָהֶם חֵלֶק לָעוֹלָם הַבָּא. שֶׁנֶּאֱמַר: וְעַמֵּךְ כֻּלָּם צַדִּיקִים, לְעוֹלָם יִירְשׁוּ אָרֶץ נֵצֶר מַטָּעַי, מַעֲשֵׂה יָדַי לְהִתְפָּאֵר:

All of the People of Israel have a portion in the World to Come, as it is stated in Scripture: "Your people – all of them – are righteous; they shall inherit the land forever; they are the shoot that I planted, My handiwork in which I glory."[1]

This introductory phrase is not found in the text of Tractate Avot. It is taken from Mishna Sanhedrin 11:1. It was inserted to serve as an introduction to be read before each chapter.

All of the People of Israel have a portion in the World to Come

The Mishna in Sanhedrin goes on to list those who do not have a portion in the World to Come; they forfeit their share because of their beliefs or behaviors. Here, the sages omit the exceptions because they wanted to make a broad and bold statement about the goodness and worthiness of every Jew, learned or ignorant, aristocrat or commoner, male or female, young or old.

World to Come

One of the articles of faith in rabbinic tradition is that the physical world is real but constitutes only a fraction of the total reality. There is a spiritual world beyond this flesh-and-blood, mortal stage. In that world,

1. Isaiah 60:21.

human beings in spiritual form (traditionally called the soul) abide in and with the Divine Presence in eternal bliss.

They shall inherit the land forever

There is a play on words here. The prophet Isaiah literally means that once the Land of Israel is restored, the Jews will inherit it forever. The sages turn that phrase to mean that every Jew, by right, inherits a portion of the land that is forever (i.e., the world of eternal existence).

The shoot that I planted... My handiwork in which I glory

Having been created by God, the People of Israel are intrinsically precious. They inherit (i.e., are given as a gift) eternal bliss. This priceless divine gift is not given to them because of their actions, but rather is bestowed as a result of God's grace and pride of parenting.

Chapter 1

Mishna 1

מֹשֶׁה קִבֵּל תּוֹרָה מִסִּינַי וּמְסָרָהּ לִיהוֹשֻׁעַ, וִיהוֹשֻׁעַ לִזְקֵנִים, וּזְקֵנִים לִנְבִיאִים, וּנְבִיאִים מְסָרוּהָ לְאַנְשֵׁי כְנֶסֶת הַגְּדוֹלָה.

Moses received the Torah at Sinai and he transmitted it to Joshua, and Joshua to the elders, and the elders to the prophets, and the prophets transmitted it to the Men of the Great Assembly.

הֵם אָמְרוּ שְׁלֹשָׁה דְבָרִים: הֱווּ מְתוּנִים בַּדִּין, וְהַעֲמִידוּ תַלְמִידִים הַרְבֵּה, וַעֲשׂוּ סְיָג לַתּוֹרָה.

The Men of the Great Assembly said three maxims: Be measured in the legal process; raise up many students; make a fence for the Torah.

Moses received the Torah at Sinai

Pirkei Avot opens with a sketch of the chain of transmission from Moses to the sages of the Mishna. This chain constitutes the sages' statement that their teaching of Torah is the authentic and unbroken continuation – and the authoritative present incarnation – of the Torah given to Moses at Mount Sinai. This is also their reply to the claims of the other groups competing for the loyalty of the Jewish people which portrayed themselves as the carriers of the true Torah.

As underscored in the Introduction, the sages had to account for the remarkable transformation in actual religious life which characterized the way of Torah as lived in rabbinically led communities. Although the sages upheld and brought with them the entirety of biblical Judaism, the rabbinic iteration of Judaism looked very different. Two hundred years earlier, people worshiped God primarily by bringing sacrifices through intermediaries, the priests, who had been elected by God to their role. God was so dominant and transcending, so electrifying in presence, that direct contact with Him was death-dealing. One entered into the "shielded" presence of God only occasionally by visiting the Holy Temple in Jerusalem and going through special purification rites first. Less of the ritual life was practiced at home. The average Jew was uneducated, and rabbis did not exist.

Two centuries later, prayer was the central medium of communication with God. The Divine Presence was "encountered" everywhere in daily living. Home rituals, such as the reenactment of the Exodus at the Passover Seder, were universal. Torah study increased as the people became ever more active religiously. With the loss of the Temple, ritual purification fell to the wayside, except in the area of relations between husband and wife.

To their credit, the sages followed God into the hitherto unknown, finding new levels of instruction in the *Torah Shebe'al Peh*; they went into exile and new cultural settings with the *Shekhina*. They opened new channels of communication with God in prayer. They and the Jewish people found renewed, covenantal interaction with God and a revitalized faith and way of life. They grasped that Judaism was a covenant between Israel and God. They understood that the Torah of Moses was transmitted to the living generation, which was responsible to obey it, live it, expand it, and carry it through the new historical circumstances. They understood that preservation and renewal were inseparable, and that both revelation and the unfolding of the Torah were continuous and seamless.

Thus the sages lived and practiced the truth, which they proclaimed in this order of transmission, that the Torah was not one set of institutions or even one body of revealed law. The Torah was a covenantal chain whose substance and rules were transmitted from generation to generation. The charge of repairing the world was applied from civilization to civilization, in whatever form was necessary. The institutions would be transmitted and innovated as needed; all were included in the infinite Torah from Sinai, whose depths would continue to be plumbed until the final goal was reached. Thus this chain of transmission (spelled out in chapters 1 and 2) refutes the Sadducees' position that the rabbinic way of life was a deviation from the classic Torah of the Jewish people.

In parallel fashion, this chain of transmission rebuts the emerging supersessionist claims of Christianity as well. As the teachings of Jesus spread among gentiles and his followers began to separate from Judaism to articulate a new religion, they claimed to be the "new Israel" or the "true Israel." They taught that Judaism had undergone a metamorphosis, that it had transformed into a new religion – a "new" testament.

At Sinai

Literally, from Sinai. This phrase attests to the divine nature of the Torah. It was not written by Moses, it was received by him. The sages teach that the Oral Torah, including the rabbinic tradition of understanding and applying the Written Torah, was also given to Moses at Mount Sinai (see Introduction): "'The Lord gave me the two stone tablets ... and on them were the exact words that the Lord had addressed to you on the mountain [Sinai]' [Deut. 9:10]. This teaches us that The Holy One, Blessed Be He, showed Moses [also] the minutiae of the Torah [the conjunctions, prepositions, and details in biblical verses that imply additional laws given over in the Oral Torah], the minutiae of the scribes [the subtle indications in the language of the Mishna from which the *Amora'im*, i.e., the sages of the Talmud, derived additional laws or spelled out further legal implications in the Mishna], and that which the scribes will innovate in the future [such as reading the Book of Esther and the other rabbinic legislation]" (Megilla 19b). The rabbinic tradition interprets the full meaning of the Written Torah; it also applies the Torah's laws, principles, and stories to later times and circumstances.

Transmitted it to Joshua

This mishna gives a thumbnail sketch of the chain of transmission of the Written and Oral Torahs. The tacit messages include: There is an unbroken chain of transmission so the later representatives and their rulings are to be given "equal" weight with the foundational Torah; Torah is the substance of an intergenerational, inter-civilizational covenant to perfect the world.

Joshua to the elders

Despite changing leaderships and variable locations, the intergenerational partnership goes on. The elders were the pre-monarchic leaders, mostly tribal, described in the biblical books of Judges and Samuel.

The elders to the prophets

In the books of Joshua and Judges, the elders appear to be mainly warriors and political leaders. The prophets, in their books, appear as individual vessels of divine revelation with a highly spiritual message, and with an authority built on transmitting the divine word. But the sages here present this *mesora* (chain of transmission) as unitary in nature. In rabbinic Midrash, the elders and prophets are associated with the chain of transmission, and their portraits are redrawn as rabbinic scholars and heads of courts.

The prophets transmitted it to the Men of the Great Assembly

The prophets primarily spoke in the Land of Israel before the Destruction of the First Temple. The Men of the Great Assembly (the name given them by the sages) led Israel in the post-Destruction period. Under this category, the sages link together later prophets such as Zechariah, Haggai, Malachi, and leaders of the returnee community such as Ezra and Nehemiah, in the Persian era of Jewish history, ca. 515–320 BCE. The latter two leaders no longer had full prophetic status, but instead were deemed to have quasi-prophetic status. Religious practices associated with them are sometimes called *divrei kabbala*; literally, words of reception, or transmission. Words uttered by those earlier in the chain of transmission are ranked higher than rabbinic ordinances in terms of legal authority.

The era of the Men of the Great Assembly continued down to Shimon the Righteous (third century BCE). During this period, there was a transition from prophetic modes of revelation to the analytic and midrashic methods of interpreting the Torah's words. These interpretive methods are developed more fully in the rabbinic schools. The Talmud credits the Men of the Great Assembly with such innovations as the shift from the ancient Hebrew script to the Assyrian orthography used in Torah scrolls today, the establishment of formal, liturgically fixed prayers, the practice of reading the Torah publicly to the congregation three times a week (the full portion on Shabbat and a smaller portion on Monday and Thursday), and the expansion of education for children and adults.

It is striking that this model of the leadership in the chain of transmission omits the role of the kings and the priests, although the prophet Malachi states: "For the lips of the priest guard knowledge, and they will seek Torah [teachings] from his mouth."[2] This omission may reflect the disillusionment with the priesthood due to corruption under the influence of Hellenism and/or the merger of priesthood with kingship during the Hasmonean dynasty. This merger violated the traditional separation of powers between the prophetic or spiritual leadership and the monarchy, and also led to the politicization and de-spiritualization of the priesthood. The sages actively opposed this union and were attacked by various rulers as a result.

Measured in the legal process

- Do not go to extremes.
- Be patient, not harsh or coercive, in applying the law to the community.
- The law works best when it moves the community moderately and steadily over time rather than trying to transform values or behaviors overnight. Revolutions often generate backlash and resistance. When the change is too drastic, it is often defeated by popular resistance, or the revolutionaries resort to harsh and tyrannical methods to impose the law.

Raise up many students

Educate the whole society. Do not let the Torah be the possession of a small, elite circle; it is meant to guide the lives of everyone.

The Men of the Great Assembly started the process of bringing Torah education to the masses. In the wake of Hellenism (and later, in exile) the masses would not stay loyal unless they were educated and brought to full understanding of and identification with the Torah. Despite the great success of popular Torah education, some sages

2. Malachi 2:7.

insisted that only a select few should be allowed into the rabbinic study house to become teachers. This was Rabban Gamliel's view when he served as *nasi* (patriarch of the Jewish community and head of the Torah academy).[3] Others held that much larger numbers of students should be admitted. Once, as a result of an inter-rabbinic controversy, Rabban Gamliel was temporarily demoted. On that day, at least four hundred new students were admitted to the academy.[4]

More generally, in the first century CE, before the Destruction of the Second Temple, the sages and their predecessors were a small group within the Jewish community. The majority of the Establishment was of aristocratic background and/or the priestly class. The Sadducees' sectarian worldview was particularly strong in these groups. The Pharisees and their successors, the sages, had to struggle for leadership of the post-Destruction community. They essentially won the competition by educating many, many students. Those students in turn won the battle for the minds and hearts of the Jews by teaching widely, by democratizing education, and by raising up many of their own students over the centuries.

Make a fence for the Torah

To protect against violations of the Torah's boundaries, one should cordon off a wider area so people will be stopped before they enter into the forbidden zone. For example, one lights Shabbat candles and starts Shabbat eighteen minutes before sunset to avoid the danger of "work" at the actual beginning of Shabbat at sunset. A second example: The sages' category of *muktzeh* (that which is off-limits to touch or handle on Shabbat) is applied to money and tools which might be used to do forbidden labor on that day. Touching the money or the tool is not intrinsically forbidden on Shabbat. However, by prohibiting the handling of those items, the sages ensured that people would not take money and go shopping or use tools to build or shape objects, both of which are types of labor prohibited on Shabbat. It should be noted that when Nehemiah came to Jerusalem during the period of return to the

3. Berakhot 28a.
4. Ibid.

Land of Israel, he found widespread violation of the Sabbath laws with regard to both commerce and the use of tools. To establish a spirit of Shabbat, it was necessary to widen the prohibition of *muktzeh*.[5]

The tactic of preemptive or preventive fences recommended here worked better in some situations or generations than in others. In some cases, fences prevented people from straying from the straight and narrow. In other cases, people felt constrained and inhibited, and some broke away. So the extent of fence-building versus teaching the individual how to walk a fine line that may test boundaries is an educational judgment to be made in every generation and culture and in almost every situation. The Men of the Great Assembly felt that in their time, the way of fences worked better.

5. Shabbat 123b.

Mishna 2

שִׁמְעוֹן הַצַּדִּיק הָיָה מִשְּׁיָרֵי כְּנֶסֶת הַגְּדוֹלָה. הוּא הָיָה אוֹמֵר: עַל שְׁלֹשָׁה דְבָרִים הָעוֹלָם עוֹמֵד, עַל הַתּוֹרָה, וְעַל הָעֲבוֹדָה, וְעַל גְּמִילוּת חֲסָדִים.

Shimon the Righteous was one of the last of the Men of the Great Assembly. He used to say: The world stands on three pillars: on the Torah, and on the divine service, and on acts of loving-kindness.

HISTORICAL BACKGROUND

Shimon the Righteous is the only member of the Great Assembly whose name we know, except for the biblical prophets and teachers included in that group. He served as High Priest and is a transitional figure from the days of prophecy and the Temple to the ever more hidden Divine Presence that took over when prophecy ceased, and later when the Temple was destroyed. For this reason, his name and memory are suffused with nostalgia and uplifting associations. Among them: As long as Shimon the Righteous was alive, the permanent fire in the Temple always burned; after his death, it became erratic. During his lifetime, the initial wood supply sufficed to burn all the sacrifices; once he died, the wood burned quickly and had to be continuously replenished.

Various traditions report Shimon the Righteous meeting and winning over Alexander the Great in the third century BCE and the Roman Emperor Caligula in the first century CE. Chronologically, of course, he could not have encountered both rulers. However, both incidents dealt with cases where the Jews were in danger of these rulers turning against them, and thus both cases of deliverance were associated with

Shimon. Some historical sources credit him with upgrading the Temple and rebuilding parts of Jerusalem during his service as High Priest.

On the Torah

The study and practice of Torah (the commandments and behaviors it prescribes) constitute the basis of a society which enables people to live in harmony with each other.

- Torah study is the foundation of a good life. "Study is the greatest of all because it brings [one] to [proper] action."[6]
- The sages made the study of Torah, i.e., education, central to their program for the Jewish people. The mitzva of *talmud Torah* (Torah study) became the core commandment of Judaism. The democratization of study inspired the masses and led them to internalize the Torah's teachings. The outcome was that the sages accomplished what the prophets with their divine communications could not: the abolition of idolatry in the community and the attainment of a much higher level of observance and faithfulness to the covenant.

On the divine service

The primary worship of God in the biblical period was through sacrifices. These included, among others, the peace offering (a celebratory, family-shared meal), sin and guilt offerings for various trespasses, and purification rites after going through certain illnesses or states of ritual impurity. However, with the Destruction of the Second Temple, this channel of communication was blocked and the age of direct revelation ended. These changes constituted more than a technical stoppage. The nature of the interaction with God underwent a transformation. Overt divine communication (i.e., prophecy) ceased. Facing the "dreadful silence" of a world without God's voice, the Men of the Great Assembly "would not let the ongoing dialogue between God and men come to an end. If God had stopped calling man… let man call God. And so

6. Kiddushin 40b.

the covenantal colloquy was shifted from the level of prophecy to that of prayer."[7] Prayer became the primary form of divine service.

On acts of loving-kindness

These include extending hospitality, visiting the sick, providing the dowry for a bride and thereby enabling her to marry, and caring for the dead (the final washing of the body, attending the funeral, escorting the deceased to his final resting place, comforting the mourners).[8] There is no minimum or maximum frequency for performing these acts. Giving something as "trivial" as a smile or a hug may save another person from despair. Paying a king's ransom to free a prisoner unjustly incarcerated, spending one's life caring for another, or giving one's life to save another are also acts of loving-kindness. Acts of charity and loving-kindness are also weighed as equal to all the other commandments, but acts of loving-kindness can go where no acts of charity can go. They can be carried out with one's body, not just with one's money; they can be extended to the rich as well as to the poor; they can be performed for the dead as well as for the living.[9]

After the Destruction of the Second Temple, R. Yehoshua turned in despair to Rabban Yoḥanan b. Zakkai, saying that now there would be no channel of atonement (i.e., it was no longer possible to give sin or guilt offerings to win divine forgiveness). Rabban Yoḥanan answered: We have an equally efficacious channel of atonement – acts of loving-kindness.[10] Rabban Yoḥanan cited the prophetic verse, "For I [God] desire loving-kindness, not sacrifice."[11] Similarly, the Talmud indicates that Shimon the Righteous' articulation of these three pillars on which the world stands replaces the earlier assumption that "the only foundation on which the world stands is the sacrifices."[12]

7. Soloveitchik, "The Lonely Man of Faith," 37.
8. Pe'ah 1:1.
9. Tosefta, Pe'ah 4; Sukka 49b.
10. *Avot DeRabbi Natan* 4:5.
11. Hosea 6:6.
12. Y. Taanit 4, end of halakha 2.

Mishna 3

אַנְטִיגְנוֹס אִישׁ סוֹכוֹ קִבֵּל מִשִּׁמְעוֹן הַצַּדִּיק. הוּא הָיָה אוֹמֵר: אַל תִּהְיוּ כַּעֲבָדִים הַמְשַׁמְּשִׁים אֶת הָרַב עַל מְנָת לְקַבֵּל פְּרָס, אֶלָּא הֱווּ כַּעֲבָדִים הַמְשַׁמְּשִׁים אֶת הָרַב שֶׁלֹּא עַל מְנָת לְקַבֵּל פְּרָס, וִיהִי מוֹרָא שָׁמַיִם עֲלֵיכֶם.

Antigonus of Sokho received [the transmission of the Oral Tradition[13]] from Shimon the Righteous. He would say: Do not be like servants who serve the master for the sake of receiving a payment. Rather, be like servants who serve the master [selflessly and] not for the sake of payment; and may the fear of Heaven be upon you.

HISTORICAL BACKGROUND

Antigonus (first half of the third century BCE) is the first noted sage with a Greek name. This was a reflection of the rising influence of Hellenism inside the Jewish community. The use of the Greek name is striking. It shows that the sages did not simply reject Greek culture; they also learned from it. They filtered its messages so that only those teachings compatible with Torah culture would get through.

Like servants who serve … for the sake of receiving a payment

God and religion should not be viewed as a vending machine in which you insert worship and obedience in order to get the good

13. Words in brackets are my additions for the purpose of making the mishna more understandable to the reader.

things in life. It is possible that Antigonus was impressed by the Hellenistic philosophical critique that everyday religionists are in it only for the payoff and that this constitutes a primitive religious position. He wanted Judaism to be a religion practiced at the highest level of religious motivation.

The sages believed that the renewed self-limitation of God which spelled the end of visible miracles and prophecy came from God's desire that humans take a higher level of responsibility in the covenant process. To be worthy of this, individuals should shift their religious psychology from a focus on reward and punishment for doing or not doing God's bidding to a state of being motivated by one's relationship with God and a desire to do good for its own sake.

Like servants ... not for the sake of payment

Unconditional love of God, i.e., obedience and actions out of intrinsic respect and not for selfish reasons, should be a religious person's ideal. The Talmud suggests that at least some students of Antigonus misinterpreted his words to mean that there is no reward and punishment in this world. As they doubted the existence of a World to Come, to them Antigonus' teaching meant that there was no judgment – and hence no Judge. Then they broke away. They started a sect known as Boethusians, which came close in philosophy to the Epicureans. They concluded that God is not involved with humans and that material existence is the only real existence.

Fear of Heaven

Since service of God should not be for the sake of reward, the category "fear of Heaven" (i.e., fear of God) cannot refer to the desire to earn admission to heaven or to escape punishment. Fear of God refers to a feeling of awe at God's majesty and wonder at the vast cosmos which He has created. Alternatively, it reflects a feeling of respect and connection to God so strong that one simply cannot do evil or hurt another out of the sense that this is inappropriate behavior in God's presence.

Mishna 4

יוֹסֵי בֶּן יוֹעֶזֶר אִישׁ צְרֵדָה וְיוֹסֵי בֶּן יוֹחָנָן אִישׁ יְרוּשָׁלַיִם קִבְּלוּ מֵהֶם. יוֹסֵי בֶּן יוֹעֶזֶר אִישׁ צְרֵדָה אוֹמֵר: יְהִי בֵיתְךָ בֵּית וַעַד לַחֲכָמִים, וֶהֱוֵי מִתְאַבֵּק בַּעֲפַר רַגְלֵיהֶם, וֶהֱוֵי שׁוֹתֶה בַצָּמָא אֶת דִּבְרֵיהֶם.

Yosei b. Yoezer of Tzereida and Yosei b. Yoḥanan of Jerusalem received the tradition from them. Yosei b. Yoezer of Tzereida says: Your home should be a meeting place for scholars. Sit in the dust at their feet, and drink their words thirstily.

HISTORICAL BACKGROUND

These two scholars (and the next four pairs of scholars quoted) are called the *zugot*, "pairs." They were co-leaders of the Jewish population; one was the *nasi*, president, or head of the Sanhedrin and community, and the other was the *av beit din*, head of the court ("vice president"). In this case, Yosei b. Yoezer was *nasi* and Yosei b. Yoḥanan was *av beit din*. Their careers run parallel to the Maccabean revolt against imposed Hellenism in the latter half of the second century BCE. Of Yosei from Tzereida we are told that he was "the *ḥasid* (pious one) in the priesthood."[14] The *ḥasidim* were an important component of the Maccabean revolt. The midrash tells us that Yosei of Tzereida was executed by the authorities along with a large group of pious priests during one

14. Ḥagiga 2:7.

of the periods when the Seleucid king reversed course and tried again to destroy the Maccabees.[15]

A meeting place for scholars

By constant association with scholars, you will become a better and wiser person, being influenced by their teachings and by their personal example as well.

Sit in the dust

Be humble in their presence; look up to them.

Drink...thirstily

Do not study passively or routinely. Studying the Torah of the sages should be done with enthusiasm and passion.

15. Genesis Rabba 65:22.

Mishna 5

יוֹסֵי בֶּן יוֹחָנָן אִישׁ יְרוּשָׁלַיִם
אוֹמֵר: יְהִי בֵיתְךָ פָּתוּחַ
לִרְוָחָה, וְיִהְיוּ עֲנִיִּים בְּנֵי
בֵיתֶךָ, וְאַל תַּרְבֶּה שִׂיחָה עִם
הָאִשָּׁה. בְּאִשְׁתּוֹ אָמְרוּ, קַל
וָחֹמֶר בְּאֵשֶׁת חֲבֵרוֹ. מִכָּאן
אָמְרוּ חֲכָמִים: כָּל הַמַּרְבֶּה
שִׂיחָה עִם הָאִשָּׁה, גּוֹרֵם
רָעָה לְעַצְמוֹ, וּבוֹטֵל מִדִּבְרֵי
תוֹרָה, וְסוֹפוֹ יוֹרֵשׁ גֵּיהִנָּם.

Yosei b. Yoḥanan of Jerusalem says: Your house should be wide open [to guests], the poor should be a constant presence [like family] in your home, and do not talk excessively with a woman. This applies to one's wife and all the more so to a friend's wife. From this insight the sages say: Whoever talks too much with a woman causes harm to himself. He will be distracted from words of Torah and in the end, he will inherit Gehenna.

Your house…wide open

- A home should be warm and inviting to all guests. The patriarch Abraham's house was open on all four sides so guests would feel welcome and enter immediately from whatever direction they came.
- "Welcoming guests is a greater act than greeting the *Shekhina* (Divine Presence)."[16] The proof is that the patriarch Abraham turned from a conversation with God and ran to invite and extend hospitality to three passersby in Elonai Mamre.[17]

16. Shabbat 127a.
17. Genesis 18:1–10.

- Rabbi Benny Lau suggests that both Yosei b. Yoezer and Yosei b. Yoḥanan are responding to the expanded challenge of Hellenism. Yosei b. Yoezer wants to focus inwardly: Fill your house with scholars and close out Hellenistic influences. Yosei b. Yoḥanan advocates opening one's home to guests and reaching out to others – meeting Hellenism in open competition.[18]

The poor… in your home

Poor people should be made to feel at home, just like family and not like objects of charity. Even if you are doing a good deed in feeding the needy, treating them as recipients of charity puts them on a lower plane.

Do not talk excessively with a woman

In a society where men and women were socially isolated from each other (and women were often segregated in their own homes), excessive socializing and talk between men and women could lead to improper thoughts and actions. This passage is a reminder of the extraordinary entrance of women into contemporary society and their rise to the dignity of public activity in the past century. It is not that there are no sexual and relational moral risks in the increased interaction between men and women. But the religious emphasis has shifted to women acting and leading in the public sphere as full participants rather than women staying home to preserve their modesty as well as that of the men. In other words, nowadays, self-control in each other's presence rather than social segregation is the key to upholding morality and modesty.

From this insight…

This final sentence seems to be a later generation's editorial comment, an expansion of the initial dictum. Some scholars have argued that talmudic attitudes toward separation between women and men (and fear of potential illicit sexual activity) were more rigorous in some generations than in others. Hence this additional note.

---

18. Binyamin Lau, *The Sages*, vol. 1 (Jerusalem: Maggid Books, 2007), 98–99.

Mishna 6

יְהוֹשֻׁעַ בֶּן פְּרַחְיָה וְנִתַּאי הָאַרְבֵּלִי קִבְּלוּ מֵהֶם. יְהוֹשֻׁעַ בֶּן פְּרַחְיָה אוֹמֵר: עֲשֵׂה לְךָ רַב, וּקְנֵה לְךָ חָבֵר, וֶהֱוֵי דָן אֶת כָּל הָאָדָם לְכַף זְכוּת.

Yehoshua b. Peraḥya and Nitai of Arbel received the tradition from them. Yehoshua b. Peraḥya says: Find yourself a teacher; win yourself a friend; and be one who judges everyone by giving them the benefit of the doubt.

HISTORICAL BACKGROUND

Yehoshua and Nitai were the co-leaders of the community (*nasi* and *av beit din,* respectively) contemporaneously with the reign of Yoḥanan Hyrcanus, the Maccabean ruler (134–104 BCE). Josephus tells us that the Pharisees (ancestors of the sages) strongly objected to the Maccabean concentration of power via uniting ruler and High Priest functions. At times, such as under the later ruler Alexander Yannai, there was open warfare between the ruler and the Pharisees. Yehoshua b. Peraḥya, the Talmud tells us, fled to Alexandria in order to avoid being killed in these clashes.[19] He returned later.

Find yourself a teacher

- To grow in wisdom, begin studying with someone who knows more than you, who can teach you from his or her own

19. Sota 47a.

experience. Then you will naturally grow toward that person's level.

- Rather than flit from teacher to teacher, find a primary teacher who can serve as an authority and consistent source of wisdom for you.

Win yourself a friend

Literally, purchase, or buy yourself a friend. To win somebody's friendship takes ongoing effort, openness, sharing, loyalty, and dependability, but the effort is worth it because a friend will validate and sustain you.

Judges everyone by… the benefit of the doubt

Many behaviors of the people in our lives (or people we come into contact with) can be interpreted negatively, even cynically, or they can be assessed positively. People often assume the worst about others' motives or intentions – out of the belief that to build themselves up and make themselves superior, they must put down others. Yehoshua b. Peraḥya believes that others deserve to be judged in the most positive light possible. This shows our true respect for them. People who judge in this way will be better people themselves and will more likely evoke the best possible behavior from others. Furthermore, the Talmud says that whoever gives others the benefit of the doubt will be judged that way by God and by others.

Giving people the benefit of the doubt creates an atmosphere of trust and safety. This encourages more honesty and openness, and more adventurous exploration, as people know they will not be put down or scorned for entertaining new possibilities.

In contemporary culture, this principle is sometimes mistakenly generalized as not judging people at all, lest they be hurt or marginalized. But absence of criticism is deadly to the formation of good judgment. It also undermines standards of good and bad or right and wrong. The key is to judge fairly and wisely, to give the benefit of the doubt, and to neither overreach and crush the other nor silence judgment and impoverish the quality of life.

There is a talmudic story that Jesus was a student of Yehoshua b. Peraḥya, who rejected him for having exhibited some bad behavior. Afterward, Yehoshua felt great remorse at the breakaway of the Jesus movement, and taught that one should never reject another person totally. Rather, when uttering a criticism, he should draw close with one hand while criticizing with the other. Rabbi Benny Lau suggests that this mishna calling for giving the other the benefit of the doubt also grows out of that earlier incident, when total condemnation led to a total break.

(In reading this story, keep in mind that this is an exercise in retrospection and nostalgia. It is doubtful that any Jewish responses to Jesus at that time would have changed the later breakaway, which was driven by the purposes of God, by the interpretations of later followers, such as Paul, and by the positive responses of gentiles.)

Mishna 7

נִתַּאי הָאַרְבֵּלִי אוֹמֵר: הַרְחֵק מִשָּׁכֵן רָע, וְאַל תִּתְחַבֵּר לָרָשָׁע, וְאַל תִּתְיָאֵשׁ מִן הַפֻּרְעָנוּת.

Nitai of Arbel says: Keep away from a bad neighbor; do not befriend an evil person; do not despair of retribution [when you see bad behavior triumph].

A bad neighbor

Such a person can harm you or influence you to join in evil.

An evil person

When you befriend a wicked person, the latter will likely draw you into evil ways. Moreover, people often unconsciously imitate the behavior of those with whom they associate.

Do not despair

Maintain your faith that "when… evildoers flourish, it [will lead to] their being destroyed."[20]

Nitai said these words when Yoḥanan Hyrcanus, the head of the Maccabean government, joined the Sadducees.[21] Rabbi Benny Lau suggests that Yehoshua b. Peraḥya and Nitai are offering two alternative

20. Psalms 92:8.

21. Zechariah Frankel, *Darkhei HaMishna* [Hebrew] (Leipzig, Germany, 1859: HebrewBooks.org), 37.

policies to the rising clash between Hellenists and Maccabees. Yehoshua suggests bringing people closer, winning them over as friends, giving them the benefit of the doubt. Nitai's proposal is to cut people off. Separate from their influence and do not despair if they temporarily seem to be winning. The key is to outlast them.[22]

22. Lau, *The Sages,* 126–131.

Mishna 8

יְהוּדָה בֶּן טַבַּאי וְשִׁמְעוֹן בֶּן שָׁטָח קִבְּלוּ מֵהֶם. יְהוּדָה בֶּן טַבַּאי אוֹמֵר: אַל תַּעַשׂ עַצְמְךָ כְּעוֹרְכֵי הַדַּיָּנִין, וּכְשֶׁיִּהְיוּ בַּעֲלֵי הַדִּין עוֹמְדִים לְפָנֶיךָ יִהְיוּ בְעֵינֶיךָ כִּרְשָׁעִים, וּכְשֶׁנִּפְטָרִים מִלְּפָנֶיךָ יִהְיוּ בְעֵינֶיךָ כְּזַכָּאִין, כְּשֶׁקִּבְּלוּ עֲלֵיהֶם אֶת הַדִּין.

Yehuda b. Tabbai and Shimon b. Shetaḥ received the tradition from them. Yehuda b. Tabbai says: [When you are a judge] do not act like a lawyer. When the parties in a lawsuit stand before you, look at them as if both sides are guilty, but when they leave you [having accepted your ruling], look at them as if they are both acquitted.

HISTORICAL BACKGROUND

There is a disagreement in the Talmud as to whether Yehuda or Shimon served as the *nasi*. This pair served in parallel with the extended reign of Alexander Yannai (102–77 BCE) and his queen, Salome Alexandra (Shlomtzion) afterward (77–67 BCE). By the end of this period, the Pharisees had regained control of the Sanhedrin and made a new alliance with the Hasmonean rulers. There is a tradition that Yehuda b. Tabbai fled to Alexandria for a while, possibly to avoid being executed as a result of the power struggles.

Shimon b. Shetaḥ played a major role in establishing proper legal procedures that would apply equally and fairly to all – king and commoner, connected and influential alike. Two highly dramatic incidents reflect his absolute integrity and courage. In one case, a servant of Alexander Yannai was tried for murder. Shimon insisted that the king must appear in court and that he must stand out of respect for the court and the Torah. Shimon's fellow judges were too frightened of the king to uphold this procedure. In the second case, Shimon's own son was convicted and sentenced to death. Shimon learned that his son had been framed by a conspiracy of evildoers, but he could not prove this. He wanted to save his son, but his son convinced him that nullification of the sentence would be interpreted as a "fix" due to familial connections. This would undermine Shimon's procedural revolution to establish unimpeachable justice. Heartbreakingly, Shimon let the process proceed.

Do not act like a lawyer

A judge should be neutral and broadminded, open to all sides of a case and the various arguments rather than allow his judgment to narrow and see the facts from the perspective of a lawyer, who is trained to be the champion of one side. It should be noted that the rabbinic courts followed a practice closer to the European tradition of judges conducting the investigation in the court case, as opposed to the Anglo-Saxon tradition which uses lawyers and the adversarial method to establish the facts.

Both sides are guilty

Be skeptical and critical when listening to the pleas of both sides.

Both acquitted

When both litigants accept a ruling in a case, they are showing obedience to and respect for the law. Therefore, both should be viewed as upstanding citizens.

Mishna 9

שִׁמְעוֹן בֶּן שָׁטָח אוֹמֵר: הֱוֵי מַרְבֶּה לַחֲקֹר אֶת הָעֵדִים, וֶהֱוֵי זָהִיר בִּדְבָרֶיךָ, שֶׁמָּא מִתּוֹכָם יִלְמְדוּ לְשַׁקֵּר.	Shimon b. Shetaḥ says: As a judge, cross-examine the witnesses thoroughly. However, be careful with what you say and how you say it, lest [the witnesses] figure out from your words how to lie [successfully].

HISTORICAL BACKGROUND

Shimon b. Shetaḥ's leadership overlaps the rule of Alexander Yannai. Alexander was the most powerful of the Hasmonean kings. During his reign, he ruled over the largest expanse of territory under Jewish government ever. Shimon had confrontations with Alexander Yannai, but survived them because of his close relationship to the queen and because the king respected his force of character. According to one tradition, Shimon was the queen's brother and she protected him. (However, at least once, Shimon fled.)

Shimon took a leading role in broadening the influence and upholding the values of rabbinic culture. This period saw a proliferation of nazirite vocations (people who took on ascetic purity practices, including drinking no wine, taking no haircuts, and avoiding contact with ritual impurity). Shimon released hundreds from this state by using rabbinic interpretations to dissolve their nazirite vows. He also led the fight against magic (witchcraft) as being based on a power incompatible with belief in a sovereign, monotheistic Deity.

Shimon is also credited with expanding Torah education for children.[23] Moreover, he made the rabbinic *ketubba* (marriage contract which guaranteed the wife financial security in case of divorce) economically viable by establishing that the money be put in escrow for the wife (if she died, her children and not their father would inherit). He also allowed the husband to use the money in business (the wife's assets were protected by a lien on all the husband's other resources).[24]

Cross-examine ... thoroughly

The Jerusalem Talmud tells that Shimon b. Shetaḥ's own son was executed due to false testimony.[25]

23. Y. Ketubbot 8:11.
24. Ketubbot 82b.
25. Y. Sanhedrin 6:3.

Mishna 10

שְׁמַעְיָה וְאַבְטַלְיוֹן קִבְּלוּ מֵהֶם. שְׁמַעְיָה אוֹמֵר: אֱהֹב אֶת הַמְּלָאכָה, וּשְׂנָא אֶת הָרַבָּנוּת, וְאַל תִּתְוַדַּע לָרָשׁוּת.

Shemaya and Avtalyon received the tradition from them. Shemaya says: Love work; hate authority [ruling over others]; do not draw the attention of the ruling power.

HISTORICAL BACKGROUND

Shemaya (*nasi*) and Avtalyon (*av beit din*) served during a stormy period of civil war over the succession in the Maccabean line (first half of the first century BCE). Unfortunately, the struggle ended with a Roman intervention and then a takeover, which left the country a protectorate of the empire.

Both men came from families of converts to Judaism, but they rose to leadership through their scholarship and teaching. One tradition traces their lineage back to Sennacherib, the Assyrian emperor who invaded the land of Judea and besieged Jerusalem.[26] That the two leading community positions were held by descendants of converts is a remarkable statement of the missionary impulse in first-century Judaism, and also of the democratization and expansion of learning in the population.

Love work

- Supporting oneself and one's family through honest labor is morally right as well as a source of dignity and independence.

26. Gittin 57b. On Sennacherib's siege, see the biblical account in II Kings, chs. 18–19.

While taking *tzedaka* is appropriate under certain circumstances, it is a form of dependency which reduces one's sense of self-worth.

- Support yourself rather than depend on charity to support your Torah study. The rabbinic ideal was to make a living from worldly work; their teaching of Torah was *pro bono*.
- Love honest work instead of gaining wealth through joining government circles and exploiting your power.
- "Whoever does not teach his son a craft [skilled, professional work] teaches him robbery."[27]
- "'The Lord your God will bless you in all the work of your hands which you do.'[28] If a person labors, [God] will bless; if [the person does] not work, then [God] will not bless."[29]

Hate authority [ruling over others]

The government of the Jewish community was corrupted by its dependency upon the Seleucid, and later, the Roman authorities. Leadership was frequently exercised by scoundrels who bought their power with bribes and sought to "earn" their bribe money back by arbitrary and exploitative rule. One may be tempted by the opportunity to make money or to advance socially by joining government circles – but the moral cost is likely to be high. The advice to hate ruling authority applies to arbitrary, unrepresentative, or tyrannical governments.

Do not draw the attention

- Corrupt ruling authorities pounce on people who appear to be successful, wealthy, etc.
- Do not seek closeness to corrupt ruling powers.

27. Kiddushin 29a.
28. Deuteronomy 16:24.
29. *Tanna DeVei Eliyahu* 14.

Mishna 11

אַבְטַלְיוֹן אוֹמֵר: חֲכָמִים הִזָּהֲרוּ
בְּדִבְרֵיכֶם, שֶׁמָּא תָחוֹבוּ חוֹבַת
גָּלוּת, וְתִגְלוּ לִמְקוֹם מַיִם
הָרָעִים, וְיִשְׁתּוּ הַתַּלְמִידִים
הַבָּאִים אַחֲרֵיכֶם וְיָמוּתוּ,
וְנִמְצָא שֵׁם שָׁמַיִם מִתְחַלֵּל.

Avtalyon says: Sages, be very careful in [choosing] your words. [If in your articulation you veer into heresy,] you may incur the penalty of exile and be sent away to a place of evil waters [heresy]. Then the disciples who follow after you will drink of these waters and die [a spiritual death]. The outcome will be that the name of Heaven will be profaned.

Sages, be very careful in [choosing] your words

This has become the proverbial talmudic dictum to think first and speak carefully, lest your words be distorted or repeated out of context. This is an especially wise directive nowadays, where slips of the tongue or spontaneous, foolish statements or misspeaking are blasted around the world via the internet.

The name of Heaven will be profaned

Human behavior that brings God or the Torah into disrepute is called desecration of the name of God. (For example, an outwardly devout person or a visibly religious representative who acts dishonorably or dishonestly.) This is considered a very serious, even unforgivable sin because it literally causes people to lose faith in God and religion.

Mishna 12

הִלֵּל וְשַׁמַּאי קִבְּלוּ מֵהֶם. הִלֵּל אוֹמֵר: הֱוֵי מִתַּלְמִידָיו שֶׁל אַהֲרֹן, אוֹהֵב שָׁלוֹם וְרוֹדֵף שָׁלוֹם, אוֹהֵב אֶת הַבְּרִיּוֹת וּמְקָרְבָן לַתּוֹרָה.

Hillel and Shammai received the tradition from them. Hillel says: Be of the disciples of Aaron [the High Priest], one who loves peace and pursues peace, loves all God's creatures, and brings them close to the Torah.

HISTORICAL BACKGROUND

Hillel (first century BCE to early first century CE) was born in Babylonia but came to Jerusalem to study with Shemaya and Avtalyon. He lived in absolute poverty, supporting himself as a woodcutter. One Friday, unable to pay the tuition, he was not admitted to the house of study. He climbed up to the roof and onto the skylight to listen to the Torah lessons. It snowed and Hillel was trapped and almost froze to death. Shabbat morning, the students detected Hillel's body blocking the skylight. They dug him out, warmed him up, and saved his life. Later he rose to become *nasi* due to the brilliance of his mind.

One year, the fourteenth of the Hebrew month of Nisan occurred on Shabbat. The question arose: "Does bringing the Paschal sacrifice override the Shabbat laws?" No one knew the answer. Hillel ruled that the sacrifice overrode the restrictions of Shabbat. According to the Babylonian Talmud, he used some of the thirteen methods of rabbinic analysis whereby laws are derived from the Torah in order to arrive at a ruling. This would imply that Hillel exercised creative leadership in expounding the Oral Law, and this constitutes his greatness.[30] By contrast, the Jerusalem Talmud insists that only when Hillel said that he heard this ruling from Shemaya and Avtalyon was his ruling accepted. This would imply that his greatness lay in being a master of tradition.

The Talmud does not give us Shammai's historical-biographical background, but it does compare the two men. Hillel is the creative originator who uses human intelligence and methods of literary analysis to apply Torah to new situations and to expand its capacity to deal with every possible challenge. For example, the development of commerce in Jewish society was blocked by the Torah law that all debts were wiped out in the sabbatical year. Hillel saw that people were no longer obeying the Torah's commandment to lend to the poor in order to avoid cancellation of the debt in the seventh year. Therefore, he established prosbol – a procedure whereby the loan could be turned over to the rabbinic court (whose debts were not nullified by the Torah in the sabbatical year). The loans were restored to the lender afterward. Thus halakhic creativity upheld the Torah law (to lend to the poor), while the halakha enabled and shaped a dynamic new economy.

For his part, Shammai upheld the inherited traditions and conserved laws handed down from time immemorial. As gatekeeper, he insisted that Torah should be taught only to individuals who were wise, modest, descendants of well-established families, and wealthy. (Another tradition reports: only to those of unimpeachable pedigree.) Hillel insisted that Torah should be taught to everyone, even people of questionable virtue. As he explained, there were many sinners in Israel who were brought closer through learning Torah, and from them emerged righteous people (*tzaddikim*), pious people (*ḥasidim*), and upright, unimpeachable people (*kasherim*).[31]

There was an important temperamental difference between the two scholars. Shammai was an elitist, and believed that people should be held to the highest standards. Some might be excluded, but to act otherwise would lead to dilution of standards, and people would not

30. Pesaḥim 66a.

31. *Avot DeRabbi Natan* 3.

elevate themselves to meet a challenge. Rather, they would "dumb down." Hillel was profoundly empathetic to people – and more modest. He urged that the Torah be offered democratically and in a user-friendly fashion. True, it would not take with everyone, but if it were offered to only a few, then even fewer people would take to it. Hillel was convinced that meeting people where they were, in a spirit of acceptance and warmth, would inspire greater efforts to rise to higher levels than would demanding superior standards in advance.

These respective approaches shaped the atmosphere of the schools that followed them. The Talmud explains why the school of Hillel was triumphant and why the tradition upholds its views over those of the school of Shammai. "They [the school of Hillel] were accommodating and humble, and they would review their own arguments and those of the school of Shammai [before deciding the law]. They even listened to the arguments of the school of Shammai before they reviewed their own arguments." [32]

Rabbi Benny Lau argues that there was also an important attitudinal difference between the two scholars and their respective adherents. Shammai and his school saw religious activity as sharply distinct from the secular and as oriented to its own standards. Hillel and his school saw holiness as possible – and desirable – in every setting, including secular activity. He and his disciples sought to bring out the sacred in daily life and mundane affairs.[33] A classic example is Hillel's comment that in going to the bathroom or taking a bath he was doing a mitzva, because preserving the body and keeping it clean honors God – for every human being is created in God's image.

Disciples of Aaron

Be a dedicated follower of Aaron the High Priest's example. In rabbinic tradition, Aaron is described as continually intervening to make peace between people. He interpreted other people's behavior in the best possible light. When people disagreed, he would mediate between the

32. Eruvin 13b.

33. Lau, *The Sages*, 203–219.

two sides, telling each party how much the other wanted to be reconciled with his adversary.

Loves peace and pursues peace

- You must love peace and desire it intensely. Otherwise, you will not generate the energy to challenge and tame the forces generating the conflict.
- Peace must be actively sought out. Words do not suffice. The obstacles and divisive factors must be assiduously and actively overcome.
- Do not stand by when people quarrel. Intervene and work with both sides to restore peace.

Loves all God's creatures

Hillel is referring primarily to people here. All human beings are equal in God's eyes. The Talmud describes how Hillel showed his love for people by exhibiting extraordinary patience even when people were tiresome and even when they imposed on him.[34]

Brings them close to the Torah

- One of the best ways to attract people to the tradition is for the person teaching and representing Torah to exude love for people, and through personal warmth draw people in.
- When people see that the teacher of Torah is a good and loving person, they assume that the Torah which shaped the teacher is good and loving. They then draw closer to the Torah out of a desire to be like him or her.

34. Shabbat 30b–31a.

Mishna 13

הוּא הָיָה אוֹמֵר: נְגַד שְׁמָא אֲבַד שְׁמֵהּ, וּדְלָא מוֹסִיף יְסוּף, וּדְלָא יָלֵף קְטָלָא חַיָּב, וּדְאִשְׁתַּמַּשׁ בְּתָגָא חֲלָף.

He would say: One who tries to inflate his reputation loses his reputation; who does not increase [his knowledge] decreases [it]; who does not study deserves to die; who exploits the crown [of Torah] shall perish.

Loses his reputation

Needy, exaggerated striving for recognition or making a great effort to impress people often leads to behaviors that evoke disrespect and dismissal from others.

Decreases [it]

If a person does not continually learn and grow, then he or she is declining both intellectually and with regard to understanding life.

Deserves to die

Torah is a source of life; the choice not to study constitutes a surrender of spiritual aspirations. The outcome will be to live an unexamined life, to dumb down, to decay spiritually. All of these are forms of death.

Exploits the crown [of Torah]

The behaviors listed in this mishna all have a paradoxical effect; they evoke an opposite reaction to the intention of the actor. In this case, instead of high achievement in Torah leading to increased respect and deeper life, the exploitation of high standing in Torah leads to loss of reputation and diminished life (i.e., "death") in status or in quality of life. Thus, he perishes.

Mishna 14

הוּא הָיָה אוֹמֵר: אִם אֵין אֲנִי לִי מִי לִי, וּכְשֶׁאֲנִי לְעַצְמִי מָה אֲנִי, וְאִם לֹא עַכְשָׁו אֵימָתָי.

He used to say: If I am not for myself, who will be for me? But when I am only for myself, what am I? And if not now, when?

If I am not for myself

It is legitimate and necessary to look out for one's own interest. Likewise, it is legitimate to give help first to one's own family and friends. The covenantal way respects the natural, human emotion of feeling the needs of one's family more intensely. It builds on this instinctive, moral sympathy and then channels those emotions outward so that all people will be brought within the universe of moral obligation. By contrast, ideologically driven, idealistic movements often disrespect these human tendencies and seek to override them in the name of a higher ideal. This masks a covert disrespect for human beings on the grounds that they do not measure up to the highest ideals.

World revolutionary movements such as Communism and Maoism attacked the family as "bourgeois" and as *a source of selfishness*. They succeeded only in weakening the natural bonds of love and affection for one's closest relatives. This degraded people's humanity and made them less humane to others as well. Starting with one's own interest and then reaching outward often leads to greater good than "idealistic" approaches that dismiss loyalty to oneself as selfish. Proof for this is that people working for themselves under capitalism out-produced and liberated more people from poverty than people working under communism, whose ideological goal was defined as ending poverty and providing economic equality for all.

When I am only for myself

Looking out *only* for oneself is selfish. Such behavior reduces both one's own standards of ethical behavior and his quality of life. Hillel affirms building on self-interest and family attachment while expanding the circle of responsibility and care to wider and wider circles. "Charity begins at home," but then it should extend outward. In sum, the key to moral behavior is balance: self-interest, yes; self-centeredness, no.

If not now, when?

- The time to act is now. Do not procrastinate; do not put off for tomorrow what you can do today.
- The Roman hedonists proclaimed: Eat, drink, and be merry, for tomorrow we die. The sages' counterpoint is: You only live once – so do a mitzva today.

Hillel is the only sage in this sequence from whom *four* sets of three wisdom sayings are quoted. Why is he featured so prominently? One possibility is that he became such a towering, central figure to the rabbinic tradition that he is given extraordinary prominence. Another is that since Hillel was the founding figure of the dynastic, patriarchal family, R. Yehuda the Prince, as editor of the Mishna and as scion of this family, chose this way to pay tribute to his great, great, great, great, great, great-grandfather.

Mishna 15

שַׁמַּאי אוֹמֵר: עֲשֵׂה תוֹרָתְךָ קֶבַע, אֱמֹר מְעַט וַעֲשֵׂה הַרְבֵּה, וֶהֱוֵי מְקַבֵּל אֶת כָּל הָאָדָם בְּסֵבֶר פָּנִים יָפוֹת.

Shammai says: Make your Torah [study] a regular habit; say little and do much; welcome every person with a smile.

Regular habit

Just as brushing one's teeth daily sustains the health of his teeth and daily exercise strengthens the heart, so does regular study add up to a knowledgeable person whose life is guided by Torah. Rabbi Israel Salanter once said: A Torah scholar (*talmid ḥakham*) is not one who studies everything, but one who studies every day. Torah study should be a way of life, not an occasional or erratic activity.

Say little and do much

A righteous person is modest in promises and pronouncements, but will over-deliver to the benefit of the other.

Welcome every person with a smile

When comparisons are made between Shammai and Hillel, Shammai is often portrayed as being stern, maybe even harsh. This is because of the talmudic stories about the three gentiles who approached these two sages expressing the wish to be converted to Judaism but asking for special arrangements. The first would-be convert asked that they teach him the whole Torah while standing on one foot (i.e., in a minute); the second one's condition was that he be required to accept only the Written Torah, not the Oral Tradition. The third stipulated that once converted, he be allowed to become the High Priest. Shammai drove all three out of his home because their requests were unreasonable and impossible to fulfill. Hillel, however, led each person to Judaism by accepting his stipulations, then educating him, without conditions. In the process of learning, they came to accept Judaism. They also realized that their demands were inappropriate or mistaken and gave them up gracefully.

Shammai's dictum in this mishna shows that he was not a harsh, unsympathetic person. Rather, he felt that diluting Judaism, or "bribing" individuals to win their allegiance, would cheapen the faith and lead to an unsuccessful conversion in the end. The Talmud sides with Hillel's approach to the outsiders. Unconditional acceptance won their trust. Once they engaged, they grew and advanced to the point where they gave up their immature expectations. Those who were turned away completely never learned what they had missed. Some who could have grown to the highest level of spirituality lost out completely. Still, this mishna shows that Hillel and Shammai differed in educational approaches, and not that one was a kind educator while the other was a harsh, unyielding teacher.

Mishna 16

רַבָּן גַּמְלִיאֵל אוֹמֵר: עֲשֵׂה לְךָ רַב, וְהִסְתַּלֵּק מִן הַסָּפֵק, וְאַל תַּרְבֶּה לְעַשֵּׂר אֻמָּדוֹת.

Rabban Gamliel says: Establish a teacher for yourself, and [thereby] depart from uncertainty and doubt; and do not repeatedly give tithes [based] on estimates.

HISTORICAL BACKGROUND

This mishna does not start with the phrase: Rabbi X received the tradition from Rabbi Y. The insertion of wisdom sayings from Rabban Gamliel in this mishna and from his son Shimon in the next two, followed by teachings from R. Yehuda the Prince (2:1) and his son, Rabban Gamliel III (2:2), constitute an interruption in the generational chain of transmission. Had the editor stuck to the generational sequence, the next sage quoted would have been Rabban Yoḥanan b. Zakkai. He played a central role in extricating the sages and their followers from Jerusalem in the final days of the Great Revolt, enabling them to rebuild their academy and Jewish life anew in Yavneh and the Galilee.

This insertion, or "interruption," most probably highlights the internal chain of transmission of the patriarchal family, i.e., Rabban Gamliel and his descendants, whose members constituted the top leadership of the rabbinic community for the next twelve generations. Throughout the period of the patriarchs, Rabban Gamliel's remarkable family united leadership in Torah scholarship and education with community responsibility (including representing Jewry to the Romans). Thus, this tribute of R. Yehuda the Prince would be a natural one for him and his circle to include here, as R. Yehuda was the fifth-generation patriarch. He achieved the highest level of Torah and communal leadership of everyone in the chain, an achievement that enabled him to edit the Mishna, and then to collect and create *Pirkei Avot.*

The fifth mishna of chapter 2 returns to Hillel and quotes more of his wisdom. It then resumes the chain of transmission, turning to Rabban Yoḥanan b. Zakkai, who received the tradition from Hillel and Shammai. It tells of Rabban Yoḥanan's five students, who played a key role in transplanting Torah and communal life after the Destruction of the Second Temple. Accordingly, Ethics of the Fathers brings wisdom from the patriarchate and the academics in each generation rather than from individual sages, as the former constitute the chain.

Rabban Gamliel was the grandson of Hillel. He is sometimes called Rabban Gamliel the Elder, because the name was used repeatedly in later generations of the family. Gamliel served as head of the Sanhedrin in the waning days of the Second Temple (first half of the first century CE). From his time on, the position of *nasi* (patriarch) became a dynastic one belonging to this family, descending from the house of Hillel. The Sanhedrin sat in the Temple itself at that time.

Rabban Gamliel exercised strong leadership despite the increasing civil unrest and clashes with the Romans. He strengthened the procedure of declaring the new month by the Sanhedrin, thus preserving an area of religious autonomy in the face of growing Roman control of national life. He also showed strong, courageous leadership in protecting women's dignity and rights. When there were situations where a husband's death could not be established by two witnesses (see Deut. 19:15), he ruled that one witness was sufficient, so that his wife would not be trapped for life and unable to remarry.[35] Similarly, he ruled that a husband could not write or cancel a *get* (bill of divorce) in the absence of his wife, in order to stop an abuse whereby husbands would cancel a *get* after writing it, leaving their wives chained to the marriage and/or delegitimizing their children from a later marriage which they had

35. Yevamot 122a.

innocently entered into, thinking that they had been freed by divorce from the first marriage.[36]

Establish a teacher

This duplicates the words of Yehoshua b. Peraḥya in mishna 6. Given the continuity of teacher and transmission of authority within the rabbinic establishment at that time, it may well be that Rabban Gamliel is simply repeating Yehoshua's principle as also being one of his core principles. Alternatively, as the translation suggests, Gamliel is calling attention to another advantage of establishing one primary teacher: to remove uncertainty and doubt about one's own judgment by depending on a superior, master teacher.

Note that Gamliel is the first scholar in this sequence who is called Rabban (a title applied to a kind of "super" rabbi). The initial scholars did not call themselves by the title Rabbi. The title emerged and was modified over the centuries. The sages of the Mishna, which is part of the Talmud and predates the Gemara, are called Rabbi (pronounced *Rabee*). The sages of the Gemara, the section of the Talmud which exposits and explores the implications of the Mishna, are called Rav. Both titles mean "master." There is no scholarly consensus as to whether the title refers to one's being a master of knowledge, of interpretation, or of exercising leadership in a fellowship or community.

36. Gittin 32a.

Mishna 17

שִׁמְעוֹן בְּנוֹ אוֹמֵר: כָּל יָמַי גָּדַלְתִּי בֵּין הַחֲכָמִים, וְלֹא מָצָאתִי לַגּוּף טוֹב מִשְּׁתִיקָה, וְלֹא הַמִּדְרָשׁ עִקָּר אֶלָּא הַמַּעֲשֶׂה, וְכָל הַמַּרְבֶּה דְבָרִים מֵבִיא חֵטְא.

Shimon, his son, says: All my life I have grown up surrounded by scholars and I have not found anything better for a person than silence; and study is not the most important [religious activity] but action is; and whoever talks too much brings about sin.

HISTORICAL BACKGROUND

Is this Shimon the Rabban Shimon b. Gamliel quoted in the next mishna? Then why are two different sets of three aphorisms given as the essential wisdom of this one person? And why is this mishna's Shimon (if he is the son of Gamliel) not given his title of Rabban? Every time the Talmud refers to Shimon b. Gamliel, it includes his title Rabban. One commentator suggests that Shimon had not yet been elected *nasi* when he stated this set of aphorisms, and thus the title Rabban was omitted. Other commentators suggest that this mishna's Shimon is not the son who succeeded Gamliel. Mishna 17 may represent a later editorial insertion.

I have not found anything better…than silence

- The best way to benefit from the company of scholars is to talk less or be silent completely.

- After watching all the scholars in his father's house, Shimon concluded that there were big talkers and there were big doers. The scholars who were more silent acted more worthily than those who spoke many words.
- Scholars talk a lot, but silence and action are more indicative of a good person.
- As long as you are talking, you cannot learn from others. To benefit from their wisdom you must be silent and listen to them. It should be noted that silence involves more than not speaking. Silence, as in meditation, expresses a decision to put aside the noise, tumult, and talking, and focus the mind. Silence allows one to become aware of what is going on inside. In order to see ourselves as we really are, we must make the shift from polished, public mode to inner, private mode. Such a silence yields insights and wisdom for life we otherwise would never obtain.

Study... action

Naturally, the sages advanced and praised the study of Torah. Still, they concluded that doing good, i.e., acting on the Torah's instructions, not studying about what to do, is the essence of Torah. Talk is cheap; action costs and counts.

Whoever talks too much brings about sin

The more you talk, the greater the likelihood of making a mistake or saying something that denigrates or hurts another. (Halakha particularly condemns gossip – speaking even truthful words that might derogate or put down another person.)

Maimonides tells of a wise man famous for his silence. When asked why he spoke so little, this righteous person answered that he had analyzed his speaking patterns and concluded that there were four categories of speech:

- Purely destructive – This category includes cursing others and filthy, degrading speech. Since there is no redeeming value in these words, one should remain silent.

- Mixed impact – For example, praising another person in front of his enemies or people jealous of that individual who will be roused by the praise to say (or do) negative counter-actions. The wise man concluded that it was better to be silent rather than to evoke antagonism against the one praised.
- Neutral – This is typical of ordinary social intercourse: descriptions of daily events or things which make matters no better and no worse. While it is permitted to say such words, since they do not really make much of a difference but only pass the time, the wise man concluded not to speak these words any more either.
- Constructive – This includes words that really have constructive effects such as good advice, directions for prayer, health, or medical treatment, teaching good values, etc. It is proper – a good deed – to speak such words.

This wise and righteous man had trained himself to assess all his words before speaking them to see if they truly fell into category 4. As a result, he found that he was speaking at least three-quarters less than in the past!

Inspired by this model, Maimonides analyzed the Torah's instructions for speaking and concluded that there were *five* categories of speech:

- Good – This is commanded speech or words that are a mitzva to say. For example, to teach and repeat Torah (as it says [Deut. 6:7]: "You shall speak of them [Torah teachings] to your children").
- Prohibited – This would be sinful speech such as lying, giving false testimony, talebearing, and gossip, all of which are expressly prohibited in the Torah.
- Low-level – These are words of no value to a person, although there is nothing improper about them either. This includes reporting daily happenings and news to no purpose. The sages call this "idle speech," since nothing bad is being said but no insight or wisdom for life is gained from speaking or hearing these words. Since it is "idle," it uses up one's life to no avail.

- "Beloved" – These are words of moral instruction: lessons on how to act properly and how to live a better life; theological instruction and philosophic understanding of experience; descriptions of good role models, which strengthen character and teach good character traits. Since these words are invaluable, Maimonides seeks to utter them and longs to hear them. He only warns that they should be compatible with one's actual behavior, so that one is not hypocritically saying one thing and doing another.
- Permitted – These are words useful in pursuing a profession and livelihood, in guiding social etiquette, in accessing need-to-know information. While it is permitted to speak these useful words, it is no mitzva. This is the category where one should speak less, in accordance with the principle: "I have not found anything better for a person than silence."

Mishna 18

רַבָּן שִׁמְעוֹן בֶּן גַּמְלִיאֵל אוֹמֵר: עַל שְׁלֹשָׁה דְבָרִים הָעוֹלָם קַיָּם, עַל הַדִּין, וְעַל הָאֱמֶת, וְעַל הַשָּׁלוֹם. שֶׁנֶּאֱמַר: אֱמֶת וּמִשְׁפַּט שָׁלוֹם שִׁפְטוּ בְּשַׁעֲרֵיכֶם.

Rabban Shimon b. Gamliel says: The world is sustained on three principles: on truth, and on law [justice], and on peace, as it says: "Render truth, justice, and peace in your gates."[37]

HISTORICAL BACKGROUND

Rabban Shimon b. Gamliel became head of the Sanhedrin after his father, and served during the period of the revolt against Rome and the subsequent Destruction of Jerusalem and the Temple (first century CE). He seems to have been a vigorous champion of the Jewish community: Josephus describes him as "full of understanding and the spirit of wisdom," who in his sagacity managed to keep societal life going in the face of difficult circumstances. The Talmud tells of one of his interventions. In order to bring down the extortionate price of sacrificial animals, Rabban Shimon suspended the Torah's requirement that every woman who gives birth (or is purified from ritual impurity) needs to bring a sacrifice. Apparently, in the course of the revolt against Rome, he was killed. Midrash Eleh Ezkera lists him as one of the ten great rabbinic martyrs of the later Hadrianic persecutions.

37. Zechariah 8:16.

Three principles

Compare the three principles on which the world stands which are suggested above, in mishna 2, by Shimon the Righteous. Perhaps there, Shimon the Righteous is talking about the metaphysical world, stressing divine worship in order to include our relationship with God, whereas here, Shimon b. Gamliel is focused on the actions needed for proper conduct of human society. That having been said, the Talmud (Shabbat 55a) nevertheless states that "truth is God's seal [or stamp]." The Talmud further states that God wants us to speak truth even to Him, and that it is appropriate to challenge Him when evil rules the world or the People of Israel is suffering, rather than to say pious words as if nothing were wrong.[38]

Robert Cover interprets Rabban Shimon's words: The world is *sustained*, meaning it continues to exist, being upheld by the operation of these three principles. Drawing on an interpretation by Rabbi Joseph Karo, he suggests that the pillars articulated by Shimon the Righteous (Torah, divine service, and acts of loving-kindness) are the building blocks in the creation of a society. Rabban Shimon's three principles (truth, law, peace) were central to the preservation of the post-Destruction Jewish community. The values paramount to building a new world are different from those of ensuring the continuity of an ongoing communal life.[39]

Truth…justice…peace

Truth is not always identical to justice, and it is often incompatible with peace. Think of the daily white lies and unspoken criticism which protect peace in the family or the workplace. The ideal society will reconcile all three principles. For the sake of peace one may yield some aspect of justice or, for the sake of justice one may override some aspect of peace. The key to a just and harmonious society lies in balance and limits. If an individual or group pursues one principle to the exclusion of the others, then there will be serious trouble. "Peace above all" leads

38. Yoma 69b.
39. Robert Cover, "Nomos and Narrative," *Harvard Law Review* 99 (1983): 4–68, cited in Jacob Milgrom, *Leviticus* (New York: Anchor Bible, 2013), 2103.

to appeasement and the loss of peace. Justice, when pursued relentlessly, while sweeping aside compromise or the established interests of others, may well lead to conflict, tyranny, or worse. The wisdom of democracy is that it distributes power and puts limits on the pursuit of any one of these principles.

Chapter 2

The main focus of chapter 2 is Rabban Yoḥanan b. Zakkai and his five disciples. Rabban Yoḥanan rose to greatness by making the decision to leave Jerusalem before it fell to the Roman siege in the year 70 CE. By then, the Zealot rebels had decided to go down fighting the Romans to the bitter end – and to take everybody else with them. Rabban Yoḥanan grasped that responsibility for transmission meant that the leadership must assure that the people and the government would not go down with the ship, but would live on to continue the next leg of the covenantal journey. He had himself smuggled out of the locked and gated walls of Jerusalem, then contacted the Romans. In exchange for assurances that his community would accept Roman rule and live in peace with them, he was granted the right to establish a new community away from Jerusalem under Rome's protection. This move – taken at great personal risk – enabled him to lead the renewal of Jewish life around the rabbinic academy in the settlement of Yavneh and the new institutions established there. The fifth, sixth, and seventh mishnas in this chapter return to the teachings of Hillel, apparently in order to show that there was a direct transmission from the great sages of the pre-Destruction period to the great sages of the post-Destruction period. One of the extraordinary accomplishments of the sages is that they overcame the rupture and the great discontinuities of the period – even as they wove a seamless web of continuity between the biblical and the rabbinic heritage.

Mishna 1

רַבִּי אוֹמֵר: אֵיזוֹ הִיא דֶרֶךְ
יְשָׁרָה שֶׁיָּבֹר לוֹ הָאָדָם,
כָּל שֶׁהִיא תִפְאֶרֶת לְעֹשֶׂיהָ
וְתִפְאֶרֶת לוֹ מִן הָאָדָם.
וֶהֱוֵי זָהִיר בְּמִצְוָה קַלָּה
כְּבַחֲמוּרָה, שֶׁאֵין אַתָּה
יוֹדֵעַ מַתַּן שְׂכָרָן שֶׁל מִצְוֹת.
וֶהֱוֵי מְחַשֵּׁב הֶפְסֵד מִצְוָה
כְּנֶגֶד שְׂכָרָהּ, וּשְׂכַר עֲבֵרָה
כְּנֶגֶד הֶפְסֵדָהּ. הִסְתַּכֵּל
בִּשְׁלֹשָׁה דְבָרִים, וְאֵין אַתָּה
בָא לִידֵי עֲבֵרָה. דַּע מַה
לְּמַעְלָה מִמְּךָ, עַיִן רוֹאָה,
וְאֹזֶן שׁוֹמַעַת, וְכָל מַעֲשֶׂיךָ
בַּסֵּפֶר נִכְתָּבִים.

Rabbi [R. Yehuda the Prince] says: What is the righteous path that a person should choose for himself? One which honors the person doing [the action] and which other people honor. Be as careful to do a minor mitzva as a major mitzva, for you do not know what is the actual reward for individual mitzvot. Always weigh the cost of doing a mitzva against its reward, and the gain in doing a sin against the loss. Look carefully at three factors, and you will never come to commit a sin. Know what is above you: a seeing eye, a listening ear, and [that] all your actions are written down [in a heavenly book].

HISTORICAL BACKGROUND

R. Yehuda the Prince (135–220 CE) was one of the greatest figures in a family which led the Jewish community for well over a century. He was the fifth generation in the family descended from Hillel, and the firstborn son of the *nasi* Rabban Shimon b. Gamliel II. R. Yehuda was one of the towering figures of the Talmud. His combination of scholarship, wealth, and political leadership was so awesome that the Talmud says that he was an icon of "Torah and greatness in one place."

He lived in Beit She'arim in the Galilee and set up a great rabbinical academy there. In time, the Sanhedrin moved its seat there. In the last twenty-five years of his life, his health waned and he moved to Tzipori in the Galilee, where the mountain air was clearer and medically prescribed for his health.

A great scholar, R. Yehuda went from school to school in order to study with the five last great students of R. Akiva, who laid down the primary structures of the Talmud. He credited R. Yaakov b. Korshai, a close associate of his father, as being his primary teacher in giving over to him the scope and significance of the Mishna and the *Baraita* (collected teachings left out of the Mishna). These teachings were still in oral form at the time. His scholarship and his status and power as the *nasi* equipped him to spearhead the project of editing and publishing, i.e., writing down, the Mishna. The respite from Roman persecution under Emperor Antoninus Pius also was helpful to his work.

While he cultivated good relations with the Roman authorities, R. Yehuda faced a looming deterioration of conditions in the Land of Israel and determined to write down and edit the teachings of the *Tanna'im* (mishnaic scholars) who preceded him. This collection became the Mishna, the core portion of the Talmud. He gathered the leading scholars for this project. Together they reviewed all the traditions, came to conclusions, excluded some material, and thus organized and published the Six Orders of the Mishna. The Mishna consists almost entirely of legal rulings without explanatory justifications or narratives.

Out of his educational vision and his conviction that the masses must be reached and inculcated with the values of the rabbinic tradition and with role models, R. Yehuda also worked on editing this special book of wisdom sayings, Ethics of the Fathers – although the work continued into the next generation. R. Yehuda treasured the Hebrew language, and insisted on speaking it in his home. The Talmud says that the maids in his house spoke such a beautiful Hebrew that various scholars came to ask them the meaning of certain rare Hebrew words.[1] R. Yehuda's commitment to Hebrew may explain the pure and fluent Hebrew of the Mishna

1. Megilla 18a.

as compared to the heavily Aramaic discourse which fills the Gemara (and which reflects the spoken language of the people at the time). The quality Hebrew in *Pirkei Avot* also associates it with the classic tradition of the Torah of Moses. By implication, it attributes status to *Pirkei Avot* and the Mishna as an authentic continuation of the biblical tradition.

R. Yehuda's achievements were so legendary that he was referred to as "Rabbi," i.e., *the* Rabbi. When the title Rabbi is used in the Mishna without further specification, that is, without a specific name, it always refers to R. Yehuda the Prince.

Righteous path

Note that Rabbi speaks of a path through life. The halakha (lit., walking) is more than a legal system. It is a way of life, guiding the individual through its twists and turns and guiding the Jews through their historical journey. Rabbi believes that concern for others' approval and awareness that God is watching works as well as or better than great piety or internalized values in assuring proper behavior.

Honors the person ... people honor

- The way you live should be respected by other people as well as by you. Appearances *are* important.
- In choosing how to walk on your life's path, be sensitive to and interested in others' judgment and not just listen to yourself. Perhaps this openness to others led R. Yehuda to one of his greatest insights: "I learned a lot from my rabbis, even more from my colleagues, and most of all, from my students."[2]
- Maimonides suggests that his "middle way" (what Aristotle calls the Golden Mean), which he recommends for developing the trait of moderation in all matters, e.g., to be neither too selfish nor too selfless, meets R. Yehuda's standard. In the *Mishneh Torah,* Maimonides writes: "One should not be an angry person with a short fuse, nor like [an emotionally] dead person who does not [allow himself to] feel, but [he should develop] a moderate

2. Makkot 10a.

> temperament." Another aphorism: "Do not be constantly in a state of hilarity and play, nor in sadness and mourning, but be quietly happy every day with a pleasant demeanor to all."[3] He writes that this middle way also fulfills the commandment, "You shall walk in [God's] ways."[4]

Be as careful to do a minor mitzva as a major mitzva

"Minor" good deeds may have enormous impact. One example: helping people before they fall into poverty or serious difficulty by lending them money or finding them a job.

Weigh the cost... against its reward

Instant gratification is not the right guide to a good life.

Look... at three factors and you will never... sin

Belief in a personal God who monitors all behavior will keep you from wrong actions.

---

3. *Mishneh Torah, Hilkhot De'ot* 1:4.
4. Deuteronomy 28:9.

Mishna 2

רַבָּן גַּמְלִיאֵל בְּנוֹ שֶׁל רַבִּי יְהוּדָה הַנָּשִׂיא אוֹמֵר: יָפֶה תַּלְמוּד תּוֹרָה עִם דֶּרֶךְ אֶרֶץ, שֶׁיְּגִיעַת שְׁנֵיהֶם מְשַׁכַּחַת עָוֹן. וְכָל תּוֹרָה שֶׁאֵין עִמָּהּ מְלָאכָה, סוֹפָהּ בְּטֵלָה וְגוֹרֶרֶת עָוֹן. וְכָל הָעוֹסְקִים עִם הַצִּבּוּר, יִהְיוּ עוֹסְקִים עִמָּהֶם לְשֵׁם שָׁמַיִם, שֶׁזְּכוּת אֲבוֹתָם מְסַיַּעְתָּם, וְצִדְקָתָם עוֹמֶדֶת לָעַד. וְאַתֶּם, מַעֲלֶה אֲנִי עֲלֵיכֶם שָׂכָר הַרְבֵּה כְּאִלּוּ עֲשִׂיתֶם.

Rabban Gamliel b. R. Yehuda the Prince says: It is good to combine Torah study with worldly occupation, for the effort needed to do both will drive out all thought of doing evil; all Torah study which is not connected with work will eventually be null and void and will bring sin in its wake; and those who work for the community should do so for the sake of Heaven, for the merit of their ancestors will sustain them and their righteousness will endure forever. [If you act that way, God says:] I credit you with great reward [and even your good intentions are counted] as if you accomplished them.

HISTORICAL BACKGROUND

This Gamliel (third century CE) was the third *nasi* named Gamliel in the family dynasty. He was a transitional figure in that his title was Rabbi and he is one of the last of the *Tanna'im*, the scholars of the Mishna. He learned Torah and engaged with the first generation of the *Amora'im*, the expositors of the Gemara who carried the title Rav. Apparently, he served as *nasi* for only a short period, and little of his teaching was handed down in the Talmud.

Combine Torah study with worldly occupation

Over the centuries, there has been conflict over the relationship between studying Torah and earning a livelihood. Full-time study (with communal support covering living expenses) would enable more concentration and more achievement in scholarship. However, most sages insisted that having work or a profession shapes a more moral, less self-interested scholar or a more spiritually independent sage. At the least, the effort exerted to master both scholarship and a profession will reduce idle time and the energy and opportunity available to be tempted into bad behavior.

Among talmudic sages, we are told that Hillel was a woodchopper and Shammai a construction worker. Other professions of sages included tailors, carpenters, blacksmiths, well-diggers, surveyors, and beer and whiskey distillers. In the Middle Ages, Maimonides famously worked as a doctor at the court of the sultan of Egypt. He had to give religious guidance and write books late at night, when he was exhausted. Nevertheless, he persisted in the work and strongly upheld the ruling that sages and teachers should support themselves with their own labor.

Torah study...not connected with work

Down the ages, the sages have come only reluctantly to permit scholars to be paid for teaching so they can live honorably. They feared that individual scholars who did not work and support themselves would be tempted to take charity. Or they might be corrupted by being supported and would not appreciate the effort and struggle needed to make a living. Therefore, they might apply the Torah wrongly or fail to understand and support laypeople's needs.

In modern times, especially in the State of Israel, a countercultural tradition of public support for full-time Torah students was developed. The outcome is that in our day and age, sixty percent of all *ḥaredi* adult males in Israel are full-time students of Torah, substantially supported by government stipends. This led to a backlash on the part of the general public, which felt that this was a burden that the economy could not carry. The future is uncertain, but some degree of return to Torah study with worldly occupation seems unavoidable.

For the sake of Heaven

Communal leadership and service done for noble motives rather than for selfish interest is of the highest order and dignity in God's eyes.

Note that these statements were made by a descendant of a family that had led the community for generations and supported itself along the way.

Mishna 3

הֱווּ זְהִירִין בָּרָשׁוּת,
שֶׁאֵין מְקָרְבִין לוֹ לָאָדָם
אֶלָּא לְצֹרֶךְ עַצְמָן. נִרְאִין
כְּאוֹהֲבִין בִּשְׁעַת הֲנָאָתָן,
וְאֵין עוֹמְדִין לוֹ לְאָדָם
בִּשְׁעַת דָּחֳקוֹ.

Be very careful of the governing people [the Romans]. They befriend a person only for their own interests. They appear to be loving friends when they are benefiting from a person, but they do not stand by a person when he is struggling.

Be very careful

Rabban Gamliel saw the exploitative and erratic behavior of the Roman authorities and their collaborators up close.

Mishna 4

הוּא הָיָה אוֹמֵר: עֲשֵׂה רְצוֹנוֹ כִּרְצוֹנְךָ, כְּדֵי שֶׁיַּעֲשֶׂה רְצוֹנְךָ כִּרְצוֹנוֹ. בַּטֵּל רְצוֹנְךָ מִפְּנֵי רְצוֹנוֹ, כְּדֵי שֶׁיְּבַטֵּל רְצוֹן אֲחֵרִים מִפְּנֵי רְצוֹנֶךָ.

He used to say: Make [God's] will as your will so that [God] may make your will as His will; nullify your own will for the sake of [God's] will so [that God] will nullify others' will in favor of your will.

God's will...your will

In Rabban Gamliel III's view, overriding personal desires and preferences for the sake of God will be reciprocated by God, who will move the divine will (and that of other people) to identify with yours. Note that making God's will one's own is a call to piety but not to fatalism, in which one accepts whatever happens and whatever state he is born into as definitive. Fate is to be acquiesced to, not resisted. But here the individual tries to "move" God to reciprocally accept his desires, dreams, and ambitions.

Having quoted wisdom from the final two generations of *Tannai'm* in the Mishna, *Pirkei Avot* returns to Rabban Yoḥanan b. Zakkai, the great leader whose vision and understanding enabled the building of rabbinic culture after the Destruction. However, apparently in order to further buttress the authority of Rabban Yoḥanan and his disciples, the chapter first cites the wisdom of Hillel, the greatest of the pre-Destruction generation. Rabban Yoḥanan b. Zakkai was the disciple of Hillel.

Mishna 5

הִלֵּל אוֹמֵר: אַל תִּפְרֹשׁ מִן הַצִּבּוּר, וְאַל תַּאֲמִין בְּעַצְמְךָ עַד יוֹם מוֹתְךָ, וְאַל תָּדִין אֶת חֲבֵרְךָ עַד שֶׁתַּגִּיעַ לִמְקוֹמוֹ. וְאַל תֹּאמַר דָּבָר שֶׁאִי אֶפְשָׁר לִשְׁמֹעַ, שֶׁסּוֹפוֹ לְהִשָּׁמַע. וְאַל תֹּאמַר לִכְשֶׁאֶפָּנֶה אֶשְׁנֶה, שֶׁמָּא לֹא תִפָּנֶה.

Hillel says: Do not separate from the community; do not be certain of yourself until the day you die; do not judge your fellow human being until you get to the same place he is in. Do not say a teaching that is impossible to understand [on the theory] that it will eventually be understood. Do not say: When I free myself up, I will study, for you may never free yourself up.

Do not separate from the community

- Being part of a community is essential for a proper and healthy life. If one becomes so self-centered as to cut loose from community in order to live only for himself, quality of life will be lost. Our very humanness shrinks when we lose our connections to a group beyond ourselves.
- If one separates even for the purpose of achieving a higher level of piety and righteousness, his judgment will become skewed and his values distorted.
- The challenge is not just to have good ideas or values, but to make them work in the life of an actual community.

Do not be certain of yourself until the day you die

People are dynamic; they can change until the last day of their lives. Furthermore, the individual is seething with impulses and feelings, both conscious and unconscious. Therefore, not until a person dies can we be certain that we have defined him correctly (even if that person is ourselves). Sometimes people turn to the good; sometimes they reverse direction toward evil in the most unexpected ways. It is wise, then, not to be complacent or convinced of one's own rectitude. It is best to view oneself and others tentatively. See everyone as open and still evolving; help them grow in the right direction.

Do not judge your fellow human being

- Only when you empathetically feel and experience the other person's life situation, needs, and conflicts will you be able to judge properly and sensitively.
- Because we are inside our own skin we tend to understand our conflicts and give ourselves the benefit of the doubt. We easily forgive our own sins. We should learn to do this for everyone.
- Do not be judgmental and do not rush to judgment. Try to enter into the other person's life situation and conflicts before passing judgment on that individual. Of course, this principle can be abused if it is pushed to the point at which to understand everything is to forgive everything. After empathy, after justifying, after being sensitive, one must make judgments. One must be able to call out evil as evil, and to uphold good as good. We are not to be paralyzed by empathy or lose our ability to discern the difference between good and evil.

Do not say a teaching that is impossible to understand

- The inability to articulate or clearly explain a teaching is frequently a sign of fuzziness in thinking or a lack of ripeness of a thought due to the failure to analyze it sufficiently.
- Do not excuse lazy thinking by reassuring yourself that eventually people will catch up with and understand your wisdom.

(The lack of clarity described here is not to be confused with one's being radically ahead of his time or with a situation where one has a truly original thought that others resist trying to understand. Do not surrender insight or creativity because the public is thinking conventionally.)

- Brilliant, original, and complex ideas can be stated with clarity, precision, and focus so that people will understand them.

When I free myself up, I will study

We often procrastinate instead of studying; or we fail to stand up for an unpopular cause, arguing that it's not the right time or that we are too busy to act. The time to study, the time to act morally, is *now*. A good decision may be hard to make, but once you make it you will know that it was right. Put off study, put off moral action, and the next thing you know, other issues crop up to make the next moment also an inopportune time to act. In the end, out of failure of will or lack of nerve, people often miss the opportunity to learn or to do the right thing. But once you study or act, you will discover that now was the right time to engage after all.

Rabbi Israel Salanter was once asked: If I have only one hour in the day to study, should I study Talmud or should I study *musar* (ethical, self-reflective, aspirational literature)? He answered: Study *musar*, because it will inspire you to find a second hour to study Talmud.

הוּא הָיָה אוֹמֵר: אֵין בּוּר יְרֵא חֵטְא, וְלֹא עַם הָאָרֶץ חָסִיד, וְלֹא הַבַּיְשָׁן לָמֵד, וְלֹא הַקַּפְּדָן מְלַמֵּד, וְלֹא כָל הַמַּרְבֶּה בִסְחוֹרָה מַחְכִּים. וּבְמָקוֹם שֶׁאֵין אֲנָשִׁים, הִשְׁתַּדֵּל לִהְיוֹת אִישׁ.

He used to say: An uncultured person cannot be truly sin-fearing; and an ignorant person cannot be truly pious; and a bashful person cannot become truly learned; and a short-tempered person cannot be a [good] teacher; nor do all who spend much time in pursuing their business become wise. And in a place where there are no men, try to be a man [i.e., a *mentsch*].

An uncultured person cannot be truly sin-fearing

If you are boorish and crude, you will not realize how roughly you are treating people, and you cannot truly fear sin or avoid acting inappropriately.

An ignorant person cannot be truly pious

If you are unlearned, you will know only the externals of the commandments or the legalities of ethical obligations, and thus will likely apply the principles formally but miss their essence. To be truly pious, you must be informed, analytical, and able to apply guidelines to real-life situations intelligently.

A bashful person cannot become truly learned

If you are afraid (or too shy) to ask questions, you will never be able to learn.

A short-tempered person cannot be a [good] teacher

- A student needs room to make mistakes and learn from them. If you are impatient and quick to anger, you will intimidate or cut off your students.
- A good teacher must evoke response and participation from his students, for that is how they grow the most. A good teacher enables students. When a student pauses, it takes enormous patience and self-restraint not to jump in at once with your superior knowledge. If you do not restrain your ego, you will constantly show off and dazzle students, but that reduces rather than elevates them.

Nor do all who spend…time in…business…become wise

People who spend all their time making a living, having no time to study, learn, reflect, or listen, will not likely attain wisdom.

In a place where there are no men

One must rise to the occasion and not be a conformist, especially when a situation cries out for leadership. It is especially urgent to step up in a moral crisis situation when no one is standing up for what is right. Take responsibility. Do not say: I am not worthy; who am I? Let some great person take the lead. Step in where there is a vacuum of leadership. That is the path of true greatness.

Mishna 6

אַף הוּא רָאָה גֻּלְגֹּלֶת אַחַת שֶׁצָּפָה עַל פְּנֵי הַמָּיִם. אָמַר לָהּ: עַל דַּאֲטֵפְתְּ אַטְפוּךְ, וְסוֹף מְטִיפַיִךְ יְטוּפוּן.	He saw a skull floating on the surface of the water. He said: Because you drowned [others,] you were drowned. And in the end, those who drowned you shall be drowned.

A skull floating

Apparently, this was a victim of violence. Perhaps Hillel recognized the face as either someone he knew or as a robber or murderer. He articulated that the murdered person had committed crimes, and these criminal acts had now been done to him. He added that the cycle of violence feeds on itself, and that the second criminal, having murdered, would be murdered in turn. Those that live by the sword shall perish by the sword.

Mishna 7

הוּא הָיָה אוֹמֵר: מַרְבֶּה בָשָׂר, מַרְבֶּה רִמָּה. מַרְבֶּה נְכָסִים, מַרְבֶּה דְאָגָה. מַרְבֶּה נָשִׁים, מַרְבֶּה כְשָׁפִים. מַרְבֶּה שְׁפָחוֹת, מַרְבֶּה זִמָּה. מַרְבֶּה עֲבָדִים, מַרְבֶּה גָזֵל. מַרְבֶּה תוֹרָה, מַרְבֶּה חַיִּים. מַרְבֶּה יְשִׁיבָה, מַרְבֶּה חָכְמָה. מַרְבֶּה עֵצָה, מַרְבֶּה תְבוּנָה. מַרְבֶּה צְדָקָה, מַרְבֶּה שָׁלוֹם. קָנָה שֵׁם טוֹב, קָנָה לְעַצְמוֹ. קָנָה לוֹ דִבְרֵי תוֹרָה, קָנָה לוֹ חַיֵּי הָעוֹלָם הַבָּא.

He used to say: The more flesh [weight], the more worms; the more wealth, the more worry; the more wives, the more witchcraft; the more maidservants, the more lewdness; the more menservants, the more thievery. [However,] the more Torah, the more life; the more sitting and studying, the more wisdom; the more counsel, the more understanding; the more *tzedaka*, the more peace. If he acquired a good reputation, he has acquired something for himself. If he acquired words of Torah, he has acquired life in the World to Come [i.e., eternal life].

More flesh … more worry … more Torah … more peace

Many of the pleasures and successes of this world bring with them side effects, i.e., increased problems: Excessive weight only feeds more worms after death; more maidservants only increases temptations to sexual corruption, etc. However, acquiring Torah brings with it a healthier and more blessed lifestyle, leading to a longer and richer life. Charity brings peace to society and fulfillment to oneself.

A good reputation ... the World to Come

A good name gives a person greater importance in his limited lifetime. Acquiring words and values of Torah brings with it an eternity of goodness and bliss.

Mishna 8

רַבָּן יוֹחָנָן בֶּן זַכַּאי קִבֵּל
מֵהִלֵּל וּמִשַּׁמַּאי. הוּא הָיָה
אוֹמֵר: אִם לָמַדְתָּ תּוֹרָה
הַרְבֵּה, אַל תַּחֲזִיק טוֹבָה
לְעַצְמְךָ, כִּי לְכָךְ נוֹצָרְתָּ.

Rabban Yoḥanan b. Zakkai received the tradition from Hillel and Shammai. He used to say: If you have learned a lot of Torah, do not give yourself so much credit for good, for this is the purpose for which you were created.

HISTORICAL BACKGROUND

Rabban Yoḥanan b. Zakkai (first century CE) was the seminal figure who assured the continuity of Judaism through and beyond the Destruction of the Second Temple. He took the decisive step of acknowledging that Jerusalem and the Temple could not be saved. He saw that the military leader of the rebellion knew that the cause was lost but was afraid to defy his activists and sue for peace. At the risk of his life, Rabban Yoḥanan had himself evacuated with his students from the Holy City to the settlement of Yavneh. There he established a rabbinic academy. He grasped that Judaism could survive the loss of the Temple with its direct access to God by shifting to "rabbinic mode," i.e., by relating to God through learning Torah instead of receiving "heavenly instructions," through communing with God through prayer in place of sacrifices, and through focusing on good deeds as a way to serve God and fellow human beings. Rabban Yoḥanan went on to lead the forging of a post-Destruction life of ongoing performance of mitzvot and commemoration of the lost rituals. He also raised up a group of disciples who became the rebuilders of Jewish faith and life.

Rabban

A special title for a great rabbi; the equivalent of "teacher-rabbi of the generation" or "a teacher's teacher." Until Rabban Yoḥanan, this title was reserved for the *nasi*, the head of the community from the descendants of Hillel. Rabban Yoḥanan was the only other person given this honorific title. It is a tribute to the central role he played in saving the Torah scholars from being trapped in the Destruction of Jerusalem in 70 CE and in creating the new Torah center in Yavneh which assured the continuity of Judaism.

Received the tradition from Hillel and Shammai

Despite the enormous disruptions and discontinuities in Jewish religion and life induced by the Destruction of the Second Temple and subsequent exile, there still existed a profound continuity and an unbroken covenantal chain. This is expressed in Rabban Yoḥanan's having received his Torah as well as the tradition directly from the rabbinic greats of the pre-Destruction period, Hillel and Shammai.

It says in the Talmud that Yoḥanan b. Zakkai was the least of Hillel's students.[5] On the one hand, this glorifies the earlier generation and age, "the good old days." On the other hand, the statement implies that a person can rise to greatness even if he is the "least" of the scholars. The lesson of Rabban Yoḥanan's life is that no one should say, "I am too small for the job." Step up and take responsibility for the situation, and you can grow and become great.

If you have learned a lot of Torah

Rabban Yoḥanan underscores the central importance of Torah study in the new, post-Destruction world by suggesting that one should never be self-congratulatory for learning a lot of Torah. Torah study is the purpose for which humans were created. Scholarship is a calling and understanding is a gift; both are earned by hard work and total application. One's ego should not swell for accomplishing what God wants.

5. Sukka 28a.

חֲמִשָּׁה תַלְמִידִים הָיוּ לְרַבָּן יוֹחָנָן בֶּן זַכַּאי. וְאֵלּוּ הֵן: רַבִּי אֱלִיעֶזֶר בֶּן הוֹרְקָנוֹס, רַבִּי יְהוֹשֻׁעַ בֶּן חֲנַנְיָה, רַבִּי יוֹסֵי הַכֹּהֵן, רַבִּי שִׁמְעוֹן בֶּן נְתַנְאֵל, רַבִּי אֶלְעָזָר בֶּן עֲרָךְ.

Rabban Yoḥanan b. Zakkai had five [primary] disciples. These are their names: R. Eliezer b. Hyrcanus, R. Yehoshua b. Ḥanania, R. Yosei the Priest, R. Shimon b. Netanel, R. Elazar b. Arakh.

Five [primary] disciples

They led in the academy at Yavneh, they spread Rabban Yoḥanan's Torah, they established Jewish religious life, and expanded the study of Torah, thus leading in the rebuilding after the great catastrophe.

הוּא הָיָה מוֹנֶה שִׁבְחָם: אֱלִיעֶזֶר בֶּן הוֹרְקָנוֹס, בּוֹר סוּד שֶׁאֵינוֹ מְאַבֵּד טִפָּה. יְהוֹשֻׁעַ בֶּן חֲנַנְיָה, אַשְׁרֵי יוֹלַדְתּוֹ. יוֹסֵי הַכֹּהֵן, חָסִיד. שִׁמְעוֹן בֶּן נְתַנְאֵל, יְרֵא חֵטְא. אֶלְעָזָר בֶּן עֲרָךְ, כְּמַעְיָן הַמִּתְגַּבֵּר.

He would recount their praises: R. Eliezer b. Hyrcanus is like a plastered cistern that does not leak a single drop of water. R. Yehoshua b. Ḥanania – blessed is the mother who gave birth to him. R. Yosei the Priest is a *ḥasid* [pious man]. R. Shimon b. Netanel is a sin-fearing man. R. Elazar b. Arakh is like an overflowing spring of water.

That does not leak

R. Eliezer combined industrious study with total recall, so he never lost a drop of the wisdom that he received from his teachers. R. Eliezer said of himself that he never spoke a word of Torah that he had not heard from his teachers. This suggests that his greatness was in preserving the traditions of the past and preventing their loss during a period of extraordinary turmoil and destruction.

Blessed is the mother

R. Yehoshua's behavior was so pleasant that people blessed his mother for raising such a person. The Talmud tells that his mother visited scholars in the study halls when she was pregnant with him, seeking blessings from the sages there. After he was born, she kept his crib in the study halls so he would absorb the sounds and wisdom of Torah study from the time he was an infant. Rabban Yoḥanan gives his mother the credit for nurturing R. Yehoshua to become a great scholar.

Ḥasid

A title which has been repeatedly reborn over the course of Jewish history. *Ḥasid* implies intense piety, a combination of fervor and devotion to God, even unto death.

An overflowing spring

While R. Eliezer b. Hyrcanus was honored for preserving everything he was taught, R. Elazar b. Arakh had a creative mind. He is celebrated for creating new insights and expanding the content and reach of Torah. In a generation of such upheaval and change, standing pat (not to mention intellectual rigidity) could not be sustained.

הוּא הָיָה אוֹמֵר: אִם יִהְיוּ כָּל
חַכְמֵי יִשְׂרָאֵל בְּכַף מֹאזְנַיִם,
וֶאֱלִיעֶזֶר בֶּן הוֹרְקָנוֹס בְּכַף
שְׁנִיָּה, מַכְרִיעַ אֶת כֻּלָּם.
אַבָּא שָׁאוּל אוֹמֵר מִשְּׁמוֹ:
אִם יִהְיוּ כָּל חַכְמֵי יִשְׂרָאֵל
בְּכַף מֹאזְנַיִם, וֶאֱלִיעֶזֶר
בֶּן הוֹרְקָנוֹס אַף עִמָּהֶם,
וְאֶלְעָזָר בֶּן עֲרָךְ בְּכַף שְׁנִיָּה,
מַכְרִיעַ אֶת כֻּלָּם.

He used to say: If all the sages of Israel were put on one side of the scale and Eliezer b. Hyrcanus was placed on the second [opposite] side, he would outweigh them all. Abba Shaul says in his [Rabban Yoḥanan b. Zakkai's] name: If all the sages of Israel were put on one scale of balance – including R. Eliezer b. Hyrcanus – and R. Elazar b. Arakh was placed on the second scale, he [R. Eliezar] would outweigh them all.

He would outweigh them all

In a time of great transformation and loss of content, which is the most important approach to assure the future? One report has it that in Rabban Yoḥanan's view, the greatest contribution was made by R. Eliezer b. Hyrcanus in preserving all the traditions of the past so they were not lost. The second report has it that in Rabban Yoḥanan's view, all the scholarship and all the preservation is outweighed by the capacity to innovate, create, and apply the Torah in new ways for unprecedented situations. Therefore, R. Elazar b. Arakh is the greatest. The Mishna does not resolve the conflicting views. An overriding argument can be made for preservation and an equally compelling case can be made for the need to innovate and meet new challenges.

Mishna 9

אָמַר לָהֶם: צְאוּ וּרְאוּ אֵיזוֹ הִיא
דֶּרֶךְ טוֹבָה, שֶׁיִּדְבַּק בָּהּ הָאָדָם.
רַבִּי אֱלִיעֶזֶר אוֹמֵר: עַיִן טוֹבָה.
רַבִּי יְהוֹשֻׁעַ אוֹמֵר: חָבֵר טוֹב.
רַבִּי יוֹסֵי אוֹמֵר: שָׁכֵן טוֹב. רַבִּי
שִׁמְעוֹן אוֹמֵר: הָרוֹאֶה אֶת
הַנּוֹלָד. רַבִּי אֶלְעָזָר אוֹמֵר: לֵב
טוֹב. אָמַר לָהֶם, רוֹאֶה אֲנִי אֶת
דִּבְרֵי אֶלְעָזָר בֶּן עֲרָךְ מִדִּבְרֵיכֶם,
שֶׁבִּכְלַל דְּבָרָיו דִּבְרֵיכֶם.

He said to them: Go forth and see what is the right path, to which a man should attach himself. R. Eliezer said: A good eye. R. Yehoshua said: A good friend. R. Yosei said: A good neighbor. R. Shimon said: To see what is coming [see beyond the moment]. R. Elazar said: A good heart. He said to them: I see R. Elazar b. Arakh's words as superior to yours, for your words [concepts] are included in his.

A good eye

- Be the type of person who does not look askance or with envy at what others have.
- Develop a generous, giving spirit.
- Do not begrudge another for what he or she has.

A good friend

Cultivating friendship is the best aid to being a good person.

A good neighbor

- Develop the trait of helpfulness or concern for those with whom you come into contact.

- Get involved in grassroots initiatives in your community.
- Develop the ability to empathize and understand people you encounter, as it is a key to living a good life.

See what is coming

- Become aware of the consequences of your actions.
- Cultivate the maturity not to be fixated on the moment and on instant gratification. The ability to delay gratification enables one to become thoughtful and responsible toward others.
- Learn to look to the future and not just to the present.

A good heart

A good heart is a synonym for goodness of character and a warm, loving attitude toward other people.

Your words are included in his

A good heart leads to all the other virtues.

אָמַר לָהֶם: צְאוּ וּרְאוּ, אֵיזוֹ הִיא דֶּרֶךְ רָעָה, שֶׁיִּתְרַחֵק מִמֶּנָּה הָאָדָם. רַבִּי אֱלִיעֶזֶר אוֹמֵר: עַיִן רָעָה. רַבִּי יְהוֹשֻׁעַ אוֹמֵר: חָבֵר רָע. רַבִּי יוֹסֵי אוֹמֵר: שָׁכֵן רָע. רַבִּי שִׁמְעוֹן אוֹמֵר: הַלֹּוֶה וְאֵינוֹ מְשַׁלֵּם, אֶחָד הַלֹּוֶה מִן הָאָדָם כְּלֹוֶה מִן הַמָּקוֹם, שֶׁנֶּאֱמַר: לֹוֶה רָשָׁע וְלֹא יְשַׁלֵּם, וְצַדִּיק חוֹנֵן וְנוֹתֵן: רַבִּי אֶלְעָזָר אוֹמֵר: לֵב רָע. אָמַר לָהֶם: רוֹאֶה אֲנִי אֶת דִּבְרֵי אֶלְעָזָר בֶּן עֲרָךְ מִדִּבְרֵיכֶם, שֶׁבִּכְלַל דְּבָרָיו דִּבְרֵיכֶם.

He said to them: Go forth and see what is the wrong path, from which a man should distance himself. R. Eliezer said: a bad eye. R. Yehoshua said: a bad friend. R. Yosei said: a bad neighbor. R. Shimon said: he who borrows and does not repay. He who borrows from a person is as if he borrows from God, as it says: "The wicked borrows and will not repay, but a righteous person is gracious and gives back."[6] R. Elazar said: a bad heart. He said: I see R. Elazar b. Arakh's words as superior to yours, for your words [concepts] are included in his.

6. Psalms 37:21.

A bad eye

Someone with this character trait begrudges and envies what others have.

A bad friend

Friendship with a bad person will lead to following his wrong path.

A bad neighbor

- A lack of concern for others and detachment from others who are nearby turns one into an uncaring, selfish person.
- One who does not join the community and looks out only for himself is irresponsible.
- A neighborhood full of such people breeds crime and civic disorder, as well as unhealthy living conditions.

He who borrows and does not repay

This reflects irresponsibility. A person with this trait has either an immature need for instant gratification or an inability to see the future or the consequences of his actions.

A bad heart

As with the positive traits discussed above, this quality, this lack of warmth and love, determines all the other bad traits.

Mishna 10

הֵם אָמְרוּ שְׁלֹשָׁה דְבָרִים.
רַבִּי אֱלִיעֶזֶר אוֹמֵר: יְהִי כְבוֹד
חֲבֵרְךָ חָבִיב עָלֶיךָ כְּשֶׁלָּךְ,
וְאַל תְּהִי נוֹחַ לִכְעֹס. וְשׁוּב
יוֹם אֶחָד לִפְנֵי מִיתָתְךָ. וֶהֱוֵי
מִתְחַמֵּם כְּנֶגֶד אוּרָן שֶׁל
חֲכָמִים, וֶהֱוֵי זָהִיר בְּגַחַלְתָּן
שֶׁלֹּא תִכָּוֶה, שֶׁנְּשִׁיכָתָן נְשִׁיכַת
שׁוּעָל, וַעֲקִיצָתָן עֲקִיצַת
עַקְרָב, וּלְחִישָׁתָן לְחִישַׁת שָׂרָף,
וְכָל דִּבְרֵיהֶם כְּגַחֲלֵי אֵשׁ.

Each of them made three statements. R. Eliezer said: Your friend's honor should be as precious to you as your own; do not be quick to anger; repent one day before your death. [He added:] Warm yourself by the fires of the sages, but be careful that their glowing coals not sear you. For their bite is [as wounding as] the bite of a fox, their sting is [as painful as] a scorpion's, their whisper is like the hiss of a fiery snake, and all their words are like coals of fire.

HISTORICAL BACKGROUND

R. Eliezer b. Hyrcanus (late first–second century CE) was of a passionate, unyielding temperament. He was driven by a sense of total commitment. He was a *baal teshuva* – a returnee to Judaism, as it were. He was the son of a wealthy land owner who declared that the last thing he wanted his son to be was a religious scholar. Eliezer defied his father, who then cut him off financially. Pressing on through poverty and deprivation, Eliezer became a leading scholar and an indispensable source because he memorized and made available for others all the traditions taught orally by the great teachers. (It was more than a century later before the traditions were written down in the Mishna.)

In Yavneh after the Destruction, he was totally convinced that he was always right in arguments with the other sages, for he claimed to never say a word of Torah that he had not heard from his teachers. Thus he refused to yield his view in the face of a majority vote for the other ruling. He invoked divine interventions to "prove" that his interpretation of Torah (and not the majority's) was the correct one. The sages finally expelled and excommunicated him despite his greatness in Torah scholarship. They were deeply grieved that they had to impose such painful discipline.

When R. Eliezer b. Hyrcanus fell into his final illness, the sages came to him on his deathbed and asked him questions of ritual purity and impurity which he alone could answer. The last word he said to them was: "pure." R. Yehoshua expressed the grief and reconciliation which they all felt, proclaiming, "The ban is over!" For days after, R. Yehoshua wept, saying that he had so many unresolved questions of law, but there was no one [like Eliezer] to ask.

Your friend's honor should be as precious to you as your own

- Love your neighbor as yourself.
- Do unto others what you would have others do unto you.
- Empathize with the other person.

Quick to anger

A bad temper repulses and/or beats down others in your life.

Repent one day before your death

- Since you do not know the day of your death – it might be today or tomorrow – repent today.
- If you act as if today is your last day on earth, you will stop sinning and regret whatever evil you did to others.
- In R. Eliezer's view, contemplating death causes people to become more caring and compassionate.

Warm yourself…be careful that their glowing coals not sear you

R. Eliezer was drawn to his teachers and other scholars, treasuring their wisdom, and he tenaciously preserved all their words. However, when he refused to accept majority rule in the academy, he was excommunicated, thereby feeling the bite and sting of the sages in their full fury.

Mishna 11

רַבִּי יְהוֹשֻׁעַ אוֹמֵר: עַיִן הָרָע וְיֵצֶר הָרָע וְשִׂנְאַת הַבְּרִיּוֹת, מוֹצִיאִין אֶת הָאָדָם מִן הָעוֹלָם.

R. Yehoshua says: The evil eye, the evil impulse, and hatred of fellow human beings shrink a person's life.

HISTORICAL BACKGROUND

R. Yehoshua b. Ḥanania (late first–second century CE) was a person of noble character and independent judgment. He lived in poverty and supported himself as a blacksmith while serving as a scholar. When he concluded that his calendar calculation was correct (as were some other important rulings), he stood up to Rabban Gamliel, the *nasi*, who sought to impose his views using the force of his political position. Yet when Rabban Gamliel ordered R. Yehoshua to appear before him on the day which was Yom Kippur by R. Yehoshua's count, the latter appeared before him rather than cause a fundamental split in the community. (The community was so upset by this abuse of R. Yehoshua that they temporarily removed Rabban Gamliel from his post as *nasi*.)

When R. Eliezer b. Hyrcanus invoked miracles to force the majority to his views, it was R. Yehoshua who faced down the divine voice which upheld R. Eliezer's view. R. Yehoshua announced (to God!): "'It [the Torah] is not in heaven [any more].'[7] Therefore, we do not pay attention to a heavenly voice!" In other words, the essence of the rabbinic tradition is that God has limited Himself and stopped sending messages directly

7. Deuteronomy 30:12.

from heaven. Instead, God has charged people with determining what He wants of us now. In seeking God's will, we must employ human logic and analyze the text, and then be bound by the conclusion of the majority.

Later, the Talmud reports that Elijah the Prophet confirmed that R. Yehoshua was right. He said that God chuckled, hearing R. Yehoshua's words, and declared: "My children have won … over Me."[8]

The evil eye

This is greed, envy, and looking down on people.

The evil impulse

This is the urge to do evil to others. Rabbinic psychology sees individuals as torn between a powerful urge to do good and a powerful urge to do evil. The human being is not fundamentally evil (as opposed to the Doctrine of Original Sin, which teaches that Adam's sin tainted human nature permanently with intrinsic evil drives that distort behavior). Nor is the fundamental goodness of all humans (as implied in the writings of Rousseau and other modern democratic theorists) a correct assumption about human nature. Rather, the human being is poised between two contradictory, internal forces. Society, family, and educational institutions should strive to create conditions that bring out the best in a person, and should act to check bad tendencies in order to encourage a free-will choice to do good.

Hatred of fellow human beings

Loving others, having loving, permanent relationships, and being married have all been shown to elicit better, healthier behaviors, and are directly correlated with a longer life. Anti-social attitudes and isolation lead to deterioration of mental and physical capacities, and to low quality of life, as well as a shorter life.

8. Bava Metzia 59b.

Mishna 12

רַבִּי יוֹסֵי אוֹמֵר: יְהִי מָמוֹן חֲבֵרְךָ חָבִיב עָלֶיךָ כְּשֶׁלָּךְ. וְהַתְקֵן עַצְמְךָ לִלְמֹד תּוֹרָה, שֶׁאֵינָהּ יְרֻשָּׁה לָךְ. וְכָל מַעֲשֶׂיךָ יִהְיוּ לְשֵׁם שָׁמָיִם.

R. Yosei says: Your friend's money should be as precious to you as your own; train yourself to study Torah, for it does not come to you as an inheritance [i.e., automatically]; all your actions should be for the sake of Heaven.

HISTORICAL BACKGROUND

Very little is known about this R. Yosei (latter half of the second century CE) other than that he was a priest and was noted for his piety. The Talmud suggests that he was involved in the study of mysticism associated with the divine chariot (*maaseh merkava*; see Ezek. 1). This is considered to be among the most powerful – and secret – of all mystical lore, so secret that it was not to be expounded in the presence of another person unless that person was a scholar and knowledgeable on the topic.[9]

Your friend's money

Friendship implies treating the other as a creature of equal dignity to oneself. According to R. Eliezer b. Hyrcanus, the dignity of equality requires one to be as concerned for the honor and respect of the other as for his own. R. Yosei adds another application of the principle of equality: being as careful with the wealth or the property of another as for one's own. In this spirit, Maimonides ruled that being as careful and prudent with

9. Ḥagiga 14b.

another's money as with one's own is a fulfillment of the commandment, "Love your neighbor [i.e., fellow human being] as yourself."[10]

Condition yourself to study Torah

Priestly status was hereditary. A prophet was chosen by God's grace without the prophet necessarily doing anything (or training) to be worthy. Becoming a scholar, however, requires action on the part of the individual. If people make the effort and train properly, they can become scholars and teachers. Thus the sages expanded and democratized the spiritual leadership of Jewry.

All your actions should be for the sake of Heaven

- A person's every act can be turned into a form of worshiping God and serving the divine plan. In the words of Proverbs 3:6: "In all your ways [i.e., behaviors], know Him." The act of eating can be an expression of animal desire or of abandon, or it can be devoted to consciously improving the quality of one's life. Eating can be regulated to show reverence for that which one eats (as in *kashrut*); food can be acknowledged as the bounty bestowed by God (through a blessing). Thus a biological function can be turned into service of God. The sages applied this concept to every human act (such as the blessing *asher yatzar* said upon relieving oneself).[11]
- Purify your behavior; look at your motives. Try to make sure that your ritual and liturgical behaviors are for the sake of God and not to show off, impress people, or gain an advantage.

---

10. *Mishneh Torah, Hilkhot Deot* 6:3.
11. Philip Birnbaum, *Ha-Siddur Ha-Shalem* [Daily Prayer Book] (New York: Hebrew Publishing Co., 1977), 13, 123.

Mishna 13

רַבִּי שִׁמְעוֹן אוֹמֵר: הֱוֵי זָהִיר בִּקְרִיאַת שְׁמַע וּבִתְפִלָּה. וּכְשֶׁאַתָּה מִתְפַּלֵּל אַל תַּעַשׂ תְּפִלָּתְךָ קֶבַע, אֶלָּא רַחֲמִים וְתַחֲנוּנִים לִפְנֵי הַמָּקוֹם, שֶׁנֶּאֱמַר: כִּי חַנּוּן וְרַחוּם הוּא, אֶרֶךְ אַפַּיִם וְרַב־חֶסֶד וְנִחָם עַל־הָרָעָה: וְאַל תְּהִי רָשָׁע בִּפְנֵי עַצְמֶךָ.

R. Shimon says: Be aware as you recite the *Shema* [*Yisrael* prayer] and the [*Amida*] prayer [the core prayer, lit., eighteen benedictions]. When you pray, do not make your prayer a fixed routine but rather the expression of compassion and pleas for mercy before God, as it says [in Scripture]: "For God is gracious and merciful, slow to anger and overflowing with covenantal love, who regrets inflicting punishment [on sinners]."[12] Do not be wicked in your own sight.

HISTORICAL BACKGROUND

This is R. Shimon b. Netanel (first century CE). We know very little about his life other than that he was a priest and that he might have married the daughter of the *nasi*, Gamliel the Elder (the first). Still, his listing among the five key disciples of Rabban Yoḥanan b. Zakkai suggests that he was an important figure.

Aware

Because prayer had become a daily practice after the Destruction of the Second Temple, R. Shimon warns that it can easily turn into rote recitation. Prayer should not become a fixed ritual, an empty form.

12. Joel 2:13.

Compassion and pleas for mercy

Prayer should be an occasion for pouring out your heart before a loving, divine parent. R. Shimon cites the prophet Joel to prove that God is not an absolute ruler who wants to be glorified by worship. (In such a case, rote recitation would prove one's obedience to Him.) Rather, God is gracious, overflowing with covenantal love. Therefore, God wants to experience our love and feelings in the words of prayer; the Lord does not want the obedient litany of an intimidated slave.

Do not be wicked in your own sight

- Do not be wicked when you are all alone, in private. Do not be a hypocrite who acts ethically and fulfills ritual laws in public in the presence of others, but does wrong and violates the law when no one is looking.
- Maimonides interprets: Do not see yourself as totally wicked and incorrigible – for then you will give up and will not repent or correct your ways.
- Always see yourself as a person of mixed tendencies and behaviors. This will assure you that you are never beyond redemption. More important, this will give you the incentive that with some extra effort, you can turn yourself to the side of good.

Mishna 14

רַבִּי אֶלְעָזָר אוֹמֵר: הֱוֵי שָׁקוּד לִלְמֹד תּוֹרָה. וְדַע מַה שֶּׁתָּשִׁיב לְאֶפִּיקוֹרוֹס. וְדַע לִפְנֵי מִי אַתָּה עָמֵל, וּמִי הוּא בַּעַל מְלַאכְתְּךָ, שֶׁיְּשַׁלֶּם לְךָ שְׂכַר פְּעֻלָּתֶךָ.

R. Elazar says: Be assiduous in learning Torah and know what answer to give to an *apikoros*; and know before whom you labor, for your employer is trustworthy to pay you the wages of your work.

HISTORICAL BACKGROUND

R. Elazar b. Arakh (latter half of the first century CE) also was involved in the study of divine chariot mysticism. Once he exposited the subject before Rabban Yoḥanan b. Zakkai, and the effect was so overwhelming that the two experienced being surrounded by a ring of heavenly fire, while the trees serenaded the wonders of creation. Later, Rabban Yoḥanan suffered the ultimate tragedy, the death of a son. Numerous students tried to console him – each pointing out a different tragic precedent: Adam, Job, Aaron the High Priest, and others all lost sons, yet ultimately they came to accept the decree. Rabban Yoḥanan rejected such comfort, saying that it only increased his pain to think of the others who also experienced tragedy. Showing his creativity, Elazar b. Arakh took a completely different tack. He spoke of God's gift to Rabban Yoḥanan – being given a son of remarkable learning and moral innocence. Despite the agony of the loss, said Elazar b. Arakh, Rabban Yoḥanan should consider the situation as if he had returned a treasure that had been only temporarily deposited with him. Rabban Yoḥanan was finally comforted.

Assiduous in learning Torah

To succeed in Torah scholarship, you must be disciplined and dedicated to regular study. Do not study like a dilettante or a lazy amateur.

Answer… an *apikoros*

Epicureans thought that there was no personal God, no reward and punishment, and, by implication, no need to practice religion. The term *apikoros* was eventually extended to cover all skeptics who crossed the line into fundamental heresy and rejection of Judaism. This mishna is an argument *for* a reasoned faith. It also suggests that one should teach students by intelligently refuting the wrong views rather than by training them to close their minds and reject wrong views out of conformity, obedience to authoritarian instruction, or ignorance and stereotype.

Know what answer to give

- It is not enough to shut out such disbelievers and not listen to them at all. Understand, analyze, and actively reject those views.
- Rather than rely on simple obedience or blind faith to stay faithful to the Torah, develop both an understanding of the justification for your own faith and the ability to refute the views of religious antagonists.
- Given the inescapable exposure to Hellenism and to skeptical philosophies, a believer should learn how to defend his faith and answer questions posed by skeptics – if not for his own sake then for the sake of other believers who are being challenged by non-believers.

Know before whom you labor

Know the nature of God. Recognize that all your work, religious and secular, is done in the sight of God, who appreciates and honors the effort and who will reward those who do good and who act honestly in work. If sometimes you feel unappreciated or it seems that you and others who live the right way are losing out while evildoers flourish, remind yourself that one day, either in this world or in the next, God will faithfully pay the wages of the good.

Mishna 15

רַבִּי טַרְפוֹן אוֹמֵר: הַיּוֹם קָצָר, וְהַמְּלָאכָה מְרֻבָּה, וְהַפּוֹעֲלִים עֲצֵלִים, וְהַשָּׂכָר הַרְבֵּה, וּבַעַל הַבַּיִת דּוֹחֵק.

R. Tarfon says: The day is short; there is a lot of work to do. The workers are lazy, the wages are high, and the owner is pressing.

HISTORICAL BACKGROUND

R. Tarfon (a Greek name) was born in the generation of the Destruction of the Second Temple to a wealthy family of priests (latter half of the first century CE). He was a student of Rabban Yoḥanan b. Zakkai for a while, and of Rabban Gamliel the Elder. He started out as a disciple of the school of Shammai, to the point where he risked his life more than once to follow their practices. Nevertheless, unlike R. Eliezer b. Hyrcanus, he was open to learning from others, and eventually became a major disciple of R. Akiva. He set up an academy and lived in the city of Lod, but joined in the deliberations in Yavneh.

R. Tarfon says

R. Tarfon's metaphor is that God put us on earth with a mission. There is more to do than there are hours in the day. People often do not push themselves; they settle for mediocre performance. Yet God asks us urgently to step up, and offers great – eternal – reward.

Mishna 16

הוּא הָיָה אוֹמֵר: לֹא עָלֶיךָ הַמְּלָאכָה לִגְמֹר, וְלֹא אַתָּה בֶן חוֹרִין לִבָּטֵל מִמֶּנָּה. אִם לָמַדְתָּ תּוֹרָה הַרְבֵּה, נוֹתְנִין לְךָ שָׂכָר הַרְבֵּה. וְנֶאֱמָן הוּא בַּעַל מְלַאכְתְּךָ, שֶׁיְּשַׁלֶּם לְךָ שְׂכַר פְּעֻלָּתֶךָ. וְדַע, שֶׁמַּתַּן שְׂכָרָן שֶׁל צַדִּיקִים לֶעָתִיד לָבוֹא.

He used to say: You are not required to complete the work, but you are not at liberty to stand idly by. If you have learned much Torah, they give you great wages. Your employer [God] is trustworthy to pay the wages of your labor, but know that the giving of the reward of the righteous happens in the World to Come.

You are not required to complete

God does not give us a mission that we cannot fulfill. Since the final Redemption is beyond the accomplishment of any sole individual, a person should not feel obligated to complete the task. Nor should one consider himself a failure if the job is not fully done; but neither should he feel at liberty to do nothing. You are commanded and expected to undertake the task of repairing the world, or, if you will, doing good with your life.

R. Tarfon's is a classic covenantal statement. Every generation knows it cannot finish the task, but begins nevertheless, for it accepts its mission. Before each generation passes, it transmits the work to another generation, which it has raised and recruited for the mission. One learns to be neither so arrogant as to believe that "if I don't do it, no one will," nor so self-effacing as to say, "What difference will my limited efforts make?" or "There is no point for me to start, since I cannot finish."

You employer is trustworthy...but know...the reward...happens in the World to Come

- God will reward the good. This is a just world, in which good is rewarded and evil is punished.
- However, it would appear that the true and exact reward for righteousness is given in the World to Come. In this world we see too many successful evildoers and unrewarded righteous people.
- Do not despair or grow cynical. Justice will be done, if not in this world then in the World to Come.

R. Tarfon practiced what he preached. He was an extremely wealthy man, and R. Akiva felt that he did not donate as much *tzedaka* money as he was capable of giving. R. Akiva approached his disciple and offered to buy for him a village or two as an investment. R. Tarfon gave him four thousand golden dinars. R. Akiva took the money and distributed it to various poor people who desperately needed the help. Soon, R. Tarfon asked: Where are the villages you were to buy for me? R. Akiva took out the Book of Psalms and read to him the verse: "[When] he gives generously to the poor, his *tzedaka* [charity, righteousness] stands forever."[13] R. Akiva's play on words contained a hint that the rate of return on money invested in buying a village would have been good, but only for short-term profit (i.e., in this world). By investing the money in *tzedaka* and helping the poor, his charity and righteousness would have an eternal, long-term return on investment (i.e., in the World to Come). R. Tarfon embraced R. Akiva's teaching, kissed his mentor, and said: "You are my master in wisdom and my friend in the ways of the world." He then gave R. Akiva more money to distribute to the poor.[14]

13. Psalms 112:9.

14. Kalla, section 21. See Soncino edition, Talmud, Minor Tractates 51A.

Chapter 3

The first two chapters of *Pirkei Avot* are focused on establishing the chain of tradition and transmission, linking the Written Torah (the Five Books of Moses and the later biblical books) with the Oral Torah (written down in the Talmud). The Talmud has two primary layers of text, the earlier Mishna, written in Hebrew in the Land of Israel, and the later commentary and expansion of the Mishna called the Gemara. Chapter 1 of Tractate Avot establishes the authority of the traditions going back to Moses at Sinai. Since the transmission is unbroken, the authority of the "later" teachers is as (tacitly) fully binding as that of Moses. Chapter 2 upholds the transmission from before the Destruction until after the catastrophe, and focuses on the generation that renewed Jewish life at Yavneh.

The next two chapters of *Pirkei Avot* are less defined. Amram Tropper suggests that the chapters continue the chronological or generational sequence but without repeating the language of transmission. He also suggests that chapters 3 and 4 are linked by a literary envelope (the opening mishna of chapter 3 and the final mishna of chapter 4) which focuses on God's final judgment of each individual at the moment of death.[1]

I submit that the themes of final judgment, and by implication, of reward and punishment in the World to Come are the crucial, although not the only, points made in these chapters. This reflects another

1. Amram Tropper, *Wisdom, Politics and Historiography: Tractate Avot in the Context of the Graeco-Roman Near East* (New York: Oxford University Press, 2004), 25. Tropper explores other organizing structures and literary units with insight and ingenuity, but they are too specialized for this commentary. See ibid., 26–50.

distinctive emphasis of the sages according to their underlying theology that God had again self-limited to call humans to a higher level of responsibility in the covenant.

As we learned, the dominating God of the Bible intervenes continuously with messages from heaven and visible miracles. The Bible is much more focused on this world, with frequent incidents of obvious reward and punishment in this life to confirm the power of God to the onlookers. One consequence of the greater hiddenness of God after the Destruction is the end of visible miracles. The model of measure-for-measure reward and punishment is much less apparent. This raises questions regarding the divine moral economy, and whether "there is no judgment and no judge," as some skeptics have argued.

The sages then turned to a model that had been all but overlooked in the biblical period: the possibility that ultimate reward and punishment truly do take place in the World to Come – beyond the mortal coil. In the Hellenistic surrounding culture within which Jewry lived and the sages worked, as well as in Parthian culture, among which the Gemara, the second and greater half of the Talmud, was fashioned, the Zoroastrian influence was strong. That religion focused on the World to Come and the afterlife, which made the idea of the World to Come far more credible – even self-evident – than it had been in the biblical period.

As profound educators, the sages spoke and taught on their students' level. Thus a book such as Ethics of the Fathers, which sought to portray the life wisdom of the sages, their moral standards and motivating factors, and their concept of how to live the individual life, would naturally incorporate a new emphasis on the World to Come and the final judgment. This teaching was to engender greater morality and integrity both in interpersonal relationships and between God and people. The tractate would be a deterrent to sin (because nothing could be hidden from God and from the final judgment). Ethics of the Fathers also tacitly dealt with the moral unease felt at living in a world where divine measure-for-measure interactions, on either a national or an individual scale, were not obvious – certainly not as visible as they were before.

The fifth chapter of *Pirkei Avot* is organized around clusters of numbers: ten generations, seven retributions, four types of students, etc. Possibly, the numbers served as a mnemonic device at a time when much of the learning circulated orally. This will be discussed further in the introduction to chapter 5.

In the end, the central purpose around which Ethics of the Fathers was edited was that it serve as an anthology of ethical and life wisdom sayings attributed to a selected list of sages from the different generations up to the closing of the Mishna, who together with other great teachers developed the rabbinic tradition. The sixty-six unique, individual scholars quoted in Ethics are a representative sample of the more than two hundred individuals whose names appear in the Mishna. Their wisdom exemplifies the values which the Mishna codifies in law and tradition.

Mishna 1

עֲקַבְיָא בֶּן מַהֲלַלְאֵל אוֹמֵר:
הִסְתַּכֵּל בִּשְׁלֹשָׁה דְבָרִים, וְאֵין
אַתָּה בָא לִידֵי עֲבֵרָה. דַּע מֵאַיִן
בָּאתָ, וּלְאָן אַתָּה הוֹלֵךְ, וְלִפְנֵי
מִי אַתָּה עָתִיד לִתֵּן דִּין וְחֶשְׁבּוֹן.
מֵאַיִן בָּאתָ, מִטִּפָּה סְרוּחָה.
וּלְאָן אַתָּה הוֹלֵךְ, לִמְקוֹם עָפָר,
רִמָּה וְתוֹלֵעָה. וְלִפְנֵי מִי אַתָּה
עָתִיד לִתֵּן דִּין וְחֶשְׁבּוֹן, לִפְנֵי
מֶלֶךְ מַלְכֵי הַמְּלָכִים, הַקָּדוֹשׁ
בָּרוּךְ הוּא.

Akavia b. Mahalalel says: Look closely at three facts and you will never come to do an act of sin: Know from where you came; where you are going; and before whom you are destined to render the account [of your life]. Where did you come from? A fetid drop. Where are you going? To a place of dirt, worms, and maggots. Before whom are you destined to render the account of your life? Before the ruler, the King of kings, The Holy One, Blessed Be He.

HISTORICAL BACKGROUND

Akavia was a first-century teacher and scholar. He was offered the post of *av beit din* (second-in-command) under Hillel – on condition that he withdraw four personal rulings which he continued to teach even though the majority of the sages rejected them. He declined Hillel's offer, saying that he would rather be deemed a fool all his life (for turning down this august position) than be deemed wicked in God's eyes even for one hour (for betraying his principles, i.e., yielding rulings based on his best judgment for the sake of getting a major communal position).

The Talmud tells another story reflecting Akavia's enormous integrity. On his deathbed, he instructed his son not to follow his four disputed rulings. His son asked why he didn't retract them earlier in his lifetime, when he was asked to by the sages. Akavia replied: I heard my rulings from a group that I judged to be the majority (so I felt bound by that view). The sages heard the opposite ruling from a group which they counted as a majority (so they felt bound by that view). I stood fast to the ruling that I received and they stood fast to the ruling that they received. But you have heard the ruling from an individual (me), who is clearly outnumbered by a majority (the sages). Therefore, it is better that you follow the majority ruling.[2]

Look closely at three facts and you will never... sin

Akavia feels that all acts of sin involve a loss of perspective. Something appears so desirable, so urgent, that all other considerations – violations of trust, disobeying God, hurting another – appear trivial by comparison. The person then pushes all the right considerations aside and sins. Someone who understands the ephemerality of earthly life and the awesomeness of God before whom one will be held accountable will never sin, because no goal or pleasure will stack up against the majesty of God and the eternity of judgment.

A fetid drop

All the microscopic cells which initiate conception quickly decay and die.

Dirt, worms, and maggots

From an eternal perspective, this earthly, bodily life is quite short, and mortal existence ends with the body in a lowly, rotted state of decomposition.

The Holy One, Blessed Be He

Akavia was ever mindful of God's presence (see Ps. 16:8). This gave him the perspective and backbone not to yield to temptation or to peer pressure but rather to live according to his principles and conscience with the greatest rectitude: "God is at my right hand; I shall never be shaken" (ibid.).

2. Mishha Eduyot 5:6, 7.

Mishna 2

רַבִּי חֲנִינָא סְגַן הַכֹּהֲנִים אוֹמֵר: הֱוֵי מִתְפַּלֵּל בִּשְׁלוֹמָהּ שֶׁל מַלְכוּת, שֶׁאִלְמָלֵא מוֹרָאָהּ, אִישׁ אֶת רֵעֵהוּ חַיִּים בְּלָעוֹ.	R. Ḥanina, the deputy High Priest, says: Pray for the well-being of the government, for were it not for fear [of its power], every man would swallow his fellow alive.

HISTORICAL BACKGROUND

The deputy High Priest stood in for the High Priest if the latter became incapacitated or ritually impure, and thus unable to carry out the High Priest's designated function (such as entering the Holy of Holies on Yom Kippur). R. Ḥanina is believed to have been a survivor of the Destruction of the Second Temple, and he is quoted giving testimony concerning certain practices followed in the Temple. He is listed in the Megillat Taanit chronicles as one of the rabbinic martyrs put to death by the Romans.

Swallow his fellow alive

- This is a Hobbesian view. Since people act out of power and selfishness, they would be in a state of perpetual warfare with each other were it not for the restraining power of the government. By this logic, as Hobbes argued, government has the right to be authoritarian and not subject to the changing will of the citizens.
- On the assumption that R. Ḥanina survived the Destruction and the experience motivated his comments, Rabbi Travis Herford

suggests the following interpretation: Even if Jews feel revulsion at the Roman government, they should accept its authority and wish it well. Without its strong hand the land would be a jungle, with each one's hand at the other's throat.[3]

- As a survivor of the Destruction, R. Ḥanina saw the evil effects of groundless hatred and civil war in bringing it. Thus he was very concerned about keeping peace and stability above all, and for this, a strong government was needed.[4]

רַבִּי חֲנִינָא בֶּן תְּרַדְיוֹן אוֹמֵר: שְׁנַיִם שֶׁיּוֹשְׁבִין, וְאֵין בֵּינֵיהֶם דִּבְרֵי תוֹרָה, הֲרֵי זֶה מוֹשַׁב לֵצִים, שֶׁנֶּאֱמַר: וּבְמוֹשַׁב לֵצִים לֹא יָשָׁב: אֲבָל שְׁנַיִם שֶׁיּוֹשְׁבִין, וְיֵשׁ בֵּינֵיהֶם דִּבְרֵי תוֹרָה, שְׁכִינָה שְׁרוּיָה בֵינֵיהֶם, שֶׁנֶּאֱמַר: אָז נִדְבְּרוּ יִרְאֵי יהוה אִישׁ אֶל־רֵעֵהוּ, וַיַּקְשֵׁב יהוה וַיִּשְׁמָע, וַיִּכָּתֵב סֵפֶר זִכָּרוֹן לְפָנָיו לְיִרְאֵי יהוה וּלְחֹשְׁבֵי שְׁמוֹ: אֵין לִי אֶלָּא שְׁנַיִם, מִנַּיִן אֲפִלּוּ אֶחָד שֶׁיּוֹשֵׁב וְעוֹסֵק בַּתּוֹרָה שֶׁהַקָּדוֹשׁ בָּרוּךְ הוּא קוֹבֵעַ לוֹ שָׂכָר, שֶׁנֶּאֱמַר: יֵשֵׁב בָּדָד וְיִדֹּם כִּי נָטַל עָלָיו:

R. Ḥanania b. Teradyon says: If two [people] sit together and no words of Torah pass between them, this constitutes sitting in the company of the insolent, as it says: "[A righteous man] does not sit in the company of the insolent."[5] But if two sit and words of Torah are exchanged between them, then the Divine Presence [*Shekhina*] is resting between them, as it says: "Then those who revere the Lord spoke to each other, and the Lord paid attention and heard it, and it was written in the book of remembrance before [the Lord] with reference to those who revere God and esteem His name."[6] This establishes that if two [people exchange words of Torah, they are rewarded, but] how do we know that even if one person sits and engages in the study of Torah, The Holy One, Blessed Be He, establishes a reward for Him? As it says: "He sits alone in silent [contemplation] and God has laid it upon him."[7]

3. Rabbi Travers Herford, *Pirke Aboth, The Ethics of the Talmud: Sayings of the Fathers* (New York: Schocken Books, 1962), 64–65.
4. Heard from Rabbi Aharon Greenberg.
5. Psalms 1:1.
6. Malachi 8:16.
7. Lamentations 3:28.

HISTORICAL BACKGROUND

R. Ḥanania b. Teradyon was one of the chief martyrs who were put to death in the Hadrianic persecutions during the Bar Kokhba revolt (ca. 130–132 CE). A man of great courage, he defied the Roman ban on Torah instruction and continued teaching his classes in public. R. Ḥanania was wrapped in a Torah and burned together with the scroll by the Romans. As he was enveloped in fire, his students asked him what he saw. He replied: "The parchment is burning, but the letters are [indestructible and] flying upward [to heaven]." His son was killed as a rebel, his wife was executed, and one of his daughters was seized and sold into prostitution.[8] Another daughter of his was Bruria, a great Torah scholar who was married to R. Meir.

No words of Torah

R. Ḥanania's love of Torah expressed itself in his final act of giving his life for the sake of teaching Torah. He finds it hard to understand how anyone can live a life that is indifferent to studying Torah and sharing its words. He concludes that to socialize without speaking any words of Torah shows that one is denying God's universal presence. It takes a certain quality of scoffing or spiritual insolence to ignore the Divine Presence.

The Divine Presence is resting between them

This mishna reflects the sages' great insight that the Destruction of the Temple signaled a change in the nature of God's presence from high-tension, sometimes even dangerous, but in a limited number of places (particularly the Temple), to a "lower-voltage," but in a wider number of places. When God self-limited, allowing the Temple to be destroyed and becoming more "hidden," one could tap into His presence by studying or exchanging words of Torah. Even if only two people studied Torah together, the Divine Presence would be discovered to be there.

Even if one person … engages in the study of Torah

If the mind of one person, sitting alone, is directed toward words of Torah, then the Divine Presence will be there.

---

8. Avoda Zara 18a.

Mishna 3

רַבִּי שִׁמְעוֹן אוֹמֵר: שְׁלֹשָׁה
שֶׁאָכְלוּ עַל שֻׁלְחָן אֶחָד
וְלֹא אָמְרוּ עָלָיו דִּבְרֵי תוֹרָה,
כְּאִלּוּ אָכְלוּ מִזִּבְחֵי מֵתִים,
שֶׁנֶּאֱמַר: כִּי כָּל־שֻׁלְחָנוֹת
מָלְאוּ קִיא צֹאָה בְּלִי מָקוֹם:
אֲבָל שְׁלֹשָׁה שֶׁאָכְלוּ עַל
שֻׁלְחָן אֶחָד, וְאָמְרוּ עָלָיו
דִּבְרֵי תוֹרָה, כְּאִלּוּ אָכְלוּ מִשֻּׁלְחָנוֹ
שֶׁל מָקוֹם, שֶׁנֶּאֱמַר: וַיְדַבֵּר אֵלַי,
זֶה הַשֻּׁלְחָן אֲשֶׁר לִפְנֵי יהוה:

R. Shimon says: Three who ate together at one table and did not say words of Torah [at that meal], it is as if they have eaten of sacrifices to the dead, as it says: "For all the tables are full of vomit and filth without *Makom*."[9] [*Makom*, place, is also one of the names of God.] But three who ate together at one table and said words of Torah at that meal, it is as if they have eaten at God's table, as it says: "He said to me: This is the table which is before the Lord."[10]

HISTORICAL BACKGROUND

R. Shimon is R. Shimon b. Yoḥai (second century CE) who grew into a saintly figure. A leading student of R. Akiva, he defied the Romans and was forced to go into hiding to avoid imprisonment or death. He stayed underground for more than a decade and learned with his son. He was religiously radicalized by the experience. The Talmud relates that when he finally came out, he initially could not tolerate people carrying on normal lives of labor and mundane activity rather than

9. Isaiah 28:8.
10. Ezekiel 41:22.

spending all their time in Torah study and devotion to God. R. Shimon said that there are three gifts which God has given to Israel which can be claimed only through [willingness to undergo] suffering: Torah, the Land of Israel, and the World to Come.[11] R. Shimon later became extraordinarily famous as the imputed author of the Zohar, the classic text of medieval Jewish mysticism.

Three … ate together … and did not say words of Torah

As according to rabbinic teaching, God is more hidden yet more present in the post-Destruction era, the table at home is tantamount to the Temple Altar; in other words, eating proper food in one's home is equivalent to eating of the sacrifices during Temple times. But failure to speak words of Torah indicates that one does not recognize the presence of God. Therefore, eating would be like the Israelites who ate of sacrifices to the dead instead of bringing their offerings to God.

Makom

God's name in rabbinic literature is *Makom,* the Place; i.e., God is the ground in which all being grows. The world is "located" within God, who sustains all of existence.

Tables … full of … filth without *Makom*

In the Midrash, the sages' commentary uses Isaiah's denunciation of the drunken feasts at which the idol-worshiping leaders of the Israelites ate their sacrifices to the dead and to chthonic deities as a critique of any feast in the rabbinic period where no Torah was spoken. The failure to say words of Torah shows that the people were oblivious to the more hidden but more present divine spirit in their midst. The key midrash is a play on words: Isaiah says the tables are full of vomit and filth, with no places (*makom*) left. The sages interpret this verse as meaning that the table is full of empty words, perhaps even of gossip and "dirt" about others. Thus it is all filth and without *Makom,* i.e., without God, who is the place of the world.

11. Berakhot 5a.

This is the table which is before the Lord

Every meal at every table in every Jewish home where properly prepared food is served, where blessings are said and Torah is shared, is equivalent to the sacrifices eaten before God in the Temple. The manifest God was encountered in a family meal at the Temple. The immanent God is encountered at a family meal in the home.

Mishna 4

רַבִּי חֲנִינָא בֶּן חֲכִינַאי אוֹמֵר: הַנֵּעוֹר בַּלַּיְלָה, וְהַמְהַלֵּךְ בַּדֶּרֶךְ יְחִידִי, וְהַמְפַנֶּה לִבּוֹ לְבַטָּלָה, הֲרֵי זֶה מִתְחַיֵּב בְּנַפְשׁוֹ.

R. Ḥanina b. Ḥakhinai says: One who is awake at night, and one who travels alone on the road, and one who clears his heart for idle thoughts forfeits his life.

HISTORICAL BACKGROUND

R. Ḥanina b. Ḥakhinai (second century CE) is listed here as a sage. However, in Sanhedrin 17b he is listed as one of four students who did not receive ordination but who were allowed to join in the discussions with the ordained rabbis in matters of halakha. Rashi suggests there that the four were not ordained because they were too young and they died young. The fact that they were unmarried may have played a role in their not being ordained (although there is an alternate tradition that Ḥanina was married[12]). According to another tradition, he was one of the ten rabbinic martyrs during the Hadrianic persecutions.

Awake at night

When everyone is asleep. He is either planning crimes or exposing himself to a world in which criminals and murderers are awake doing their evil work while respectable people sleep.

---

12. Ketubbot 62b.

Travels alone

- Unaccompanied travel on deserted roads is dangerous.
- Given the dangers on the roads, most people travel in groups or with guards. Thus the lone traveler is likely up to no good.

Clears his heart for idle thoughts

If one is not thinking constructively and making life-affirming plans, then his idle thoughts easily turn him to bad actions or illegitimate pleasures.

Forfeits his life

- He will commit deadly sins.
- She risks her life by traveling in dangerous places.
- He is spiritually killing himself by wasting his life.

Mishna 5

רַבִּי נְחוּנְיָא בֶּן הַקָּנָה אוֹמֵר: כָּל הַמְקַבֵּל עָלָיו עֹל תּוֹרָה, מַעֲבִירִין מִמֶּנּוּ עֹל מַלְכוּת וְעֹל דֶּרֶךְ אֶרֶץ. וְכָל הַפּוֹרֵק מִמֶּנּוּ עֹל תּוֹרָה, נוֹתְנִין עָלָיו עֹל מַלְכוּת וְעֹל דֶּרֶךְ אֶרֶץ.

R. Neḥunia b. Hakana says: Anyone who accepts the yoke of Torah upon himself, they remove from him the yoke of the government and the yoke of worldly pursuits. But anyone who throws off the yoke of Torah, they put on him the yoke of the government and the yoke of worldly pursuits.

HISTORICAL BACKGROUND

R. Neḥunia was born in Emmaus (first century CE). He was the teacher of R. Yishmael, R. Akiva's great interlocutor, and taught Yishmael a special method of Torah analysis known as *clal u'frat*. He was gentle and forthcoming in his relationships with people. He once testified about himself: "I never in my life sought respect through the degradation of my fellow." He always immediately forgave anyone who troubled or vexed him.[13] He supported the *nasi*, Rabban Shimon b. Gamliel II, when other sages sought to oust him. He remained a close associate of the *nasi* and became a primary teacher of R. Yehuda the Prince.

---

13. Megilla 28a.

Accepts the yoke of Torah … they remove from him the yoke of the government and … worldly pursuits

- Obedience to God is resistance to tyrants.
- Whoever accepts the rule of God in a genuine, deeply personal way, is liberated from fear of government (even of dictators), and is released as well from the tyranny of making a living.
- These comments may refer to actual exemptions from taxes and to financial subsidies given to scholars to enable them to concentrate on their learning.

Throws off the yoke of Torah

Human nature abhors a vacuum. If one throws off the limits implied by Torah ethics and laws, he frequently becomes not a free spirit or freethinker but a slave to human governments and human written rules and conventions.

Mishna 6

רַבִּי חֲלַפְתָּא בֶּן דוֹסָא אִישׁ כְּפַר חֲנַנְיָה אוֹמֵר: עֲשָׂרָה שֶׁיּוֹשְׁבִין וְעוֹסְקִין בַּתּוֹרָה שְׁכִינָה שְׁרוּיָה בֵינֵיהֶם, שֶׁנֶּאֱמַר: אֱלֹהִים נִצָּב בַּעֲדַת־אֵל: וּמִנַּיִן אֲפִלּוּ חֲמִשָּׁה, שֶׁנֶּאֱמַר: וַאֲגֻדָּתוֹ עַל־אֶרֶץ יְסָדָהּ: וּמִנַּיִן אֲפִלּוּ שְׁלֹשָׁה, שֶׁנֶּאֱמַר: בְּקֶרֶב אֱלֹהִים יִשְׁפֹּט: וּמִנַּיִן אֲפִלּוּ שְׁנַיִם, שֶׁנֶּאֱמַר: אָז נִדְבְּרוּ יִרְאֵי יהוה אִישׁ אֶל־רֵעֵהוּ, וַיַּקְשֵׁב יהוה וַיִּשְׁמָע: וּמִנַּיִן אֲפִלּוּ אֶחָד, שֶׁנֶּאֱמַר: בְּכָל־הַמָּקוֹם אֲשֶׁר אַזְכִּיר אֶת־שְׁמִי, אָבוֹא אֵלֶיךָ וּבֵרַכְתִּיךָ:

R. Ḥalafta b. Dosa of Kfar Ḥanania says: Ten who sit together and occupy themselves with the Torah, the *Shekhina* rests among them, as it says: "God stands in the godly congregation."[14] How do we know that if five [participate, God is also present]? As it says: "He has founded His band upon the earth."[15] How do we know that if three [participate, God is also present]? As it says: "In the presence of the judges, God judges."[16] How do we know that even if two [participate, God is also present]? As it says: "Then those who revere God spoke to each other, and the Lord paid attention and heard."[17] How do we know that even if one [participates, God is also present]? As it says: "In every place where I have My name mentioned, I will come to you and bless you."[18]

14. Psalms 82:1.
15. Amos 9:6.
16. Psalms 82:1.
17. Malachi 3:16.
18. Exodus 20:20.

HISTORICAL BACKGROUND

R. Ḥalafta b. Dosa (second century CE) was from Kfar Ḥanania, a settlement in the Galilee. Rashi states that R. Ḥalafta's family originally came from Babylonia.[19]

Congregation

Ten adult males make up a *minyan* in a congregation coming together for a ritual purpose.

Band

A band implies a group of less than ten, but more than three. Since the purpose is a holy one, i.e., the study of Torah, God is seen as having established the group.

In the presence of the judges

There are three judges in the standard, first-level rabbinical court. This proves that God participates in a group of three who have come together for a holy purpose.

19. Yoma 66b.

Mishna 7

רַבִּי אֶלְעָזָר אִישׁ בַּרְתּוֹתָא אוֹמֵר: תֶּן לוֹ מִשֶּׁלּוֹ, שֶׁאַתָּה וְשֶׁלְּךָ שֶׁלּוֹ. וְכֵן בְּדָוִד הוּא אוֹמֵר: כִּי־מִמְּךָ הַכֹּל, וּמִיָּדְךָ נָתַנּוּ לָךְ:

R. Elazar of Bartota says: Give to God [and you give] of His [God's], for you and yours are God's. And so David said: "All things come from You; it is a [gift] from Your hand that we have given to You."[20]

HISTORICAL BACKGROUND

R. Elazar of Bartota (second century CE) was a student of R. Yehoshua b. Ḥanania and a colleague of R. Akiva. He was a person of legendary goodness and generosity who would give away his last penny to help the poor. He taught that one who gives *tzedaka* does an act greater than bringing all the different types of sacrifices. His proof text was: "To do righteousness [*tzedaka*] and justice is more admired by God than sacrifice."[21] The Talmud says that the treasurers of the communal welfare fund, when out raising money to help the needy, would run away when they saw R. Elazar of Bartota coming, for fear that he would give beyond his means in order to help others. Once he was carrying his daughter's dowry money with him when he discovered that an orphaned boy and girl had no money to get married. He gave them the dowry money,

---

20. I Chronicles 29:14.
21. Proverbs 21:3.

saying they needed it more than his daughter (since orphans have no one to turn to).

Give to God of [God's]

Acts of charity and financial outlay for religious purposes should not be seen as taking money out of our pockets to give to another. Rather, God has given us all that we possess. We are only giving back a fraction of the goodness bestowed on us.

רַבִּי יַעֲקֹב אוֹמֵר: הַמְהַלֵּךְ בַּדֶּרֶךְ וְשׁוֹנֶה, וּמַפְסִיק מִמִּשְׁנָתוֹ וְאוֹמֵר, מַה נָּאֶה אִילָן זֶה, מַה נָּאֶה נִיר זֶה, מַעֲלֶה עָלָיו הַכָּתוּב כְּאִלּוּ מִתְחַיֵּב בְּנַפְשׁוֹ.

R. Yaakov[22] [b. Korshai] says: He who is walking on the way and going over his [Torah] and interrupts his study and says: "How beautiful is this tree! How beautiful is this furrowed field!" Scripture considers him as if he is guilty of a mortal sin.

HISTORICAL BACKGROUND

R. Yaakov b. Korshai lived in the late second century CE and is said to have been a grandson of R. Elisha b. Avuya, R. Meir's teacher. Elisha broke away from rabbinic Judaism and became a skeptic. R. Yaakov was a primary associate of the *nasi* Rabban Shimon b. Gamliel II, and a key teacher of the *nasi*'s son, R. Yehuda the Prince. It says in the Talmud that two sages set an intellectual trap for Rabban Shimon b. Gamliel II by challenging him at his public lecture, trying to show him up as ignorant of the obscure laws of ritual impurity found in Tractate Uktzin. (They were trying to force the *nasi* out of office.) R. Yaakov learned of the plot, tipped off R. Shimon, and prepped him on all the laws involved. Being well prepared, the *nasi* prevailed over his inquisitors, thus foiling the plot.

Interrupts his study and says, "How beautiful!"

The point is that interrupting Torah study is a terrible act, even if done to admire beauty. Since the Torah never suggests that pausing while learning Torah is a capital offense, various traditional commentators offer a rationale for R. Yaakov's statement:

22. Some texts attribute this saying to R. Shimon b. Yoḥai.

- Ḥe was walking alone on a dangerous road (see mishna 4, above), but the merit of learning Torah was protecting him. By stopping his Torah study, he exposed himself to danger.
- It is a mitzva to admire nature and even to say a blessing over beautiful, natural phenomena such as a rainbow, or when the trees first blossom in the spring, or when tasting a fruit. However, here the sin is to break off from Torah study in order to appreciate beauty, thus pitting God's beautiful revelation against God's beautiful nature. There are two books of revelation – Torah and nature ("The heavens tell the glory of God and the firmament proclaims God's handiwork"[23]). The two do not contradict each other since they have one Creator. Each should be accorded its own respect and studied in its own time.

23. Psalms 19:1.

Mishna 8

רַבִּי דוֹסְתַּאי בְּרַבִּי יַנַּאי מִשּׁוּם רַבִּי מֵאִיר אוֹמֵר: כָּל הַשּׁוֹכֵחַ דָּבָר אֶחָד מִמִּשְׁנָתוֹ, מַעֲלֶה עָלָיו הַכָּתוּב כְּאִלּוּ מִתְחַיֵּב בְּנַפְשׁוֹ, שֶׁנֶּאֱמַר: רַק הִשָּׁמֶר לְךָ וּשְׁמֹר נַפְשְׁךָ מְאֹד, פֶּן־תִּשְׁכַּח אֶת־הַדְּבָרִים אֲשֶׁר־רָאוּ עֵינֶיךָ: יָכוֹל אֲפִלּוּ תָקְפָה עָלָיו מִשְׁנָתוֹ, תַּלְמוּד לוֹמַר: וּפֶן יָסוּרוּ מִלְּבָבְךָ כֹּל יְמֵי חַיֶּיךָ: הָא אֵינוֹ מִתְחַיֵּב בְּנַפְשׁוֹ, עַד שֶׁיֵּשֵׁב וִיסִירֵם מִלִּבּוֹ.

R. Dostai b. Yannai, in the name of R. Meir, says: [With regard to] one who forgets a single item of his learning, Scripture considers it as if he has committed a mortal sin, as it says: "But be very careful and protect your soul very much lest you forget the things which your eyes have seen."[24] You might think that forgetting is a sin even if one's study just became too hard for him. Therefore, the teaching goes on to state: "Lest they depart from your heart all the days of your life."[25] This implies that he is not mortally guilty until [unless] he sits down and [deliberately] removes them from his heart.

HISTORICAL BACKGROUND

Little is known of R. Dostai b. Yannai's (second century CE) halakhic teachings, but numerous aggadic statements in his name are preserved. (He stated that when one gives a small coin to a poor person, he has achieved the merit of greeting the *Shekhina*.[26]) He had a wry sense of

24. Deuteronomy 4:9.
25. Ibid.
26. Bava Batra 10a.

humor. Once he was asked why Jerusalem was not blessed by God with hot water springs as Tiberias was. He answered: So that the pilgrims could never say: "It was worth going to Jerusalem just for the hot water springs!"[27]

In the name of R. Meir

R. Dostai heard this teaching from R. Meir. The sages consider it a mitzva to credit the person who originated an idea. If you credit the source, you bring redemption to the world. The proof text is that Esther reported the plot of Bigtan and Teresh against Aḥashverosh to the king in Mordekhai's name, even though she might have gotten more personal credit by not attributing her source. When King Aḥashverosh had the chronicle read during his night of sleeplessness, Mordekhai was credited, and this was a turning point in the events. The king's gratitude led him to honor Mordekhai, which saved him from Haman's gallows and started the evil vizier's rapid descent.[28] Another incentive to giving credit to prior teachers is that attribution confirms that this Torah has been handed down as a tradition from generation to generation, which adds to its prestige and authority.

One who forgets a single item of his learning… as if he has committed a mortal sin

Throughout the Talmud, upholding learning is the highest value and rejecting Torah study is seen as a terrible sin that will lead to many other wrongful behaviors.

One's study just became too hard for him

We are only human. Forgetting is not a sin. Only deliberate rejection of Torah study and knowledge is sinful behavior.

27. Pesaḥim 8b.

28. Esther 2:21–23; 6:1–13.

Mishna 9

רַבִּי חֲנִינָא בֶּן דּוֹסָא אוֹמֵר: כָּל שֶׁיִּרְאַת חֶטְאוֹ קוֹדֶמֶת לְחָכְמָתוֹ, חָכְמָתוֹ מִתְקַיֶּמֶת. וְכָל שֶׁחָכְמָתוֹ קוֹדֶמֶת לְיִרְאַת חֶטְאוֹ, אֵין חָכְמָתוֹ מִתְקַיֶּמֶת.

R. Ḥanina b. Dosa says: Everyone whose fear of sin has first priority over his wisdom, his wisdom will endure. Everyone whose wisdom takes priority over his fear of sin, his wisdom will not endure.

HISTORICAL BACKGROUND

R. Ḥanina b. Dosa (first century CE) and his wife are described in the Talmud as pious people of simple faith whose good, generous nature and self-abnegation made them worthy of miracles: "The whole world is fed by the merit of My son Ḥanina [b. Dosa], and My son Ḥanina's [needs are] personally satisfied with a measure of carob fruits from Friday to Friday."[29] He prayed with such concentration and power that people turned to him to pray for desperately ill children. His concentration was so total that we are told that once during his prayer a poisonous snake bit him but he did not even notice. With some humor, the Talmud tells that R. Ḥanina was unaffected, but the snake died (such is the protective power of elemental piety). "Woe to a person who is bitten by a viper, but woe to a viper who bites [Ḥanina] ben Dosa."[30] The Talmud states that when R. Ḥanina passed away, miracle-makers ceased to be. These mishnas are the only theological statements by R. Ḥanina b. Dosa

29. Taanit 24b.
30. Y. Berakhot 9a.

quoted in the Talmud. All the other references are to his prayers and acts of piety.

Fear of sin has first priority over his wisdom

This is a paradox. One would think that if wisdom is put as one's highest priority, then it will constantly grow and endure. Putting fear of sin first sounds like placing piety ahead of study and knowledge so that the outcome will be second-class wisdom. No, says R. Ḥanina. Torah knowledge is intended to inculcate fear (i.e., reverence) of God. If that virtue is solidly anchored in the person, then he will treasure and preserve the wisdom of Torah. If the person heaps up knowledge but does not give fear of God any priority or adequate weight, then his wisdom will be evaluated as much less important. Ultimately, it will be downgraded, neglected, and forgotten.

הוּא הָיָה אוֹמֵר: כָּל שֶׁמַּעֲשָׂיו מְרֻבִּין מֵחָכְמָתוֹ, חָכְמָתוֹ מִתְקַיֶּמֶת. וְכָל שֶׁחָכְמָתוֹ מְרֻבָּה מִמַּעֲשָׂיו, אֵין חָכְמָתוֹ מִתְקַיֶּמֶת.

He used to say: Anyone whose [good] deeds exceed his wisdom, his wisdom will endure. Anyone whose wisdom exceeds his [good] deeds, his wisdom will not endure.

[Good] deeds exceed his wisdom

- As above, Torah wisdom is a matter of life-and-death importance to people whose good deeds exceed their wisdom. If they study Torah but their knowledge outweighs their good deeds, they will not grasp the true value and importance of Torah wisdom. This means that the wisdom is unlikely to endure.
- One who does not do many good deeds may likely be someone who does many bad deeds. Then God would reject his Torah study and it will not endure. "To the wicked, God said: What are you doing reciting My laws and mouthing My covenant? Yet you hate My discipline and cast My words behind you!"[31]

---

31. Psalms 50:16–17.

Mishna 10

הוּא הָיָה אוֹמֵר: כָּל שֶׁרוּחַ הַבְּרִיּוֹת נוֹחָה הֵימֶנּוּ, רוּחַ הַמָּקוֹם נוֹחָה הֵימֶנּוּ. וְכָל שֶׁאֵין רוּחַ הַבְּרִיּוֹת נוֹחָה הֵימֶנּוּ, אֵין רוּחַ הַמָּקוֹם נוֹחָה הֵימֶנּוּ.

He used to say: Anyone who is liked by his fellow human beings is liked by God; anyone who is not liked by human beings is not liked by God.

Liked by his fellow human beings … liked by God

- One can be harsh, judgmental, etc. in the name of piety and loyalty to God. R. Ḥanina believes that God wants pious people to be kind, loving, and accepting of others, so their religiosity will make them liked by fellow human beings.
- If you love God you should love human beings, who are created in the image of God. Thereby, you will win people's affection.
- It is an oxymoron to love God and be hateful toward others. Such behavior also brings God into disrepute with human beings.

רַבִּי דוֹסָא בֶּן הַרְכִּינָס אוֹמֵר: שֵׁנָה שֶׁל שַׁחֲרִית, וְיַיִן שֶׁל צָהֳרַיִם, וְשִׂיחַת הַיְלָדִים, וִישִׁיבַת בָּתֵּי כְנֵסִיּוֹת שֶׁל עַמֵּי הָאָרֶץ, מוֹצִיאִין אֶת הָאָדָם מִן הָעוֹלָם.

R. Dosa b. Harkinas says: Sleeping [late] in the morning, drinking wine in the afternoon, [constant, immature] talking with children, and sitting in the meeting places of the unlearned shorten a man's life.

HISTORICAL BACKGROUND

R. Dosa b. Harkinas – both the son and the father carry Greek names. Dosa (first century CE) was a contemporary of Rabban Yoḥanan b. Zakkai, but outlived him. In his old age, he was too frail to go to the house of study, and his colleagues at Yavneh would come to his home to solicit his judgment and knowledge.

Sleeping in the morning

- This suggests a disordered life – up all night and sleeping late in the day.
- Sleeping late means missing the deadlines to say the morning prayers, or failing to attend school, or coming late to work. All this will lead to bad behavior, loss of a job, etc. This can have an effect on one's longevity.

Drinking wine in the afternoon

This refers to problem drinking, not to taking an aperitif at a friendly social gathering. Alcoholism and/or neglect of work will have further social and economic consequences, and can ultimately shorten life.

Talking with children

Excessive talking with children reflects immaturity and an inability to carry on adult conversation. An inability to socialize with peers leads to an inability to bond with peers. Social isolation leads to depression, which can have life-threatening consequences.

Sitting in the meeting places of the unlearned

- To constantly rub shoulders with a group is to be influenced by it.
- This passage may also reflect the tensions in relations between the sages and the unlearned. R. Akiva once mentioned that when he was an illiterate laborer, he once said that if he could get his hands on a Torah scholar he would bite him fiercely.

Shorten a man's life

In the United States, lower levels of education are correlated with unhealthy lifestyles, such as higher rates of smoking, obesity, high blood pressure, and poor nutrition patterns – all of which lead to a shorter life.

Mishna 11

רַבִּי אֱלְעָזָר הַמּוֹדָעִי אוֹמֵר:
הַמְחַלֵּל אֶת הַקֳּדָשִׁים, וְהַמְבַזֶּה
אֶת הַמּוֹעֲדוֹת, וְהַמַּלְבִּין פְּנֵי
חֲבֵרוֹ בָּרַבִּים, וְהַמֵּפֵר בְּרִיתוֹ
שֶׁל אַבְרָהָם אָבִינוּ, וְהַמְגַלֶּה
פָּנִים בַּתּוֹרָה שֶׁלֹּא כַהֲלָכָה,
אַף עַל פִּי שֶׁיֵּשׁ בְּיָדוֹ תּוֹרָה
וּמַעֲשִׂים טוֹבִים, אֵין לוֹ חֵלֶק
לָעוֹלָם הַבָּא.

R. Elazar of Modi'in says: He who profanes sacred objects, [or] shows contempt for the festivals, [or] puts his friend to shame publicly, [or] breaks the covenant of our Father Abraham, [or] distorts the Torah interpretation [to arrive at a wrong ruling], even if he has Torah and good deeds in his hand, will have no share in the World to Come.

HISTORICAL BACKGROUND

R. Elazar of Modi'in, (the Hasmoneans' city of origin) is known as Elazar HaModa'i in the Talmud. He survived the Destruction of the Second Temple and played an important role at Yavneh in the early second century CE. (After difficult debates on various Torah subjects, the *nasi*, Rabban Gamliel II, was wont to say: We still need the Modi'in man's judgment.) Tragically, he was killed by his nephew Bar Kokhba, the leader of the Jewish revolt against Rome, due to a false report that R. Elazar was guilty of treason by conspiring with the Romans to let them into the city of Beitar. In fact, R. Elazar was deeply devoted to the Jewish cause. The Talmud sees Bar Kokhba's reckless behavior in killing his uncle as the culminating act of his arrogance and growing megalomania, which emerged in the course of the initially successful rebellion and in light of the publicly expressed expectation that Bar Kokhba was the Messiah.

Profanes sacred objects ... shows contempt for the festivals
Such behaviors degrade sacred objects and values, as well as erode respect for them. Therefore, acting in this contemptuous manner cancels out the merit of Torah study and good deeds one has accrued. One who behaves in this way despite his erudition and performance of mitzvot will be condemned when he stands for judgment in the World to Come.

Shows contempt for the festivals
Some commentators interpret this as disrespect for the intermediate days of the festivals (of Passover and Sukkot). Since these days do not carry the prohibitions of work prescribed for the full festival days, there is room for variation and individual judgment in observing them. However, the person who exploits the delegation of authority to his own judgment in order to belittle and degrade these days is engaging in sinful behavior.

Puts his friend to shame publicly

- This is one of the gravest sins a person can commit. The Talmud explains it as morally equivalent to actual murder, pointing out that the humiliated person turns red and then white, as if someone had spilled his blood. A person's dignity is shattered when he is humiliated in front of other people. If a person misbehaves, it is a mitzva to correct or criticize him: "You shall surely correct your friend" (Lev. 19:17). However, the criticism should be done privately and respectfully so the offender will learn and improve but not be hurt.[32] To criticize and/or shame a person publicly turns the act of chastising into a grave sin, just about the gravest there is (murder of the soul). Consequently, "it is better to throw oneself into a flaming oven rather than to shame someone publicly."[33]

---

32. Arakhin 16b.
33. Bava Metzia 58b.

- The act of shaming the friend was masked as a good deed – to rebuke sin or to uphold the public good. But in fact it was an act of character assassination and an assault on the other's dignity. You can fool the public by doing such an act as if it were for the sake of good, but you cannot fool God, who sees right through it to the evil intentions which drive it. Therefore, God will punish the sinner by depriving him of his share in the World to Come.

Breaks the covenant of... Abraham

This is someone who rejects circumcision, which is the mark of the covenant given initially to our forefather Abraham. He is unwilling to stand up for the covenant or stand out as a Jew. He seeks to hide the fact that he is Jewish, and therefore forfeits the portion of the World to Come which every Jew obtains simply by being Jewish. (See Introduction.)

Distorts... interpretation [to arrive at a wrong ruling]

He perverts the legitimate process of interpretation in order to justify a wrong application of the Torah. This deliberate distortion and misleading of others is a form of lying, and a grave sin because it pollutes the understanding of Torah. By appearing to be an acceptable interpretation, a ruling of this type may prevent the other from properly analyzing and applying the Torah correctly. Or the veneer of the process of deriving the halakha may intimidate the other into accepting this misapplication of Torah. As above, the gravity of the sin is deepened because it uses the cover of Torah to make wrong into right. God will not be tricked; He will punish this crime.

No share in the World to Come

This does not mean that he will be suffering in Gehenna for eternity. *Tosafot* say that there is a maximum of twelve months of suffering in the World to Come, even for such serious misbehaviors. Publicly shaming another person is so grave a sin that one is permanently placed in Gehenna. However, after the twelve-month period, the sinner is neither tormented nor enjoys the extraordinary spiritual pleasures of heaven. Sinners exist in a kind of unfeeling, unchanging, spiritual no-man's-land, deprived but not suffering.[34]

34. Ibid., and *Tosafot* ad loc., s.v. *ḥutz migimel sheyordin.*

Mishna 12

רַבִּי יִשְׁמָעֵאל אוֹמֵר: הֱוֵי קַל לְרֹאשׁ וְנוֹחַ לְתִשְׁחֹרֶת, וֶהֱוֵי מְקַבֵּל אֶת כָּל הָאָדָם בְּשִׂמְחָה.	R. Yishmael says: Be suppliant to a superior, submissive under compulsory service, and welcome everybody cheerfully.

HISTORICAL BACKGROUND

R. Yishmael b. Elisha (late first–second century CE) was a priest. His grandfather was the High Priest who was tortured to death by the Romans alongside Rabban Shimon b. Gamliel I. According to another account, his father also served as High Priest. The Talmud reports that as a child, R. Yishmael himself was held as a prisoner of war in Rome, but that R. Yehoshua b. Ḥanania heard about him and obtained his release in return for a large ransom. He grew up and became a highly respected scholar and close colleague of R. Akiva, who called him "my brother."

R. Akiva represented the school of mystical interpretation which read the Torah as "out of this world" and full of hidden meanings. R. Yishmael represented a school which stressed the plain sense meaning in its interpretation. R. Akiva insisted that every word in the Torah was fraught with messages, and that in a sentence, the presence of prepositions such as "*et*" implied additional laws. R. Yishmael countered that "the Torah speaks the language of people" (so that not every phrase is refined and burnished and loaded with messages). Nor is the Torah written in strict chronological order, he said; therefore he objected to attempts to draw inference from the sequence of passages and topics.

A talmudic source credits R. Yishmael with expanding Hillel's interpretive principles which can be used to derive halakha from the

Torah from seven to thirteen.[35] He is also credited as the author of *Mekhilta* on Exodus, a collection of halakhic midrashim. Among his halakhic maxims were: "The burden of proof is on he who seeks to be strict" and "Saving a life overrides all but three commandments of the Torah, because of the principle: 'You shall keep My laws and My rules which a person shall do, and *live by them*' (Lev. 8:6), not die by them."[36]

Be suppliant to a superior

Be flexible and bending with a superior, who is more powerful than you. This is prudent advice. Do not start up with a lion.

Submissive under compulsory service

- Even when service is imposed, just do it. Do not fight it in vain. Just get it over with.
- There is an alternative translation of these two sentences: Be bending (i.e., respectful) toward an older person; be easygoing and kind to a young person. (The word *tishḥoret* comes from the word *shaḥor,* black. This refers to one with dark hair, i.e., a young person.)

Welcome everybody cheerfully

- This is a form of respecting and honoring the other.
- The spirit of cheer also reflects an attitude of optimism and hope toward life.
- Encountering another person brings anticipation that something good will happen.
- My optimism and cheerfulness raise the spirits of another person or a group. Thus, I am giving a gift to others with my good mood.

35. Tosefta, Sanhedrin 7:5; *Torat Kohanim,* Leviticus 1.
36. Sanhedrin 74a.

Mishna 13

רַבִּי עֲקִיבָא אוֹמֵר: שְׂחוֹק וְקַלּוּת רֹאשׁ מַרְגִּילִין אֶת הָאָדָם לְעֶרְוָה. מָסֹרֶת סְיָג לַתּוֹרָה, מַעְשְׂרוֹת סְיָג לָעֹשֶׁר, נְדָרִים סְיָג לַפְּרִישׁוּת, סְיָג לַחָכְמָה שְׁתִיקָה.

R. Akiva says: Jesting and levity accustom a person to sexual immorality; the tradition is a fence [*siyag*] for the Torah; tithings are a fence for [protecting] wealth; vows are a fence for self-restraint; silence is a fence for wisdom.

HISTORICAL BACKGROUND

R. Akiva b. Yosef is one of the greatest sages of the Talmud. He was particularly influential with his development of a methodology to derive more meanings and messages by close readings of every word, every letter, and even every jot and tittle (curlicue) on the Hebrew letters in a Torah scroll.

R. Akiva was the child of converts. He grew up in a poor, landless family (they were like migrant workers), and was illiterate until adulthood. Raḥel, the daughter of Kalba Savua, the wealthiest man in Jerusalem, met Akiva as a poor shepherd, loved him, married him, and inspired him to go to the academy and become a scholar. Disowned by her father for marrying Akiva, Raḥel put him through school for years, living in complete poverty and supporting him. He rose to become the greatest teacher of his generation.

R. Akiva supported the Bar Kokhba rebellion in 132–135 CE and hailed its leader, Shimon bar Kosiba, as the long-awaited Messiah and deliverer of Israel. He gave him the name Bar Kokhba (son of the star), associating him with the pronouncement of the non-Jewish prophet

Balaam: "A star rises from Jacob" (Num. 24:17), which was interpreted as a messianic text. The rebellion succeeded in temporarily driving the Romans out of Jerusalem, but the empire brought up reinforcements and crushed the insurrection. During the repression that followed, the Romans killed leading Torah scholars and sought to suppress Torah study. R. Akiva continued teaching Torah in defiance of the Roman interdict. He recruited new students, including some who became the mainstays of the Mishna. R. Akiva was captured and, after a period of imprisonment, he was tortured and put to death. He died with the words of the *Shema* prayer on his lips: "You shall love the Lord your God with all your heart, with all your soul, and with all your might."

R. Akiva says

This entire mishna is about the role of boundaries and limits in protecting values and good behavior.

Jesting and levity accustom a person to... immorality

Inappropriate humor and off-color language can be used to soften up hesitation on the part of a seducer or a potential seducee's resistance. To assure proper behavior, fence off – do not use – raunchy language and frivolous come-ons.

Tradition is a fence for the Torah

If scholars and students are guided by the sages' tradition and rules of exegesis, the Torah will be more protected against misapplication and misuse.

Tithings are a fence for wealth

- Generosity in giving charity is a fence; it protects, one's wealth. This is because God will reciprocate the charity.
- Society will be better off and less likely to lash back at the wealthy if they are generous with their money.

Vows are a fence for self-restraint

When you want to limit yourself beyond the Torah's legal requirements, then taking on an additional restriction through a vow may carry you through a situation where the will is weak and a little voice is whispering: The Torah does not require this boundary; why should you control yourself?

Note that the Talmud is ambivalent about vows even as it is hesitant about voluntary restraints that go beyond Torah prohibition. According to one opinion, the additional vow goes beyond the letter of the law but helps the individual reach a higher spiritual level. According to an opposing opinion, "Do not be overly righteous" (Eccl. 7:16). Taking on more may reflect some type of excess (pride, urge, ambition), and the extra burden may make a violation of the standard requirement more likely. Also, one is denying to himself what God did not deny him. According to one talmudic view, a person will have to answer at the final judgment for every (legitimate) pleasure passed up in this life.[37]

Silence is a fence for wisdom

- Silence enables listening; listening enables one to absorb wisdom from others.
- Remaining silent means speaking less. Speaking less means that one is less likely to say foolish things. This will protect his reputation for being wise.
- Practicing silence means that not every bit of wisdom we have should be spoken publicly or applied to every issue. People tend to apply their wisdom repeatedly to each successive situation, especially when the previous ones had favorable outcomes. Eventually, the wisdom will be applied to a situation where the outcome was unfavorable. Therefore, falling silent – sensing the limits of one's wisdom and reining it in before it is applied one step or situation too far – is a form of wisdom. Paradoxically, such silence protects wisdom by asserting its limits.

37. Y. Kiddushin 4, last paragraph.

Mishna 14

הוּא הָיָה אוֹמֵר, חָבִיב אָדָם שֶׁנִּבְרָא בְצֶלֶם, חִבָּה יְתֵרָה נוֹדַעַת לוֹ שֶׁנִּבְרָא בְצֶלֶם, שֶׁנֶּאֱמַר: כִּי בְּצֶלֶם אֱלֹהִים עָשָׂה אֶת־הָאָדָם: חֲבִיבִין יִשְׂרָאֵל שֶׁנִּקְרְאוּ בָנִים לַמָּקוֹם, חִבָּה יְתֵרָה נוֹדַעַת לָהֶם שֶׁנִּקְרְאוּ בָנִים לַמָּקוֹם, שֶׁנֶּאֱמַר: בָּנִים אַתֶּם לַיהוה אֱלֹהֵיכֶם: חֲבִיבִין יִשְׂרָאֵל שֶׁנִּתַּן לָהֶם כְּלִי חֶמְדָּה, חִבָּה יְתֵרָה נוֹדַעַת לָהֶם שֶׁנִּתַּן לָהֶם כְּלִי חֶמְדָּה שֶׁבּוֹ נִבְרָא הָעוֹלָם, שֶׁנֶּאֱמַר: כִּי לֶקַח טוֹב נָתַתִּי לָכֶם, תּוֹרָתִי אַל־תַּעֲזֹבוּ:

He used to say: The human being is beloved, for he was created in the image [of God]; even greater love [was shown by God] in that the human being is informed that he was created in the image [of God], as it says: "For in the image of God, God created the human being."[38] The People of Israel are beloved, for they were designated as children of God; even greater love was shown to them in that they were informed that they were designated as the children of God, as it says: "You are the children of the Lord your God."[39] The People of Israel are beloved, for they were given a precious instrument [the Torah]; even greater love was shown to them in that they were informed that they were given a precious instrument with which the world was created, as it says: "For I have given you good instruction; do not forsake my Torah [i.e., My teaching]."[40]

38. Genesis 9:6.

39. Deuteronomy 14:1.

40. Proverbs 4:2.

The human being is beloved

- God created humanity out of love. God is infinite and beyond personal need, thus God created out of desire to have an object of love. By implication, all of creation is an act of love on God's part. But humanity is especially beloved because this form of life is so developed that it is God-like (in the image of God). This inner capacity of consciousness (understanding, emotional, intuitive) enables humanity, in a limited but nevertheless God-like way, to understand God as He is. This prepares human beings to relate to and reciprocally love God. As a result, God loves them even more.
- Human beings are beloved because they were created in the image of God. According to Tractate Sanhedrin 37a, anything created in the image of God is endowed with three intrinsic and inalienable dignities: infinite value (saving one life is equivalent to saving a whole world), equality, and uniqueness (images created by human beings such as on currency or stamps can be replicated and mass-produced, but each human being created by God is like no other). The latter quality is the mark of being created in God's image, for even identical twins are not completely identical. Uniqueness bespeaks human free will, which enables individual, divergent responses from every person in every situation. Honoring equality and uniqueness implies democracy. Respecting the dignity of uniqueness implies rejecting stereotypes and unfair generalizations.
- When one recognizes the other as an image of God and experiences that person's inner dignity, uniqueness, value, and equality, he will come to love the other as an image of God. R. Akiva is suggesting that this cycle starts with God's creating life out of divine love.

Even greater love…the human being is informed

- Every person is born with the intrinsic dignities of being infinitely valuable, equal, and unique. But if society systematically denies those dignities, for instance by legally enslaving people or by systematic degradation of outsiders, etc., then individuals may not know their own value. Outsiders and outcasts also frequently internalize the contempt shown by others. On the other hand, if people are informed that they have these intrinsic qualities, they are more likely to experience their inner worth and assert their rights. That is why the spread of democratic ideology evoked worldwide, anti-colonialist revolts.

- R. Akiva is suggesting that revelation is also an act of divine love. The Torah teaches people their dignities: their right to live, their right to justice, their right to be treated with equality and kindness, etc.

The People of Israel...children of God

To experience God's love makes one beloved. The People of Israel experienced God's love as a caring parent, for example when God appeared to the patriarchs and matriarchs and during the liberation from slavery in Egypt. They experienced God's love as a doting, protective father ("as an eagle stirs up its nest, hovering over the young eaglets *to feed them*"[41]) and as an embracing, concerned mother ("as a person is comforted by his mother when he is hurt, so will I comfort you"[42]). Every loved child feels beloved. Note that all human beings are children of God. Israel's experience of this phenomenon serves as a model for their loving all other human beings.

Even greater love...they were informed

As above, by the Israelites' being told that they were the children of God, they were given a new sense of their preciousness and dignity. As Moses initially told Pharaoh: "Thus says the Lord, Israel is My firstborn child...send My child free to serve Me." In time, the Israelites came to understand and expect the rights of a free people.

---

41. Deuteronomy 32:11.
42. Isaiah 66:13.

Beloved ... they were given a precious instrument

Giving the Torah, and indeed, all revelation, was an act of love. When you love someone, you give them a precious gift. You want them to live a happy, fulfilled, and good life. That is what the Torah is: the guide to a good life.

A precious instrument

Why is the Torah called an instrument?

- Some commentators interpret that the Torah was God's instrument with which He created the world, and hence it is precious for that reason.
- The Torah was given as an instrument with which to guide the life of the individual, to shape society, and to repair the world. It is not an end in itself but a means which God has given us to make a better life for us, for our family, for our society, and for our world.

Even greater love ... they were informed

- God expresses extra love for Israel by telling them how precious and delightful the Torah is. To know a truth – not just as a notion but as a deeply felt, experienced truth – increases its salience and impact on the person.
- Having been told to use the Torah as a tool, when we learn to wield it with greater effect we get even better results.

Mishna 15

הַכֹּל צָפוּי, וְהָרְשׁוּת נְתוּנָה, וּבְטוּב הָעוֹלָם נִדּוֹן, וְהַכֹּל לְפִי רֹב הַמַּעֲשֶׂה.	Everything is foreseen, and free will is given to humans. And the world is judged with [God's quality of] goodness. And all is decided [in God's judgment] according to the amount of good deeds.

Everything is foreseen... free will is given

R. Akiva mentions both sides of a paradox. God is omniscient, and therefore knows the future and all that will happen. Logically, this means that humans cannot experience free will and do the unexpected, because that would mean that God would not know the outcome in advance. Yet R. Akiva insists that free will also exists. Neither truth should be denied just because logic suggests that there is a contradiction between them. Reality eludes logical categories and should not be denied out of a mistaken desire for consistency: "Consistency is the hobgoblin of little minds."[43]

With this mishna, R. Akiva illustrates the richness and pluralism of rabbinic thinking. One group of sages rules "it is pure," and another group rules that the same entity is impure. The same goes for kosher and non-kosher, true and false. Yet "both are the words of the living God" (Eiruvin 13b). The limits of logic and reason should be recognized, especially given the limits of the human mind. Furthermore, life experiences, and indeed all of reality, should be accepted in their complexity and often contradictory states rather than be filtered or denied due

43. Ralph Waldo Emerson.

to philosophical or ideological blinders. And no less important: Make room for the pluralism of God's creation and human understanding.

The world is judged with God's…goodness

- God could judge the world in a spirit of harshness and retribution, with strict justice, or in a spirit of goodness, kindness, and compassion. R. Akiva insists that God employs the attributes of divine love and goodness in judging the world and the human beings in it.
- Judgment can be the expression of goodness and compassion. It teaches people what is right and what is wrong, so they learn to live a good life. In the absence of judgment, bad behaviors continue, and sin and evil may fester and become more deadly and dangerous. If I love another, I will offer that person my best judgment in order to help him or her.
- Implied in R. Akiva's teaching is the concept of providence, that God is attentive to every moment and every action of every human being. (Maimonides argues that humans are the only living species that is the object of individual providence.)

All is decided according to the amount of good deeds

A human being is judged on balance. No one is perfect. There is no one "righteous in the land who does only good and never sins."[44] God makes allowances for human weakness. A judgment of innocence or acquittal is based on a person's having done more good deeds than bad. Maimonides says that if one does one more good deed than bad over a lifetime, he is considered a *tzaddik*, a righteous person.[45]

Two factors offset this. First, sometimes a person does an act so heroic, so lifesaving, so precious, that he earns the World to Come with this one act, in one hour – even though he may have done many more bad deeds in his lifetime. In other words, not just quantity, but quality counts. Secondly, there is a rabbinic concept of *zekhut avot*, the merit of

44. Ecclesiastes 7:20.

45. *Mishneh Torah, Hilkhot Teshuva* 3:1, 4.

one's ancestors. They may have done so much good for the world that their "surplus" of good may be dipped into for the benefit of a favorable judgment on their descendants. People are part of families, social networks, and communities. Those connections increase (or decrease) the individual's contributions to the world.

R. Akiva's presumption here is that the world is run on providential lines, and all that occurs to a person is a true reflection of his behavior. The Talmud goes further, expressing R. Akiva's view that everything that occurs in the world is right. His dictum was: "Whatever the All-Merciful does [in this world] is for the good."[46] He himself once experienced a series of setbacks on a journey. He could not get lodgings in the town in which he arrived and therefore passed the night in a nearby field. During the night, the wind blew out his candle, his rooster was eaten by a feral cat, and his donkey was devoured by a passing lion. After each incident he insisted that "whatever the All-Merciful does is for the good." Sure enough, a group of brigands invaded the town, robbing and abducting all of its inhabitants – but R. Akiva, in the field without the candle's light to illuminate him to the brigands and without animals to make noise and betray his whereabouts, went undetected. He repeated that this proved his principle that whatever the All-Merciful does *in this world* is for the good.

By this standard, it would appear that there can be neither suffering of the innocent nor triumph for the wicked in this world. This appears to be a simplistic affirmation coming from a person who upheld in all its raw contradiction the concept that there is both divine free knowledge and human free will.

Apparently, in order to assure that we not turn R. Akiva into a simplistic Candide, the Talmud tells us that R. Akiva himself was tortured to death by the Romans for the crime of teaching Torah at a time when it was proscribed by them. First (on Yom Kippur), they tore off his flesh with iron combs. Then they sold the pieces in the marketplace as meat. The Talmud testifies that the angels were so revolted by this manifest injustice that they cried out to God: "This is Torah, and this is its reward [for a life of teaching it]?"

46. Berakhot 60b.

In another story, the Talmud tells us that Moses' spirit visited R. Akiva's academy. Moses is dazzled by Akiva's brilliance in Torah scholarship, and then is deeply shocked when he discovers his grisly fate. Moses then protests: "This is Torah, and this is its reward [for studying and teaching it]?" The only answer he receives from God is: "Be silent! So it has come to My mind!"[47] In other words, the fate of the innocent who suffer unjustly in this world is an inscrutable decree of God. Thus the Talmud leaves us torn by the paradoxes of faith and doubt, of trust and protest, which correspond to R. Akiva's theological paradoxes that make up this mishna.

Of course, one could apply Akiva's teaching in this mishna only to the afterlife. In that world, no innocents are tortured and no evildoers are lording it over everyone else.

47. Ibid., 61b; Menaḥot 29b.

Mishna 16

הוּא הָיָה אוֹמֵר: הַכֹּל נָתוּן בְּעֵרָבוֹן, וּמְצוּדָה פְּרוּסָה עַל כָּל הַחַיִּים. הֶחָנוּת פְּתוּחָה, וְהַחֶנְוָנִי מַקִּיף, וְהַפִּנְקָס פָּתוּחַ, וְהַיָּד כּוֹתֶבֶת, וְכָל הָרוֹצֶה לִלְווֹת יָבֹא וְיִלְוֶה. וְהַגַּבָּאִין מַחֲזִירִין תָּדִיר בְּכָל יוֹם, וְנִפְרָעִין מִן הָאָדָם מִדַּעְתּוֹ וְשֶׁלֹּא מִדַּעְתּוֹ, וְיֵשׁ לָהֶם עַל מַה שֶּׁיִּסְמֹכוּ. וְהַדִּין, דִּין אֱמֶת. וְהַכֹּל מְתֻקָּן לִסְעוּדָה.

He used to say: Everything is given on pledge [collateral], and a net is spread out over all living creatures. The shop is open, the shopkeeper extends credit, the ledger is open, and the hand writes. Whoever wants to borrow can come and borrow, and the collectors go around continuously every day and they collect from people, with consent or not. And they have a basis for their claims and the judgment is a true judgment, and everything is prepared for the feast.

Everything is given on pledge

God enables people to live on trust. Newborns have done nothing and contributed nothing to the world, but God extends them "credit" to live, against the collateral of their future contributions to society and to the world.

A net is spread out over all ... creatures

- No one can escape this world with his debt unpaid.
- Death is inevitable, so live accordingly, with this in mind.

The shop...the shopkeeper...the ledger...the hand

People have free will. They can buy, sell, and exchange deeds, relationships, values, and purposes, in any manner they see fit. God lets them make these choices, but everything is recorded and people are held accountable for all their actions. People may forget. Society may overlook what was done. But God remembers all and overlooks nothing.

The collectors go around...every day

- The final debt is collected daily.
- There is a continuous process of give and take, of reward and punishment, of actions and consequences. Some people notice and some do not.

They have a basis for their claims

Here too, R. Akiva insists that people generally get their just deserts even though they may not see it that way.

Judgment is...true

In the end, R. Akiva affirms that God is good and that he, Akiva, accepts whatever life brings.

Everything is prepared for the feast

- A feast for the righteous in the World to Come has been prepared, no matter their fate in this world.
- As above, according to R. Akiva, our own actions produce what we experience in our own lifetime, for better or for worse.

Mishna 17

רַבִּי אֶלְעָזָר בֶּן עֲזַרְיָה אוֹמֵר: אִם אֵין תּוֹרָה אֵין דֶּרֶךְ אֶרֶץ, אִם אֵין דֶּרֶךְ אֶרֶץ אֵין תּוֹרָה. אִם אֵין חָכְמָה אֵין יִרְאָה, אִם אֵין יִרְאָה אֵין חָכְמָה. אִם אֵין דַּעַת אֵין בִּינָה, אִם אֵין בִּינָה אֵין דַּעַת. אִם אֵין קֶמַח אֵין תּוֹרָה, אִם אֵין תּוֹרָה אֵין קֶמַח.

R. Elazar b. Azaria says: If there is no Torah, there will be no worldly occupation [*derekh eretz*]; if there is no worldly occupation, there will be no Torah. If there is no wisdom, there will be no [true] fear [of God]; if there is no fear [of God], there will be no [true] wisdom. If there is no knowledge, there will be no understanding; if there is no understanding, there will be no knowledge. If there is no flour [i.e., bread], there will be no Torah; if there is no Torah, there will be no flour [bread].

HISTORICAL BACKGROUND

R. Elazar b. Azaria (first century CE) was a major figure in Yavneh, where the sages, initially led by Rabban Yoḥanan b. Zakkai, renewed Jewish life and launched the eventually dominant rabbinic culture. He was a popular figure because he was learned and deeply pious, yet humble, and while he was extremely wealthy, he lived modestly. He was elected *nasi* in place of the deposed Rabban Gamliel, although he was only eighteen years old at the time. The reason is that of all the candidates, he alone was learned, well-to-do, and scion of a distinguished family. (He was a tenth-generation, direct descendant of Ezra the Scribe, who led the community of Jews from Babylonia and Persia who returned to

Jerusalem.) Moreover, as R. Elazar was not identified as an opponent of Rabban Gamliel, his election reduced the deposed *nasi*'s humiliation.

No Torah ... no worldly occupation

The sages were conflicted with regard to the tension between a life of Torah study and a life of worldly occupation, i.e., earning a living. Some felt that studying Torah should be all-consuming: "You shall meditate on it day and night."[48] Earning a living could weaken Torah scholarship in two ways: there would not be enough time to master the ocean of knowledge, and earning a living would distract from learning and disturb moral judgment. The alternate position argued that earning a living by labor or a profession was an essential value in the Torah: "When you eat the fruit of the labor of your own hands, you are fortunate and well-off." You are *fortunate* in this world, and *well-off* in the World to Come.[49] Proponents of work feel that when full-time Torah study requires that a scholar be supported by the community, this turns the Torah into "a shovel with which to dig [for a living],"[50] i.e., studying Torah would be done for the support money instead of for pure, idealistic reasons.

R. Elazar argues that both positions offer too stark a dichotomy; to take either side exclusively would be to embrace a false either/or. If the person does not study Torah, then his professional work will not succeed, perhaps because he will lack a moral compass or perhaps because God will not show favor to the person who neglects Torah. But if there is no worldly work, the person will not succeed in learning Torah, perhaps because the anxiety of not having an income will destroy concentration or perhaps because the Torah study will be tainted by being dependent on others' bounty. All this may distort or pervert judgments made by the scholar. R. Elazar is arguing that a healthy balance of Torah study and work in a person's life will strengthen both enterprises.

The argument over pure Torah study supported by community funding versus scholars earning a living through business or profession has persisted down to modern times.

48. Joshua 1:8.

49. Psalms 128:2; Berakhot 8a.

50. *Pirkei Avot* 4:5.

No Torah... no worldly occupation

An alternative interpretation would translate *derekh eretz* as appropriate conduct, meaning proper etiquette in society or possibly the right way of living and working. In the nineteenth century, Rabbi Samson Raphael Hirsh translated this concept into the *Torah im derekh eretz* way of life, which combined Torah knowledge with living in modern culture and civilization so that religious Jews could live properly in the new society.

No wisdom... no fear [of God]

Much of this mishna consists of values and concepts which in the conventional view are in conflict. However, R. Elazar believes that these polar qualities develop best when both are present and interact in the person's life to strengthen each other. Some believe that fear of God is a matter of blind faith and obedience, of simple piety. Therefore, too much thinking, wisdom, and analysis undermines it. Some argue that piety is the enemy of wisdom; faith and obedience engender fanaticism and drive wisdom out. R. Elazar insists that wisdom leads to true fear of God. Absence of thought or wisdom will lead to authoritarianism, wrong moral conclusions, and wrong applications of religious principles. Together, fear of God leads to wisdom in sizing up (or limiting) the choices of human systems and authorities. Similarly, wisdom leads to proper reverence for and awe of God, not to narrow-minded or blind zealotry.

No knowledge... no understanding

The way to understanding is by amassing knowledge, sifting through it, and arriving at a deeper insight. The road to knowledge is closed unless one has some understanding. Without it, one will miss the forest for the trees or will collect masses of facts but will be left with no patterns or meaningful insights.

No flour... no Torah

One school offers the argument that poverty leaves the person free of material pursuits and moral temptation, so living a poor lifestyle is good for the potential Torah scholar. R. Elazar argues that without adequate resources to support Torah study, neither a scholar nor a Torah institution will succeed. Similarly, without amassing knowledge of Torah, individuals will not succeed in making money, either because they lack moral guidance or have failed to sharpen their mind, or because God will not reward such a person with worldly success.

R. Elazar was willing and able to live with tensions and to balance conflicting claims rather than suppress them.

הוּא הָיָה אוֹמֵר: כָּל שֶׁחָכְמָתוֹ מְרֻבָּה מִמַּעֲשָׂיו, לְמָה הוּא דוֹמֶה, לְאִילָן שֶׁעֲנָפָיו מְרֻבִּין וְשָׁרָשָׁיו מֻעָטִין, וְהָרוּחַ בָּאָה וְעוֹקַרְתּוֹ וְהוֹפַכְתּוֹ עַל פָּנָיו. שֶׁנֶּאֱמַר, וְהָיָה כְּעַרְעָר בָּעֲרָבָה, וְלֹא יִרְאֶה כִּי־יָבוֹא טוֹב, וְשָׁכַן חֲרֵרִים בַּמִּדְבָּר, אֶרֶץ מְלֵחָה וְלֹא תֵשֵׁב: אֲבָל כָּל שֶׁמַּעֲשָׂיו מְרֻבִּין מֵחָכְמָתוֹ, לְמָה הוּא דוֹמֶה, לְאִילָן שֶׁעֲנָפָיו מֻעָטִין וְשָׁרָשָׁיו מְרֻבִּין, שֶׁאֲפִלּוּ כָּל הָרוּחוֹת שֶׁבָּעוֹלָם בָּאוֹת וְנוֹשְׁבוֹת בּוֹ, אֵין מְזִיזִין אוֹתוֹ מִמְּקוֹמוֹ. שֶׁנֶּאֱמַר: וְהָיָה כְּעֵץ שָׁתוּל עַל־מַיִם, וְעַל־יוּבַל יְשַׁלַּח שָׁרָשָׁיו, וְלֹא יִרְאֶ כִּי־יָבֹא חֹם, וְהָיָה עָלֵהוּ רַעֲנָן, וּבִשְׁנַת בַּצֹּרֶת לֹא יִדְאָג, וְלֹא יָמִישׁ מֵעֲשׂוֹת פֶּרִי:

He used to say: A person whose wisdom [i.e., knowledge of Torah] is greater than his [good] deeds, to what can we compare him? To a tree whose branches are many but whose roots are few. [Therefore,] when the wind comes, it uproots the tree and blows it over, as it says: "He shall be like a Tamarisk in the desert; he shall not [live to] see when good comes. He shall dwell in the parched places in the desert, a soil that is salted and uninhabited."[51] But a person whose [good] deeds outnumber his wisdom [knowledge of Torah], to what can we compare him? To a tree with few branches but with extensive roots, for even if all the winds in the world come and blow on it, the tree shall not be moved, as it says: "And he shall be like a tree planted by the water that shall send forth its roots by the flowing river, and it shall not see when the hot wind comes. And its leaf shall be [ever] green, and in a year of drought it shall not be troubled, and it shall never move away from bearing fruit."[52]

51. Jeremiah 17:6.
52. Ibid., v. 8.

Whose wisdom is greater than his [good] deeds

Good deeds and virtuous character are fundamental. They should be the root out of which Torah knowledge, wisdom, and authority grow. Otherwise, one's Torah is theoretical and will not be applied to life. If a person's moral structure is top heavy, then hard times – or great temptations – may easily overthrow the intellectual knowledge of what is right or wrong and what is true piety.

Whose [good] deeds outnumber his wisdom

When grounded solidly in good deeds and virtue, Torah wisdom can flourish and maintain itself in the face of counter-forces and pressures or temptations. It will continue to bear the fruit of more good deeds and wisdom.

Mishna 18

רַבִּי אֱלְעָזָר בֶּן חִסְמָא אוֹמֵר: קִנִּין וּפִתְחֵי נִדָּה הֵן הֵן גּוּפֵי הֲלָכוֹת, תְּקוּפוֹת וְגִימַטְרִיָּאוֹת פַּרְפְּרָאוֹת לַחָכְמָה.

R. Elazar Hisma says: The laws governing the bird offerings and the openings of menstruation are fundamental halakhot. Calculating the seasons [i.e., astronomy] and [*gematria*] are desserts to [a meal] of wisdom.

HISTORICAL BACKGROUND

R. Elazar Ḥisma was a student of R. Yehoshua b. Ḥanania and Rabban Gamliel, and became an important figure in the following generation in Yavneh's rabbinic leadership (first half of the second century CE). He was a mathematician and a bit of a scientist. He was extremely poor and lived a life of deprivation and poverty until the *nasi*, Rabban Gamliel, became concerned for him and created a position for him at the academy in Yavneh. R. Eliezer received the name Ḥisma (strong or strengthened) after an embarrassing incident. He was leading the prayer service, and stopped because he did not know how to lead the congregation further. Instead of withdrawing out of shame, he resumed studying and developed his aptitude to lead properly. Then he returned and led that service. In honor of his strength of character, he was named Ḥisma.

Bird offerings

These were brought by women after purification from non-menstrual blood.[53]

53. Leviticus 15:29–30.

Openings of menstruation

- Knowing the source of blood which a woman sheds is critical to determine whether in fact she is ritually impure as a menstruant or not.
- Some interpret this word not as openings but as referring to the calculations of the period of menstruation.

Offerings ... menstruation

These may appear to be of negligible significance, but they should be dealt with seriously as expressions of fundamental halakhot.

Calculating the seasons

- Calculating when the equinoxes fall.
- More broadly, mathematical projections of the dates and hours when astronomical events will occur.

Gematria

- Every Hebrew letter has a numerical equivalent. For instance, *aleph* equals 1, *yud* equals 10, *tzaddi* equals 90, and so on. In *gematria,* each letter in a word or phrase is totaled and decoded in order to discern additional Torah messages and teachings.
- Others are of the opinion that R. Elazar is referring to geometry, another mathematical science, here.

Seasons ... *gematria*

These calculations are tangential to Torah study, whereas the smallest halakhic issues are not. R. Elazar, who was known for his mastery of astronomy and physics, might have been building the prestige of Torah study by suggesting that the least, i.e., "smallest" of halakhot is like the main course of a meal, whereas astronomy and geometry are like dessert – sweet, fulfilling, but not life-sustaining. Alternatively, he might have been upholding astronomy and geometry (mathematics) as adding spice, that is, interesting and stimulating insights to classic Torah wisdom.

Chapter 4

Mishna 1

בֶּן זוֹמָא אוֹמֵר: אֵיזֶהוּ חָכָם, הַלּוֹמֵד מִכָּל אָדָם, שֶׁנֶּאֱמַר: מִכָּל־מְלַמְּדַי הִשְׂכַּלְתִּי, כִּי עֵדְוֹתֶיךָ שִׂיחָה לִי: אֵיזֶהוּ גִבּוֹר, הַכּוֹבֵשׁ אֶת יִצְרוֹ, שֶׁנֶּאֱמַר: טוֹב אֶרֶךְ אַפַּיִם מִגִּבּוֹר וּמֹשֵׁל בְּרוּחוֹ מִלֹּכֵד עִיר: אֵיזֶהוּ עָשִׁיר, הַשָּׂמֵחַ בְּחֶלְקוֹ, שֶׁנֶּאֱמַר: יְגִיעַ כַּפֶּיךָ כִּי תֹאכֵל אַשְׁרֶיךָ וְטוֹב לָךְ: אַשְׁרֶיךָ בָּעוֹלָם הַזֶּה וְטוֹב לָךְ לָעוֹלָם הַבָּא. אֵיזֶהוּ מְכֻבָּד, הַמְכַבֵּד אֶת הַבְּרִיּוֹת, שֶׁנֶּאֱמַר: כִּי־מְכַבְּדַי אֲכַבֵּד, וּבֹזַי יֵקָלּוּ:

Ben Zoma says: Who is [truly] wise? One who learns from everyone, as it says: "I drew understanding from all my teachers, for Your testimonies are my [constant] meditation."[1] Who is [truly] strong? One who controls his impulses, as it says: "Better [i.e., stronger] one who is slow to anger than one who is mighty, and one who controls his spirit [is better] than one who conquers a city."[2] Who is rich? One who is happy with his portion [in life], as it says: "When you eat the fruits of the labor of your own hand, you are fortunate and well-off."[3] You are [fortunate] in this world, and [well-off] in the World to Come. Who is honored? One who honors all human beings, as it says: "Those who honor Me, I shall honor; those who scorn Me, shall be made light of."[4]

1. Psalms 119:99.
2. Proverbs 16:32.
3. Psalms 128:2.
4. I Samuel 2:30.

HISTORICAL BACKGROUND

Ben Zoma's full name was Shimon ben Zoma, but he is almost universally referred to as Ben (son of) Zoma in the Talmud (first half of the second century CE). He was one of four great scholars who never received ordination – possibly because they were too young (and he died young). In his lifetime, he had many students and a popular following, as he was recognized to be a great expositor of the texts.[5]

Ben Zoma was one of four great scholars who undertook the study of mysticism, and one of the principal players in a mysterious incident. The Talmud reports that they entered the Pardes – the garden of mystical delights – and immersed themselves to such a degree that they were deeply affected. In the language of the Talmud, "Ben Azzai looked [into the garden] and died; Ben Zoma looked and was damaged; Elisha b. Avuya looked and lost his faith. Only R. Akiva exited the garden intact and whole."[6] The Talmud suggests that Ben Zoma became demented.

Wise... learns

A wise person is not defined as someone who has learned everything, but one who is learning all the time and from everyone. No one is too young or too old, too educated or too illiterate, too famous or too unknown, to be able to teach you. Remain open to learning from everyone you encounter.

Strong... controls his impulses

- It takes more internal strength to control one's temper and restrain himself than to lift weights or to lash out verbally.
- True strength is defined by the trait of self-control; power is best exercised with self-restraint.
- Weak people bear down on others whom they perceive to be weaker than they are. The truly strong have no need to lord it over others.

5. Sota 49a.
6. Ḥagiga 14b.

Rich ... happy with his portion

- No matter how wealthy one is, the desire for more (or envying others who have more) can make a person feel poor or deprived.
- The feeling of being rich, like the feeling of happiness, is relative to expectations. If I am happy with and accepting of what I have, then whatever my level of personal assets, I am rich.
- Pursuing and heaping up wealth can become all-consuming and deprive a person of all other pleasures in life. He or she may sacrifice family, integrity, and honesty in the process of attaining wealth, and be left poor in many other contexts.

Is honored ... honors

In all four cases mentioned in this mishna, the conventional wisdom would suggest going out and seeking the desired goal (wisdom, strength, wealth, honor). Ben Zoma's paradoxical answer is: No. All four achievements involve an internal process. If you honor others, they will reciprocate. Respect for others evokes respect for you. Pursuit of honor often yields a tainted or coerced recognition which is contradicted by the contempt or disrespect that people feel for one who demands it.

Those who honor Me, I shall honor

An alternative interpretation to the simple meaning of this verse would be: We show honor to God by honoring the image of God in each and every human being. In turn, God honors us for honoring creation.

Mishna 2

בֶּן עַזַּאי אוֹמֵר: הֱוֵי רָץ לְמִצְוָה קַלָּה וּבוֹרֵחַ מִן הָעֲבֵרָה. שֶׁמִּצְוָה גּוֹרֶרֶת מִצְוָה, וַעֲבֵרָה גּוֹרֶרֶת עֲבֵרָה. שֶׁשְּׂכַר מִצְוָה מִצְוָה, וּשְׂכַר עֲבֵרָה עֲבֵרָה

Ben Azzai says: Run to [do] a minor mitzva as [you would] a major [mitzva], and run away from [doing] a transgression; for [doing] one mitzva draws another mitzva [in its wake], and [doing] a transgression draws another transgression [in its wake]. This is because the reward for [doing] a mitzva is another mitzva, and the reward for [doing] a transgression is another transgression.

HISTORICAL BACKGROUND

Like Ben Zoma, Ben Azzai's first name was Shimon and he is always referred to as the son of his father, i.e., Ben Azzai. Also like Ben Zoma, Ben Azzai was never ordained a rabbi despite a lifetime of devoted Torah study. This may reflect the fact that both sages never married, or it could be a side effect of the Roman ban on ordination, or reflect a fear that the Romans would go after an ordained rabbi. Ben Azzai was a student of R. Yehoshua b. Ḥanania, and a colleague and friend of R. Akiva (first half of the second century CE). Their most famous disagreement was over the question: What is the fundamental principle (*klal gadol*) of the Torah, that is, what is the foundational concept from which all the other teachings of the Torah can be derived, or toward which the sages all strive to lead the faithful? R. Akiva said: "Love your neighbor as yourself"[7]

7. Leviticus 19:18.

summarizes the whole Torah. Ben Azzai said that humanity's being created in the image of God[8] is even more fundamental.[9]

Ben Azzai's dedication to and persistence in Torah scholarship was so legendary that the Talmud states: "With Ben Azzai's death, assiduous students of Torah ceased to be."[10] The Talmud puts down the reason for his short life to his study of mysticism. He and three colleagues entered the "Pardes," or garden of mystical study, and as the cryptic account states: "Ben Azzai looked and died."

The Talmud reports that Ben Azzai was briefly engaged to R. Akiva's daughter but they never married, for he feared that the burden of supporting a family would prevent him from learning Torah. Yet he himself declared that with regard to one who does not engage in having children, it is as if he spills blood and reduces the presence of the image of God in the world. Since Judaism is strongly family oriented and considers having children a mitzva, he was chastised by his colleagues and friends. His only reply to his critics was: "My soul is totally seized with the desire for Torah."[11]

Run to do a minor mitzva

No mitzva is minor. The good deed or action may appear to be trivial, but it leads to another mitzva, perhaps even a "greater" mitzva. The same is true with sins. An inappropriate act may appear to be unimportant, but it sets in motion a train of behavior which may lead a person all the way down the wrong path.

The reward for a mitzva is another mitzva

- One good deed leads to another.
- By implication, the reward of a mitzva is not to be sought in the World to Come. The true reward of doing good is that it leads you to do more and more good in this world. A good deed is its

---

8. See Genesis 5:1–2, 1:27.
9. Y. Nedarim 9:4.
10. Sota 49a.
11. Yevamot 63b.

own reward. Ben Azzai is trying to lead people from the regnant expectation of reward and punishment in this life and the psychology of serving God to get instrumental reward. The sages understood God's self-limiting as a move to reduce the psychology of serving the divine on a *quid pro quo* basis. In stepping up the human role in the covenant, God was trying to lift up the quality of religious service, i.e., to do mitzvot – and all good actions – for their own sake (and for the sake of one's relationship to God).

Mishna 3

הוּא הָיָה אוֹמֵר: אַל תְּהִי בָז לְכָל אָדָם, וְאַל תְּהִי מַפְלִיג לְכָל דָּבָר. שֶׁאֵין לְךָ אָדָם שֶׁאֵין לוֹ שָׁעָה, וְאֵין לְךָ דָבָר שֶׁאֵין לוֹ מָקוֹם.

He used to say: Do not deprecate any person and consider nothing to be beyond possibility, for there is no person who does not have his hour [the moment when he contributes], and there is nothing which does not have its place [in the world].

Do not deprecate any person

- Any and every person can and will make a contribution through his life and actions.
- Do not dismiss anyone as irrelevant. The person you deem now as unimportant or without talent may rise to importance and greatness, and you will live to regret looking down on him. In the Midrash, R. Tanḥuma says that if one curses, deprecates, or degrades another human being, it is as if he has cursed, deprecated, or degraded God, because that human being is made in His image.[12]

12. Genesis Rabba 24:7.

Nothing which does not have its place

- There is a profound order in the cosmos and meaning for its constituents. That which you dismiss as trivial may yet have tremendous importance when the right circumstances come together.
- There is an ecology between living things and their environment. One change, omission, or disruption can turn into a cascade of loss.

Mishna 4

רַבִּי לְוִיטַס אִישׁ יַבְנֶה אוֹמֵר: מְאֹד מְאֹד הֱוֵי שְׁפַל רוּחַ, שֶׁתִּקְוַת אֱנוֹשׁ רִמָּה.	R. Levitas of Yavneh says: Be very humble [and of lowly spirit], for all the aspiration of the human being [ends in] a worm.

HISTORICAL BACKGROUND

The Talmud gives no biographical information on R. Levitas, but apparently he was a *Tanna* of the third generation of Yavneh scholars, ca. mid-second century CE.

Be… [of lowly spirit]… for the human being [ends in] a worm

R. Levitas believes that the inescapable fate of death turns all human aspirations into vanity; they are an illusion terminated in death and decay. This is one perspective (consider the alternative angle in mishna 3:1, above, where awareness of death drives us to do good deeds). R. Levitas' view is comparable to the morning prayer that says that God is infinite and great, and that all human matters fade into nothingness by comparison: "All heroes are as nothing before You; the famous as if they never existed, the wise as if they know nothing, and the intelligent as if they have no understanding. For most of their actions are empty gestures, and the days of their lives are vain in Your presence – and the superiority of the human over the animal is zero, for all is vanity."[13]

13. Birnbaum, *Ha-Siddur Ha-Shalem*, 23.

Perhaps R. Levitas was so overwhelmed by this insight that he fell silent – for this is the only statement made in his name in the entire Mishna. However, some of the maxims in the collection known as *Pirkei DeRabbi Eliezer* are attributed to him. Alternatively, although R. Levitas left very few maxims and he was not a leading sage, R. Yehuda the Prince, the editor of the Mishna, includes him and his saying because his is an important voice in the chorus of views on the interplay between death and the meaning of life.

רַבִּי יוֹחָנָן בֶּן בְּרוֹקָא אוֹמֵר: כָּל הַמְחַלֵּל שֵׁם שָׁמַיִם בַּסֵּתֶר, נִפְרָעִין מִמֶּנּוּ בַגָּלוּי. אֶחָד שׁוֹגֵג וְאֶחָד מֵזִיד בְּחִלּוּל הַשֵּׁם.

R. Yoḥanan b. Beroka says: Whoever profanes the name of God in secret [actions], they will punish him publicly. When it comes to profanation of the name, whether it be done unintentionally or intentionally, [the sin is considered equally great].

HISTORICAL BACKGROUND

R. Yoḥanan b. Beroka was of the third generation of *Tanna'im* (the earliest rabbinic scholars who formulated the Mishna) in Yavneh. He was a student of R. Yehoshua b. Ḥanania, alongside R. Elazar Ḥisma, who became his friend and colleague. He seems to have been particularly sensitive to women's issues. Among his rulings are that a father is obligated to support his daughters and not just his sons;[14] that women are equally obligated in the mitzva to be fruitful and multiply, which is not the majority view in the Talmud;[15] and that one need be careful not to excessively degrade a woman in the course of the legal process of testing a woman accused of adultery.[16]

Profanation of the name

This refers to an act that leads to disrespect for God or religion, such as murdering in the name of God, or actions by a religious figure that contradict his or her religious message. These erode the fundamental respect for God and for religion. Since belief in God and in the Torah

14. Tosefta, Ketubbot 4:8.
15. Yevamot 65b.
16. See Numbers 5:18ff.; *Sifrei, Naso* 41.

is based on teachings given by religious figures and leaders, such contemptible behavior is catastrophic to faith, and hence is designated a profanation or desecration of the name of God. This is the ultimate sin; some say it is unforgivable and no repentance helps, for the act undermines basic belief in God and the essential credibility of the faith. Therefore, even if done secretly, such actions will be punished by God in public (and devastating) ways.

Likewise, sometimes a permitted action should not be done because it will lead to disrespect for God and loss of the Torah's credibility.

Unintentionally or intentionally

In the case of other sins, a person who did wrong unintentionally is considered much less culpable than one who performed evil acts willfully. However, when the deed undermines belief in God and the Torah, the perpetrator's motivation makes no difference. When the results are so negative that they drive other people away from God and from the good life, then even unintentional acts are treated as heinous and unforgivable, because they have the same negative impact as do intentional evil acts.

Mishna 5

רַבִּי יִשְׁמָעֵאל בְּנוֹ אוֹמֵר:
הַלּוֹמֵד עַל מְנָת לְלַמֵּד,
מַסְפִּיקִין בְּיָדוֹ לִלְמֹד וּלְלַמֵּד.
וְהַלּוֹמֵד עַל מְנָת לַעֲשׂוֹת,
מַסְפִּיקִין בְּיָדוֹ לִלְמֹד וּלְלַמֵּד,
לִשְׁמֹר וְלַעֲשׂוֹת.

R. Yishmael, his son, says: One who studies Torah with the intention of teaching others will be enabled to learn and teach. One who studies with the intention of [carrying out the Torah in all his actions] will be enabled to learn and teach and observe and carry out [the Torah].

HISTORICAL BACKGROUND

R. Yishmael (first–second century CE) studied Torah with his father, R. Yoḥanan b. Beroka, and with other sages in Yavneh. He became a good friend of the *nasi*, Rabban Shimon b. Gamliel II.

Intention of teaching... intention of [carrying out]

The sages consistently rate carrying out the mandates and way of life recommended in the Torah as being of higher value than learning Torah only as an intellectual exercise (even though that is a praiseworthy activity).

רַבִּי צָדוֹק אוֹמֵר: אַל תִּפְרֹשׁ
מִן הַצִּבּוּר, וְאַל תַּעַשׂ עַצְמְךָ
כְּעוֹרְכֵי הַדַּיָּנִין, וְאַל תַּעֲשֶׂהָ
עֲטָרָה לְהִתְגַּדֵּל בָּהּ, וְלֹא
קַרְדֹּם לַחְפֹּר בָּהּ. וְכָךְ הָיָה הִלֵּל
אוֹמֵר: וּדְאִשְׁתַּמֵּשׁ בְּתָגָא חֳלָף.
הָא לָמַדְתָּ, כָּל הַנֶּהֱנֶה מִדִּבְרֵי
תוֹרָה, נוֹטֵל חַיָּיו מִן הָעוֹלָם.

R. Tzadok says: Do not separate from the community; do not act as a lawyer yourself; do not make [the Torah a] crown to glorify yourself with, nor a shovel to dig with. And this is what Hillel used to say: One who exploits the crown [of Torah will] perish. Thus you have learned that whoever makes a profit from the words of the Torah removes his life from the world.

HISTORICAL BACKGROUND

R. Tzadok (first century CE) is probably the sage who we are told fasted for decades trying to avert the heavenly decree that the Temple would be destroyed. He was a priest, and he took the lead in protesting the spilling of innocent blood when one priest stabbed another for daring to precede him on the ramp leading up to the sacrificial altar. Apparently, this act – or the lack of response to his protest – convinced R. Tzadok that the Temple process was so ethically compromised that it was rejected by God and the building was designated for destruction. All his fasting could not avert the impending doom. By the year of the Destruction, R. Tzadok was so weak and ill that Rabban Yoḥanan b. Zakkai asked the Romans for a team of doctors to treat him lest he die. He agreed to be evacuated by R. Yoḥanan with the Romans' permission.

Do not separate

This remark was attributed earlier to Hillel (mishna 2:5) and is interpreted there.

Do not act as a lawyer

This remark was attributed earlier to Yehuda b. Tabbai (1:8) and is interpreted there. Some manuscripts of Tractate Avot do not include these remarks, which duplicate the original statements.

A shovel to dig with

An alternative reading for this text is: "A dish to eat."

Makes a profit from the words of the Torah

- The Torah should be revered as a source of inspiration, guidance, and conversation with God. It should not be used or exploited for personal gain.
- One must learn to love Torah for its own sake and as the word of God, not as a source of personal or career advancement. It could be that as the sages' movement strengthened and won over more and more communities, the sages grew more concerned

that this new form of rabbinic Judaism might attract careerists and people motivated by selfish and material interests.

Removes his life from the world

- Shortens his life.
- Forfeits all or some of his life in the World to Come.

Mishna 6

רַבִּי יוֹסֵי אוֹמֵר: כָּל הַמְכַבֵּד אֶת הַתּוֹרָה, גּוּפוֹ מְכֻבָּד עַל הַבְּרִיּוֹת. וְכָל הַמְחַלֵּל אֶת הַתּוֹרָה, גּוּפוֹ מְחֻלָּל עַל הַבְּרִיּוֹת.

R. Yosei says: Whoever honors the Torah will himself be honored by his fellow human beings. Whoever dishonors the Torah will himself be dishonored by his fellow human beings.

HISTORICAL BACKGROUND

R. Yosei b. Ḥalafta (whose father was also a *Tanna*; see 3:6) was one of the five young students whom R. Akiva recruited and taught after losing tens of thousands of students in the aftermath of the Bar Kokhba uprising (mid-second century CE). R. Yosei was one of the handful to receive ordination from R. Yehuda b. Baba. R. Yehuda defied the Romans' proscription of the act of ordination in order to prevent the chain of rabbinic transmission from being broken. He was executed by the Romans for this. R. Yosei was very influential because of the force of his mind, and is cited hundreds of times in the Mishna. He supported himself as a tanner, a difficult and foul-smelling job. He married his late brother's childless wife in fulfillment of the Torah's law of *yibbum* (levirate marriage) and they had five sons together – all of whom became scholars.

R. Yosei was very well-liked, in part because of his pleasant temperament and personal modesty and in part because he showed great respect for the views of his colleagues. He worked to unify views and to compromise so that there would be no divisive arguments separating communities. R. Yehuda the Prince was one of his students. He was also a leader in articulating a deeper understanding of the incorporeality of God together with a strong sense of the *Shekhina*, the Divine Presence of God, being closer and more intimately involved with the People of Israel. In later generations, he was called a holy person.

Whoever honors the Torah will...be honored

- A person who shows respect for the Torah and its teachings will be a better person and will win the respect of his fellows.
- Whoever honors the Torah is ennobled, and this show of respect in turn ennobles his fellows and inspires them to honor him.

Mishna 7

רַבִּי יִשְׁמָעֵאל בְּנוֹ אוֹמֵר: הַחוֹשֵׂךְ עַצְמוֹ מִן הַדִּין, פּוֹרֵק מִמֶּנּוּ אֵיבָה וְגָזֵל וּשְׁבוּעַת שָׁוְא. וְהַגַּס לִבּוֹ בְּהוֹרָאָה, שׁוֹטֶה, רָשָׁע וְגַס רוּחַ.

R. Yishmael says: Whoever holds back from legal suits removes enmity, theft, and vain oaths from himself. Whoever is haughty in handing down legal rulings is foolish and arrogant.

HISTORICAL BACKGROUND

R. Yishmael was the first of the five scholarly sons of R. Yosei b. Ḥalafta. He studied Torah with his father, whom he highly respected. Most of his halakhic rulings are quoted from his father. He resided in Tzippori in the Galilee. R. Yishmael lived into the third century CE and became a confidante of R. Yehuda the Prince. He served as an officer of the court under the Romans. This was criticized by others, who saw such actions as a form of collaboration, even accusing him of being a *moser*, one who delivers Jews to an (illegitimate) government authority for punishment. Apparently, R. Yishmael felt there was no choice but to work with the Romans so that they would let up on the political pressure and allow the Jewish community to live some semblance of a normal life.

The Talmud tells of R. Yishmael's absolute integrity. His sharecropper used to bring him fruit from his, R. Yishmael's, orchard every Friday. One week the farmer showed up with the usual fruits on Thursday. R. Yishmael asked him why he brought the produce a day earlier than usual. The farmer replied that he was scheduled to appear before R. Yishmael in a suit with another claimant that day, so he thought that he could take care of both matters at the same time. R. Yishmael responded that regretfully he could not accept the fruit and that he must recuse himself from serving as a judge in this case. He understood the Torah's prohibition against a judge taking a bribe because the money corrupted his judgment in a broader context. He felt instinctively that the slight benefit he was receiving from his tenant could subtly – perhaps unconsciously – distort his judgment. Therefore, he withdrew as a judge in the case.

Holds back from legal suits

- The sages preferred to settle disputes by arbitration and compromise rather than by legal suits, as once people go to court, they tend to harden their positions and often lie and perjure and, in effect, steal from the other.
- The second half of the mishna is clearly dealing with a judge's behavior. This suggests that we interpret this first clause as follows: Try to avoid serving as a judge because you will invariably end up being hated and will inevitably transfer property from the real owner to the wrong person , thus perpetrating a miscarriage of justice.

Haughty in handing down legal rulings

Disputes are rarely a matter of black or white. Given the subjectivity and vulnerability of the legal process, judges should be very humble when handing down each ruling. Any judge who is absolutely convinced that he is right beyond question in his rulings proves that he is arrogant, and likely is either a fool or a wicked person.

Mishna 8

הוּא הָיָה אוֹמֵר: אַל תְּהִי דָן יְחִידִי, שֶׁאֵין דָּן יְחִידִי אֶלָּא אֶחָד. וְאַל תֹּאמַר קַבְּלוּ דַעְתִּי, שֶׁהֵן רַשָּׁאִין וְלֹא אַתָּה.

He used to say: Do not be the sole judge; there is only one who is capable of being the sole judge. Do not say [to the others]: Accept my [personal] view, for they may say it but you may not.

The sole judge

It is better to exchange views. One refines judgment by exploring the arguments with others. Truth is best arrived at as a distillation of a wide range of opinions and by a process of clarification. The only one whose judgment is infallible and singular is God. Human judges need to know their limits. They should listen to the other viewpoints to the maximum and always speak tentatively, i.e., this is my best judgment and the conclusion is on balance... and the evidence and conclusions are not 100 percent the way I think. (Note that even the lower rabbinic Jewish courts were composed of more than one sitting judge.)

Do not say: Accept my [personal] view

Do not try to impose your personal view on the other judges. They may make this request of the others if they so choose – but you should not, as this pressure is improper. The most likely way to arrive at sound judgment is to listen and learn from the others, not to silence or shout down the others by the force of your personality.

Mishna 9

רַבִּי יוֹנָתָן אוֹמֵר: כָּל הַמְקַיֵּם אֶת הַתּוֹרָה מֵעֹנִי, סוֹפוֹ לְקַיְּמָהּ מֵעֹשֶׁר. וְכָל הַמְבַטֵּל אֶת הַתּוֹרָה מֵעֹשֶׁר, סוֹפוֹ לְבַטְּלָהּ מֵעֹנִי.

[R. Yonatan] says: Whoever fulfills the Torah in a state of poverty will, in the end, fulfill it when he is rich. Whoever nullifies the Torah when he is rich will, in the end, nullify it when he is in a state of poverty.

HISTORICAL BACKGROUND

R. Yonatan was a fourth-generation *Tanna* (second century CE) and a student of R. Yishmael b. Elisha, R. Akiva's great colleague. This is the only place where he is quoted in the Mishna, but he is quoted frequently in the *Mekhilta* on the Book of Exodus and *Sifrei* on the Book of Numbers. These collections of *midreshei halakha* (halakhic interpretations and applications of Torah verses) were gathered and edited in the school of R. Yishmael.

The Talmud recounts that at one point R. Yonatan and three other colleagues decided that they must leave the Land of Israel to escape the Roman persecution that followed in the wake of the Bar Kokhba uprising. When they reached the borders, however, they could not bear to leave, and they turned back.[17]

17. *Sifrei, Re'eh* 80.

Fulfills the Torah in ... poverty

- Poverty makes it difficult to study and to observe the commandments, either because of the temptation to cut corners or because it costs money to observe the Torah. If you nevertheless persist in learning when you are poor, you will find it even easier to study Torah when your economic conditions improve.
- If you show the strength of character to observe the commandments when you are poor, you will find the strength of character to observe them when you face temptations and obstacles to observing the Torah which flow from being wealthy.

Nullifies the Torah when he is rich

- If you nullify the Torah even though you have the margins and comfort of being rich, then you will surely nullify it when you are in a state of poverty, with all its economic and other pressures.
- If you lack the strength of character to uphold the Torah when you are in a comfortable financial position, you will likely not live up to its standards when you are poor and under pressure financially.

Torah in ... poverty ... Torah when ... rich

The Talmud says that when a person faces the final, true judgment, neither the stresses and strains of poverty nor the pressures and temptations of wealth can serve as an excuse for not studying (or for nullifying) Torah. After all, Hillel lived in utter poverty and sometimes could not afford tuition, yet he persevered and became the greatest scholar of his generation. At the other extreme, R. Elazar b. Ḥarsom served as High Priest and inherited a gigantic fortune (including a thousand villages and a thousand seagoing ships), yet he totally devoted himself to learning Torah.

Mishna 10

רַבִּי מֵאִיר אוֹמֵר: הֱוֵי מְמַעֵט בְּעֵסֶק וַעֲסֹק בַּתּוֹרָה, וֶהֱוֵי שְׁפַל רוּחַ בִּפְנֵי כָל אָדָם. וְאִם בָּטַלְתָּ מִן הַתּוֹרָה, יֵשׁ לְךָ בְּטֵלִים הַרְבֵּה כְּנֶגְדְּךָ. וְאִם עָמַלְתָּ בַּתּוֹרָה, יֶשׁ לוֹ שָׂכָר הַרְבֵּה לִתֶּן לָךְ.

R. Meir says: Reduce your business activity and occupy yourself with the [study of] Torah. Be humble in the presence of every person. If you have been idle from Torah [study], you will find many causes to be [further] idle [from Torah.] But if you work hard at [studying] Torah, [God] has much reward to give you.

HISTORICAL BACKGROUND

R. Meir (139–163 CE) is one of the Talmud's greats. He was a descendant of a family which originated from a convert to Judaism. According to one talmudic source, the family could trace its ancestry back to the Roman emperor Nero. R. Meir was married to Bruria, daughter of R. Ḥanania b. Teradyon. She was a brilliant woman who was a Torah scholar in her own right.

R. Meir is one of the most widely quoted sages in the Mishna. Moreover, if a law is recorded anonymously in the Mishna, one can assume that it reflects the ruling of R. Meir in accordance with the teachings of his teacher, R. Akiva. It seems that R. Meir was so influential because he produced a preliminary collection of rulings (based on the rulings of R. Akiva) which was utilized by R. Yehuda the Prince when his group definitively redacted the Mishna. Although R. Meir is reputed to be the author of innumerable parables and wise sayings, this mishna is the only cluster of his sayings incorporated into the original Tractate Avot. (Chapter 6 was added later.)

One talmudic tradition recounts that R. Meir was ordained by R. Yehuda b. Baba, who was martyred by the Romans during the Hadrianic persecutions.[18] Seven individuals were ordained at that time. These are the sages who are quoted in mishnas 12–17 of this chapter. Another tradition suggests that R. Meir was one of the five younger scholars trained and ordained by R. Akiva to replace the thousands of Torah scholars who perished during the uprising against Rome.[19] Both traditions point to the fact that R. Meir became one of the builders of the Mishna and rebuilders of Jewish religious life in the settlement of Usha after the devastating Roman suppression of the Bar Kokhba rebellion.

Driven by their conviction that learning Torah was the highest form of serving God and that every Jew should be invited to join in this vocation, the members of this group succeeded in widening the appeal of Torah study and its presence among the Jewish public. Their many accomplishments came about thanks to the power and inspiration of their thinking, the magnetism of their personalities, and their ability to reach out to everyone regardless of family background or social standing. (R. Meir ruled that a *mamzer*, an illegitimate and therefore unmarriageable person, who was a Torah scholar should be given priority over a High Priest who was an ignoramus.[20]) The group's formidable talents were supported by their total dedication and by their willingness to be martyred if that is what it took.

R. Meir made a living as a scribe, writing Torah scrolls, mezuzas, and the passages that go inside tefillin. Despite his extraordinary intellect, he became somewhat controversial. He was so brilliant and analytical that he was able to argue both sides of a case – even to the point where he could convince people that something was ritually pure despite the fact that it was actually impure. (The Talmud says that he could bring 150 proofs that a crawling reptile was pure, although in fact it is an icon

18. Sanhedrin 14a.
19. Yevamot 62b.
20. Horayot 13a.

of an absolutely impure creature in halakha.) His colleagues reacted against this skill and often overruled his brilliance, since they did not entirely trust it. Moreover, he was a student of R. Elisha b. Avuya. When R. Elisha lost his faith and became an Epicurean, the other sages shunned him. R. Meir, however, remained devoted to his teacher. He continued to quote him, speak to him, and try to keep him connected. When people objected to his continuing contact with R. Elisha (for fear that it would lead him astray), he insisted that he was capable of getting the fruit (i.e., substance of the wisdom) from R. Elisha and throwing away the peel (the disbelief with which the teaching was surrounded).

When R. Elisha was on his deathbed, R. Meir came to visit him. He urged his teacher to repent and return to the faith. Elisha at first told him that he had heard a heavenly voice proclaim that the path of repentance was open to every sinner except him. (Given his original standing as a *Tanna*, he had committed unforgivable sins not only in breaking with the faith but in publicly desecrating the Shabbat and violating sexual prohibitions as well.) R. Meir insisted that it was not too late. He cited the verse: "You [God] return man to dust, and say, 'Return [repent], you mortals.'"[21] He explained the rabbinic interpretation of dust (*daka* in Hebrew – interpreted as *dikhdukha,* the [final] flickering [of the soul]). This last minute of life was the moment when God called for repentance. At this, R. Elisha wept copiously – and passed away.[22] R. Meir was convinced that his teacher had repented and died a faithful Jew. The Talmud suggests that after R. Meir and R. Yoḥanan died, there were heavenly signals that R. Elisha b. Avuya had finally been forgiven and taken into Paradise.

There is also a talmudic account of a feat of derring-do whereby R. Meir rescued his sister-in-law, R. Ḥanania b. Teradyon's other daughter, who had been seized by the Romans and sold into prostitution. As a result, he had to go into hiding in exile for a while. Perhaps this tradition of a miraculous rescue accounts for the later generations associating R. Meir with wonder-working. One of the great Diaspora charitable funds in support of Jewish people living in the Land of Israel down to

---

21. Psalms 90:3.
22. Ḥagiga 15a–b.

the twentieth century was called the fund of R. Meir Baal HaNeis – R. Meir the Wonder-Worker.

Reduce your business ... and occupy yourself with the Torah

The Talmud rules that a father is obligated to teach his son Torah *and* a trade or profession whereby he can make a living.[23] Like other sages, R. Meir supported himself with a trade. Still, he warned that to become a Torah scholar, one must minimize business activity and maximize Torah study.

Be humble

Your scholarship will grow if you listen in order to learn from everyone, instead of being self-confident or arrogant and feeling no need to listen to others.

Idle ... [further] idle

Torah study is a discipline. Every time the muscle of study is exercised, it becomes stronger. Every time one gives in to a feeling of tiredness or laziness, or yields to a distraction and does not use the study muscle, the muscle is weakened. The capacity of persistence is eroded by this failure. This increases the likelihood of being distracted or of getting lazy and passing up on Torah study the next time as well.

---

23. Kiddushin 30b.

Mishna 11

רַבִּי אֱלִיעֶזֶר בֶּן יַעֲקֹב אוֹמֵר: הָעוֹשֶׂה מִצְוָה אַחַת, קוֹנֶה לּוֹ פְּרַקְלִיט אֶחָד. וְהָעוֹבֵר עֲבֵרָה אַחַת, קוֹנֶה לּוֹ קַטֵּגוֹר אֶחָד. תְּשׁוּבָה וּמַעֲשִׂים טוֹבִים, כִּתְרִיס בִּפְנֵי הַפֻּרְעָנוּת.

R. Eliezer b. Yaakov says: Whoever does one mitzva acquires one advocate for himself. Whoever commits one sin acquires one accuser for himself. Repentance and good deeds serve as a shield in the face of calamity.

HISTORICAL BACKGROUND

R. Eliezer b. Yaakov was one of the last students of R. Akiva (before R. Akiva was murdered by the Romans in 137 CE), and was active in the rebuilding of rabbinic culture and schools in Usha after the Hadrianic persecutions.

There is an earlier R. Eliezer b. Yaakov who lived through the Destruction of the Temple and is cited in the Talmud as an expert on its dimensions and some of its practices. However, the sages who are the source of mishnas 12, 14, 15, 16, and 17 in this chapter are contemporaries of the second R. Eliezer b. Yaakov. Therefore, we can assume that the source of this mishna's teaching is the fourth-generation *Tanna* R. Eliezer.

Advocate... accuser

- Every human action, good or bad, will testify for or against the person in the final judgment.

- No action is wasted or ephemeral. There is a permanent record of every action, which plays a role in determining one's ultimate fate.

Repentance and good deeds

- Do not despair that you have lost your standing as a good person if you sin. No such person exists: "There is no righteous person in the world who does only good and will never sin."[24] The good person is the one who recognizes and admits having done wrong, then repents and undertakes good deeds to make up for the past.
- Repentance and good deeds stop and reverse the sequence of evil set in motion by bad behavior. Thus they avert an extension of one's sin that could have, if unchecked, led to calamity.

A shield in the face of calamity

- The language here suggests that there is reward and punishment in this world. God brings calamity on the wicked. One who repents and does good deeds averts such terrible events in his life.
- The Hebrew word *puranut,* which is translated here as calamity, can also be translated as retribution. Maimonides interprets this aphorism as a statement about the World to Come. There God punishes evil deeds. However, repentance and good deeds save one from retribution in the World to Come.

רַבִּי יוֹחָנָן הַסַּנְדְּלָר אוֹמֵר: כָּל כְּנֵסִיָּה שֶׁהִיא לְשֵׁם שָׁמַיִם, סוֹפָהּ לְהִתְקַיֵּם. וְשֶׁאֵינָהּ לְשֵׁם שָׁמַיִם, אֵין סוֹפָהּ לְהִתְקַיֵּם.

R. Yoḥanan the shoemaker says: Every assembly for the sake of Heaven will have a permanent outcome. But [every assembly] which is not for the sake of Heaven will not have a permanent outcome.

24. Ecclesiastes 7:20.

HISTORICAL BACKGROUND

R. Yoḥanan was one of the rabbis ordained in secret to carry on the rabbinic tradition in the face of Roman persecution. He was originally from Alexandria and was described as a typical Alexandrian: aggressive, outspoken, convinced that he was right. He was one of R. Akiva's closest students. He managed to stay in touch with and even learn from his master during the period when R. Akiva was imprisoned by the Romans before they killed him. At one point, the Roman persecution was so fierce that R. Yoḥanan and R. Elazar b. Shamua decided to go study Torah outside of the Land of Israel in order to escape the troubles. However, when they reached the border at Sidon, they turned back because they could not bear to leave the land.

Assembly for the sake of Heaven

A gathering like the convocation at Mount Sinai whereby the Israelites accepted the Torah – or indeed any coming together for the sake of God and goodness – is an assembly for the sake of Heaven. R. Yoḥanan believes that gatherings to organize on behalf of Torah or making God's world better will have a lasting effect. God blesses the good with permanence.

However, an assembly for the purpose of exercising amoral power, political or otherwise, or an assembled group that seeks to take advantage of people or to create policies and rules that go against God's plan for the world, is an assembly that is not for the sake of Heaven. This type of gathering, even if it generates a lot of attention and pomp, will prove to be ephemeral. "If God will not build a house, its builders will toil in vain."[25] This statement would have particular resonance, as the sages came to Usha to reestablish the academy and to guide Jewish life after the Bar Kokhba uprising failed.

25. Psalms 127:1.

Mishna 12

רַבִּי אֶלְעָזָר בֶּן שַׁמּוּעַ אוֹמֵר: יְהִי כְבוֹד תַּלְמִידְךָ חָבִיב עָלֶיךָ כְּשֶׁלָּךְ, וּכְבוֹד חֲבֵרְךָ כְּמוֹרָא רַבָּךְ, וּמוֹרָא רַבָּךְ כְּמוֹרָא שָׁמָיִם.

R. Elazar b. Shamua says: May the honor of your student be as dear to you as your [own] honor; and your colleague's honor as [dear to you] as your reverence for your teacher; and reverence for your teacher [as sacred to you] as reverence for Heaven.

HISTORICAL BACKGROUND

R. Elazar b. Shamua was also one of the handful of rabbis ordained when the Roman persecution in the aftermath of the Bar Kokhba revolt threatened to stamp out the rabbinic leadership (mid-second century CE). He set up a very important study house which attracted large numbers of students – possibly because his scholarship embraced Midrash, halakha, Aggada, and Tosefta,[26] whereas most yeshivas studied only one or two of these categories of rabbinic literature. He fiercely loved the Land of Israel. At the peak of the Roman persecution, after wavering, he determined not to leave the land, proclaiming that the mitzva of settling in the land was to be weighed as equal to all the other mitzvot in the Torah.[27]

R. Elazar was known for his respect for all human beings (to which this mishna testifies), including gentiles.[28] He was a modest,

26. *Avot DeRabbi Natan* 28.

27. *Sifrei, Re'eh* 80.

28. See Ecclesiastes Rabba 11.

self-effacing man of whom it is said that he never in his whole life had a conflict with his friends, neither in words nor in deeds. *Midrash Eleh Ezkera* ("These I Remember") lists him as one of the ten great, rabbinic martyrs of the Hadrianic persecutions. He was 105 years old when the Romans came for him, and they killed him on Yom Kippur.

The honor of your student... as your [own] honor

- Show proper respect for your students. Do not treat them as inferior. Treat them as you would want a colleague to treat you.
- Showing respect for your students (although they are of a lesser degree of scholarly standing) should be just as important in your eyes as your colleagues' showing the proper level of respect to you.

Colleague's honor... reverence for your teacher

The title for teacher, Rav (Rabbi), means master. Therefore, treat a teacher with the reverence due to a superior.

By contrast, one might assume that the relationship to a colleague-friend (the two being more equal) is more relaxed. R. Eliezer says no. Treat your colleague-friend with the same level of reverence as that with which you treat your teacher. Friendship should not reduce your sense of awe at the greatness of your colleague. Honor your colleague-friend as if it is as serious an obligation as the reverence you are expected to show a teacher.

Reverence for your teacher... reverence for Heaven

Commentators hesitate to take literally the equation of reverence for a teacher and reverence for God. By that logic, this saying would be interpreted as: Show reverence for your mentor (albeit to a lesser degree) with the same pleasure and faithfulness that you show reverence for God. The lower level of reverence that is owed your teacher should not lead to taking the obligation lightly.

There is good reason to take the equation of reverence for God and reverence for one's teacher more literally. A teacher introduces the student to the word of God and serves as a direct conduit to experiencing Him. This was the great rabbinic accomplishment – to discover

God's will and communicate God's presence everywhere in the post-Destruction world. By rabbinic insight, hearing the voice of the master is hearing the voice of God.

Furthermore, the sages revealed hitherto unknown levels of meaning in the Bible. R. Akiva learned from his teacher, Naḥum of Gimzo, who drew forth distinct (new) laws from every conjunction word in the Torah (such as *et*, an untranslatable preposition introducing a direct object, and *rak*, which means "only"). From this teaching, R. Akiva drew the conclusion: "With regard to the verse, 'You should fear [*et*] the Lord your God' (Deut. 10:20), the *et* here is intended by the Torah to add the sage to the category of the one to be feared."

There is the literal equation of fear of God and fear of one's teacher. However, the same talmudic passage adds that another sage who derived laws from every *et* in the Torah fell silent when he came across the *et* in the above verse. Obviously, he felt that the application (equating reverence for a teacher and reverence for God) was excessive, and bordered on the heretical.[29]

Still, when it comes to "revelation" today, the rabbi-teacher is now the voice of God, more so than the voice of God which no longer speaks to us directly. Thus Rava makes the following comment: "People who stand up before a Torah scroll when it is brought into the room but who remain seated before a great Torah sage are foolish. For in the Torah scroll it is written, 'He shall be flogged forty times [and no more].'[30] And the rabbis reduced [the forty lashes] by one, and that number of lashes, thirty-nine, is the sentence that is carried out."[31] In other words, the sages' interpretation in practice determines the content of the word of God, making their authority actually greater than the Torah scroll's authority. Of course, there is a danger here that the fear and awe of a teacher will be inculcated and treated as equal to fear of God. If this statement is taken literally, respect for great scholars can become a form of idolatry, i.e., one ends up obeying or worshiping a human authority as if he were an absolute authority like God.

29. Pesaḥim 22b.
30. Deuteronomy 25:3.
31. Makkot 22b.

Mishna 13

רַבִּי יְהוּדָה אוֹמֵר: הֱוֵי זָהִיר בְּתַלְמוּד, שֶׁשִּׁגְגַת תַּלְמוּד עוֹלָה זָדוֹן.

R. Yehuda says: Be very careful in your teaching, for an error in teaching is equivalent to [teaching] an intentional sin.

HISTORICAL BACKGROUND

R. Yehuda b. Ilai was one of the leaders in the rebuilding of communal life and rabbinic Torah in Usha after the Hadrianic persecutions (second century CE). The son of a *Tanna,* he grew up in Usha and studied with his father, but he also learned from most of the great teachers of the generation: R. Tarfon in Lod, R. Eliezer, R. Yehoshua b. Ḥanania, and most of all, R. Akiva. He was one of the students ordained in secret by R. Yehuda b. Baba during the Hadrianic persecutions. Despite the fact that his teacher was martyred by the Romans for this courageous deed, R. Yehuda was inclined to work with them rather than disparage them. The Romans' reciprocal positive attitude toward him may have aided him in his work. The Talmud describes him as the chief spokesman for Jews everywhere.[32] More than six hundred halakhot are quoted in his name in the Mishna.

R. Yehuda was recognized as a truly pious person, so that whenever anecdotes are told about the behavior of "a *ḥasid,*" the assumption is that it is a reference to R. Yehuda b. Ilai. The Talmud tells many stories of his kindness, his trustworthiness, his giving the benefit of the doubt,

32. Shabbat 33b.

and his warmth toward all kinds of people (even the *am haaretz,* the uncultured, whom many sages treated with disdain). He was famous for taking a myrtle wreath and dancing in honor of the bride at weddings, singing the song: "She is a beautiful and pious bride" – as recommended by Hillel – to the point where other sages complained that his celebration was excessive. Some questioned his behavior as a violation of the laws of modesty in relations between the sexes. R. Yehuda explained that the spirit and enthusiasm of giving joy to the bride and groom so took over his emotions that they removed any trace of eroticism or sexuality in his contact with the bride. (Rebuking the critics, the Talmud states that after his death a flame in the shape of a myrtle wreath hovered over his grave.) Although R. Yehuda lived in poverty much of his life, he unfailingly stressed the dignity and importance of work.

Equivalent to [teaching] an intentional sin

Normally the gravity of willful, wrong behavior, i.e., an intentional sin, is considered to be much greater than doing an unintentional transgression, and the punishment is much greater as well. However, if a teacher does not study properly, he may make the wrong deduction and teach that which is prohibited as permitted or that which is wrong as right. In turn, his students, having been instructed improperly, will transgress unintentionally. The teacher is guilty of a kind of reckless endangerment. By not paying attention, by not thoroughly analyzing, he is putting his students in spiritual jeopardy. Just as in drunken driving, the accident that follows smacks of deliberate sin, so the reckless behavior of the teacher is equivalent to deliberate, evil action.

רַבִּי שִׁמְעוֹן אוֹמֵר: שְׁלֹשָׁה כְתָרִים הֵן, כֶּתֶר תּוֹרָה וְכֶתֶר כְּהֻנָּה וְכֶתֶר מַלְכוּת, וְכֶתֶר שֵׁם טוֹב עוֹלֶה עַל גַּבֵּיהֶן.

R. Shimon says: There are three crowns [that people can earn and wear]: the crown of Torah, the crown of priesthood, and the crown of royalty. But the crown of a good name rises above them all.

R. Shimon is R. Shimon b. Yoḥai. He was one of R. Akiva's primary students. Active in Yavneh and Usha, he had a special love for Torah and for the Land of Israel, and many of his statements in praise of both are found in the Talmud. He was credited with many miracles (which may have paved the way for the later Zohar to be attached to his name). Despite his checkered history with the Romans, he was sent as a member of a delegation to Rome to solicit an end to the persecutions. He went and was successful.

The crown of Torah

Achieving great knowledge of Torah is like being crowned a great king: "Rabbis are called kings."[33]

The crown of priesthood

The priest had an honored, special place in Israelite society. Priests received special gifts from the public. Much of the priests' special standing disappeared once the Temple was destroyed. They lost their role as mediators between Israel and the Divine Presence via the Jewish people's sacrificial offerings. However, priests are called up first to the Torah; they are expected to abide by certain Torah restrictions such as not having direct contact with the dead (except for immediate relatives) and not marrying divorcées and women in other restricted categories.

The crown of royalty

This is kingship.

A good name

This is a good reputation.

The crown of a good name rises above them all

"A good name is better than good oil."[34] A good name is earned over a lifetime by the excellence of one's behavior. This intrinsic, earned dignity (recognized by peers) is more precious and more ennobling than crowns reflecting external accomplishments, media celebrity recognition, or genetic endowment.

---

33. Gittin 62a.
34. Ecclesiastes 7:1.

Mishna 14

רַבִּי נְהוֹרַאי אוֹמֵר: הֱוֵי גוֹלֶה לִמְקוֹם תּוֹרָה. וְאַל תֹּאמַר שֶׁהִיא תָבוֹא אַחֲרֶיךָ, שֶׁחֲבֵרֶיךָ יְקַיְּמוּהָ בְּיָדֶךָ. וְאֶל־בִּינָתְךָ אַל־תִּשָּׁעֵן:

R. Nehorai says: Exile [yourself] to a [faraway] place of Torah [if necessary]; and do not say that it [the Torah] will come after you, for it is your colleagues who make it your permanent possession; and "do not rely on your own understanding [alone]."[35]

HISTORICAL BACKGROUND

R. Nehorai was a fourth-generation *Tanna* (second century CE) and participated in the life and learning of Usha. He so treasured Torah that he quarreled with the sages' statement that a father is obligated to teach his son a craft whereby to earn a living. He said that he would instead teach his son Torah because its rewards are unfailing in this world, and unlike material work, it also brings reward in the World to Come.

Exile [yourself] to a place of Torah

To study in a community with a well-established Torah academy is a major advantage for mastering Torah. Therefore, it is worth going to the ends of the earth (i.e., into exile) in order to be in a place that can enrich one's learning so much.

35. Proverbs 3:5.

Do not rely on your own understanding

Participating in a learning community, exchanging views with colleagues, and the give-and-take of Torah study all lead to a greater understanding and mastery of Torah than isolated, individual study. The classic rabbinic study method still practiced in contemporary yeshivas is the *ḥavruta,* whereby two or more students read through a text and analyze it together.

Mishna 15

רַבִּי יַנַּאי אוֹמֵר: אֵין בְּיָדֵינוּ לֹא מִשַּׁלְוַת הָרְשָׁעִים וְאַף לֹא מִיִּסּוּרֵי הַצַּדִּיקִים.

R. Yannai says: We can grasp neither the tranquil lives of the wicked nor the suffering of the righteous.

HISTORICAL BACKGROUND

Very little is known about the *Tanna* R. Yannai (first half of the third century CE), but he was probably a fourth- or fifth-generation scholar. This heartbreaking statement is the only one in the Mishna that is directly attributable to him.

The tranquil lives of the wicked ... the suffering of the righteous

- It is a spare, sober comment on the disparity in this world when one sees the wicked prosper and the righteous suffer. This view is particularly striking because it departs from the two dominant answers offered by the sages of the Mishna to the problem of evil and innocent suffering. R. Yannai neither offers the reassurance that reward in the future life will restore justice nor insists that all experiences in this world are providential and match up with one's behavior (i.e., measure-for-measure).

  R. Yannai's view may be compared with Jeremiah's outcry (12:1): "Why does the way of the wicked prosper?" which is a sub-theme in Scripture. This voice pleads that all is not well with the world and wants to know why bad things happen to good people. One can also refer to the Book of Job, which challenges the dominant view that everything that happens in this world is the direct outcome of (and divine response to) the individual's personal behavior.

It appears that R. Yannai is urging that the best policy is not to revolt or despair but rather to practice silent acceptance of the world as it is, refraining from expressing pious assurances that all is right with the world.

- An alternative explanation: The average person lives a life that is a mixture of good and bad, never achieving the tranquility of the purely wicked, who in their brazenness are at ease with their evil behavior, or the purity of the truly righteous, who are able to live with their suffering. This is what makes our suffering so upsetting.

R. Matya b. Ḥeresh says: Be the first to greet everyone [when you encounter them]; better to be a tail to lions than a head to foxes.

רַבִּי מַתְיָא בֶּן חָרָשׁ אוֹמֵר: הֱוֵי מַקְדִּים בִּשְׁלוֹם כָּל אָדָם, וֶהֱוֵי זָנָב לָאֲרָיוֹת, וְאַל תְּהִי רֹאשׁ לַשּׁוּעָלִים.

HISTORICAL BACKGROUND

R. Matya b. Ḥeresh (second century CE) fled the Land of Israel at the beginning of the Bar Kokhba revolt and ended up in Rome, where he stayed for the rest of his life.

Be the first to greet

Greeting your fellow human being is a statement of respect and friendship. Saying hello may appear to be only a conventional gesture, but the message is, in fact, significant. Greeting the other is an affirmation that he or she is an image of God, a human being deserving engagement. "Hello" means: I know you are there and I acknowledge you.

R. Matya's deeper meaning is that being the first to greet deepens the greeting because it affirms the equality of the other. Since you are equal in my eyes (no matter how important my social status), I will speak first, lest you approach me as an inferior would approach a superior, asking for recognition.

A tail to lions... a head to foxes

It is better to be one of the followers in a superior group, because you will be stretched by the model. You will develop from exposure to people who are of such high quality that you must grow in order to keep up with them. If you are the head of a group of inferior quality, you will decline toward their standard and will not grow from the interchange.

Mishna 16

רַבִּי יַעֲקֹב אוֹמֵר: הָעוֹלָם הַזֶּה
דּוֹמֶה לִפְרוֹזְדוֹר בִּפְנֵי הָעוֹלָם
הַבָּא. הַתְקֵן עַצְמְךָ בַּפְּרוֹזְדוֹר,
כְּדֵי שֶׁתִּכָּנֵס לַטְּרַקְלִין.

R. Yaakov [b. Korshai] says: This world is like a vestibule before the World to Come; fix yourself up in the vestibule so that you can enter into the main room.

[For biographical information on R. Yaakov b. Korshai, see 3:7.]

This world is like a vestibule

Life in this world is short. Therefore, mortal existence should be lived as a preparation for eternal life in the World to Come.

Fix yourself up

- Live the kind of life that will earn you eternal paradise.
- If you live an evil life or a self-centered life during your years on earth, you are exchanging eternal bliss for short-term pleasure or advantage. This is a bad bargain.

The central importance of life in the World to Come is a classic rabbinic theme. The Torah focuses on the importance of life in this world. The primary reward for good deeds, ranging from those perceived as trivial (sending away a mother bird before gathering in the fledglings) to the weightiest (respecting father and mother), is being granted a longer life on this earth (compare Deut. 22:7 with ibid., 5:16). Obedience to God is rewarded primarily with rain and good harvests. Disobedience is punished with military defeats and conquest by oppressors. Yet the Bible does not consider an individual's life in this world the be-all and end-all of life. There is continuity of existence beyond the grave.

The sages shifted their teaching emphasis to the eternal existence of the human being: the soul's eternal life of bliss with God. The motivation to perform good deeds and the reward for carrying them out are more focused on the World to Come (as in this mishna). Each age has its own focus and distinctive motivators of behavior.

Mishna 17

הוּא הָיָה אוֹמֵר: יָפָה שָׁעָה אַחַת בִּתְשׁוּבָה וּמַעֲשִׂים טוֹבִים בָּעוֹלָם הַזֶּה, מִכֹּל חַיֵּי הָעוֹלָם הַבָּא. וְיָפָה שָׁעָה אַחַת שֶׁל קוֹרַת רוּחַ בָּעוֹלָם הַבָּא, מִכֹּל חַיֵּי הָעוֹלָם הַזֶּה.

He used to say: One hour of repentance and good deeds in this world is better than all the life of the World to Come. But one hour of tranquil bliss in the World to Come is better than all the life of this world.

One hour of repentance and good deeds in this world is better than ... the World to Come

In this world you are a complete human being, a body and a soul. When you do good or repent from evil in this world there is a deeper, more totally human pleasure in these worldly activities. In this moment, when you are acting at the highest level, you receive a deeper fulfillment than you will in all of eternity – because there, only the soul dimension exists.

One hour ... in the World to Come is better than ... this world

On the other hand, the spiritual bliss is so sweet in the World to Come that one hour gives more satisfaction than all the physical pleasures of the entire mortal life. In *Halakhic Man*, Rabbi Joseph B. Soloveitchik cites this mishna as capturing a profound, paradoxical truth of the Torah.[36] The religious person should focus totally on living this

36. Soloveitchik, *Halakhic Man*, 30, 33ff., 41ff.

worldly life properly and fully. The Torah is all about living one's mortal, flesh-and-blood life to the fullest. This is the true existence with God. On the other hand, we should be aware of and gladdened by the expectation of eternal joy in a future spiritual existence with God. (But this is like a bonus; it should not be the driving force of the religious life.)

Mishna 18

רַבִּי שִׁמְעוֹן בֶּן אֶלְעָזָר
אוֹמֵר: אַל תְּרַצֶּה אֶת חֲבֵרְךָ
בִּשְׁעַת כַּעְסוֹ, וְאַל תְּנַחֲמֶנּוּ
בְּשָׁעָה שֶׁמֵּתוֹ מֻטָּל לְפָנָיו,
וְאַל תִּשְׁאַל לוֹ בִּשְׁעַת
נִדְרוֹ, וְאַל תִּשְׁתַּדֵּל לִרְאוֹתוֹ
בִּשְׁעַת קַלְקָלָתוֹ.

R. Shimon b. Elazar says: Do not try to pacify your friend in the hour when he is in a rage; and do not comfort him in the hour when his dead lies [unburied] before him; and do not question him in the hour when he is making a vow; and do not make an effort to see him in the hour of his disgrace.

HISTORICAL BACKGROUND

R. Shimon b. Elazar was a primary student of R. Meir and a colleague and associate of R. Yehuda the Prince (second century CE). He gave over many of his teachings in the name of R. Meir. He credited his knowledge of Torah to the years of apprenticeship when he followed R. Meir and studied his teachings and behavior. He once said, tongue in cheek, "I held onto R. Meir's walking stick with my hand, and it taught me much understanding and wisdom." He lived to a ripe old age and was the grandfather of Rav Yoḥanan, one of the most important *Amora'im* in the Gemara, the part of the Talmud which was developed following the editing and closure of the Mishna. As a young child, Rav Yoḥanan was given rides on his grandfather's shoulders. He heard his grandfather's Torah and began to absorb it.

Do not try

All four cases cited by R. Shimon point to the issue of mixed messages: the overt message of our words and actions versus the contradictory subtext of the actual effects of our intervention with another. In other words, our good intentions are contradicted by the facts on the ground. We are saying the right things, but due to insensitivity to the other person's state, our actions are having the opposite effect. There is a negative impact on the other. R. Shimon's point is that proper communication is intrinsically covenantal, i.e., two-way. The speaker and the listener both affect the message of the interchange. In all interactions with others, we must take into account his or her needs and state of mind. Communication is not just about us; it is about the other as well.

Pacify... when he is in a rage

The overt intention is to calm the other. However, speaking – even soothingly – to someone when he or she is in a rage frequently pours fuel on the fire, enraging the other further. Before speaking, wait for the person to use up all his rage and thereby become more open to listening.

Comfort him... when his dead lies [unburied]

When the deceased lies unburied before the mourner, the wound of loss is raw; the feelings of devastation and void are explosive. To offer comfort in such a moment is premature. One is actually adding to the mourner's feelings of loss and maybe even violating his sense of relationship and deep connection to the deceased by expecting him to turn from grief so quickly.

Question him... when he is making a vow

When someone is making a vow, i.e., renouncing or taking on some special obligation, to question him in the very act – whether it be to offer to nullify it or to seek to define its parameters – is to go against the grain of his intense personal feelings. This may drive him into an extreme extension of the oath, or it may cause you to come across as dismissive of the pledge and trifling with the emotions that drove this urgent act. We can apply this today with regard to how we react to a person taking on a diet or commitment to exercise, or even a new Jewish practice. Even if in the past, that individual has failed at this very undertaking, do not demonstrate an attitude of disrespect toward his intentions or capacity to follow through.

See him in the hour of his disgrace

Here again, the outward intention is to help the other. But to push one's way in to see the person in the very moment of his disgrace or intense vulnerability is to violate his privacy. On the conscious level one seeks to help, but unconsciously he may be pushing to see (with unadmitted satisfaction) the degradation and disgrace of another. In the end, you might add to the sufferer's state of residual shame that will last beyond the moment. The victim will feel that one more person saw him at his worst.

It may be entirely legitimate and helpful to be with someone in a moment of rage, loss, or disgrace. If you are there at such a moment, stand in solidarity with him or embrace him to give him support. However, to push yourself in when others do not want you to be there, or to insist on seeing them when they are in pain or disgrace, or to insinuate yourself in to speak words of comfort or explanation prematurely is to violate the other's dignity. As in the case of Job's friends, your words may turn into criticism and, intentional or not, into mockery, thus adding insult to injury.

Mishna 19

שְׁמוּאֵל הַקָּטָן אוֹמֵר:
בִּנְפֹל אוֹיִבְךָ אַל־תִּשְׂמָח,
וּבִכָּשְׁלוֹ אַל־יָגֵל לִבֶּךָ: פֶּן־
יִרְאֶה יהוה וְרַע בְּעֵינָיו,
וְהֵשִׁיב מֵעָלָיו אַפּוֹ:

Shmuel the Small says: When your enemy falls do not rejoice; when he stumbles do not be glad, lest the Lord see [your celebration] and it be wrong in His eyes, and [as a rebuke to you, God] will turn away His wrath from him [your enemy].

HISTORICAL BACKGROUND

Shmuel the Small was a second-generation *Tanna* active under the *nasi* Rabban Gamliel I at Yavneh (late first–second century CE). At the *nasi*'s request, he formulated the blessing against the *minim* (heretic sectarians, or possibly the Jewish Christians), which was incorporated into the *Amida* (central prayer) permanently. It is likely that he was called "the small" in tribute to his modesty. When he died, he was eulogized: "Woe [for the loss of the] pious one; woe [for the loss of the] modest one; a [true] disciple of Hillel." He was also celebrated for his righteousness and good character. Once he took responsibility for an embarrassing act which in fact he did not do, in order to protect the actual perpetrator from public humiliation. His saintliness was so great that the Talmud states that he was worthy of receiving direct, divine instruction, but did not receive it because the generation was not worthy of it.

Note: In the twentieth century, the great Rav Kook, then-chief rabbi of Palestine, stressed the centrality of love of all Jewish people and all of humanity. He taught the importance of reconciling elements in the tradition that come across as hostile to gentiles or non-religious Jews.

He wrote that only someone like Shmuel the Small could be assigned to write this prayer of rejection of the *minim*, because his modesty, saintliness, and kindness could be trusted to put a limit on the expression of hostility to the heretics. Were a lesser person given the assignment, anger and hatred would likely have taken over, turning the religion into a merciless or cruel foe of the other.

Shmuel the Small says

This entire statement is taken word for word from Proverbs 24:17–18. Perhaps Shmuel said this piece of wisdom so frequently that it was associated with him as a saying with which he totally identified.

[God] will turn away His wrath from him

Some of the sages were extremely sensitive to the concept of retribution, sometimes called measure-for-measure: the idea that all the incidents in an individual's life come about in response to previous behavior. In this case, Shmuel says: Curb your joy at the fall of your enemy, lest God bring retribution on you for finding joy in someone else's misfortune. God could respond by commuting the enemy's punishment.

Mishna 20

אֱלִישָׁע בֶּן אֲבוּיָה אוֹמֵר:
הַלּוֹמֵד יֶלֶד, לְמָה הוּא דוֹמֶה,
לִדְיוֹ כְּתוּבָה עַל נְיָר חָדָשׁ.
וְהַלּוֹמֵד זָקֵן, לְמָה הוּא דוֹמֶה,
לִדְיוֹ כְּתוּבָה עַל נְיָר מָחוּק.

Elisha b. Avuya says: He who learns when he is young, to what is it likened? To ink written on new paper. And he who learns when he is old, to what is it likened? To ink written on erased [blotted] paper.

HISTORICAL BACKGROUND

Elisha b. Avuya was a great teacher. He was the primary sage of one of the leading lights of the Mishna, R. Meir. Elisha became an apostate from rabbinic Judaism. Anecdotes in the Talmud suggest that his encounter with the death and suffering of righteous people drove him to rebel against the tradition. Another source implies that his entry into the Pardes (see 4:1) was so explosive that it undermined his faith (as it damaged the health of Ben Azzai and the mind of Ben Zoma). Elisha's disciple, R. Meir, remained loyal to him, and stayed in contact with him despite his falling away. It is noteworthy that the historical record was not erased, and this teaching was preserved in his name in Tractate Avot.

Young…old

It is better and easier to learn Torah as a child, when the mind is not as clogged and the openness to improvement and new thoughts is at its peak. One can learn Torah in old age, but "the paper has been erased." The mind is not as pristine, as sharp, or as retentive as it was in childhood.

רַבִּי יוֹסֵי בַּר יְהוּדָה אִישׁ כְּפַר הַבַּבְלִי אוֹמֵר: הַלּוֹמֵד מִן הַקְּטַנִּים, לְמָה הוּא דוֹמֶה, לְאוֹכֵל עֲנָבִים קֵהוֹת וְשׁוֹתֶה יַיִן מִגִּתּוֹ. וְהַלּוֹמֵד מִן הַזְּקֵנִים, לְמָה הוּא דוֹמֶה, לְאוֹכֵל עֲנָבִים בְּשׁוּלוֹת וְשׁוֹתֶה יַיִן יָשָׁן.

R. Yosei b. Yehuda of Kfar HaBavli says: One who learns from the young, to what can he be compared? To one who eats unripe grapes and drinks wine that [is not aged, i.e.,] comes directly from the winepress. One who learns from elders, to what may he be compared? To one who eats ripe grapes and drinks wine that is aged.

HISTORICAL BACKGROUND

R. Yosei b. Yehuda of Kfar HaBavli probably lived in the mid-second century CE and was a student of R. Elazar b. Shamua. R. Yehuda the Prince mentions that when he went to study under R. Elazar, he found R. Yosei already studying there. Kfar HaBavli is in the northern Galilee, approaching Sidon.

Learns from the young...learns from elders

R. Yosei points to the paradox whose first half has been stated by Elisha b. Avuya. It is better to start studying when one is young, for then his learning capacities are at their peak. However, when it comes to being taught, it is better to find a teacher who is older, because the teacher's wisdom grows from studying over the years and from the cumulative wisdom bestowed by life's experiences.

רַבִּי אוֹמֵר: אַל תִּסְתַּכֵּל בַּקַּנְקַן, אֶלָּא בְּמַה שֶׁיֵּשׁ בּוֹ. יֵשׁ קַנְקַן חָדָשׁ מָלֵא יָשָׁן, וְיָשָׁן שֶׁאֲפִלּוּ חָדָשׁ אֵין בּוֹ.

R. Yehuda the Prince says: Do not look at the pitcher but at its contents. [Sometimes] there is a new pitcher full of old [wine] and [sometimes there is] an old pitcher which does not have even new wine in it.

Pitcher...wine

R. Yehuda concludes the discussion of the advantages of youth versus those of age. When it comes to studying and teaching, he says: Do not judge the teacher or the student by the container (whether the body is old or young). A youth can have wisdom, and sometimes the old may have neither wisdom nor even common sense.

Mishna 21

רַבִּי אֶלְעָזָר הַקַּפָּר אוֹמֵר: הַקִּנְאָה וְהַתַּאֲוָה וְהַכָּבוֹד, מוֹצִיאִין אֶת הָאָדָם מִן הָעוֹלָם.

R. Elazar HaKappar says: Envy, lust, and [excessive] ambition shorten a person's life.

HISTORICAL BACKGROUND

R. Elazar HaKappar (second century CE) was a late fifth-generation *Tanna* who was in contact with R. Yehuda the Prince. While in this mishna he opposes seeking the wrong kind of experiences, he nevertheless taught elsewhere that it was not right to practice excessive denial or asceticism. His proof text was that the Torah requires the nazirite to bring an expiatory sacrifice when he finishes his term of consecration.[37] This type of offering is a statement of guilt (or punishment for sin) for the "sin" of having denied himself the pleasure of wine. Says R. Elazar: Avoid giving in to bad urges and life-shortening actions. At the same time, however, it is wrong to deny yourself any or all legitimate pleasure.

Envy, lust, and [excessive] ambition

These drive a person to irresponsible, sometimes reckless, sometimes highly dangerous behaviors which not infrequently can endanger his life or health. Moreover, these types of behaviors cause high stress, which can shorten a person's life.

37. See Numbers 13:6ff.

Mishna 22

הוּא הָיָה אוֹמֵר: הַיִּלּוֹדִים לָמוּת, וְהַמֵּתִים לְחָיוֹת, וְהַחַיִּים לִדּוֹן, לֵידַע וּלְהוֹדִיעַ וּלְהִוָּדַע, שֶׁהוּא אֵל, הוּא הַיּוֹצֵר, הוּא הַבּוֹרֵא, הוּא הַמֵּבִין, הוּא הַדַּיָּן, הוּא הָעֵד, הוּא בַּעַל דִּין, הוּא עָתִיד לָדוּן. בָּרוּךְ הוּא, שֶׁאֵין לְפָנָיו לֹא עַוְלָה וְלֹא שִׁכְחָה, וְלֹא מַשּׂוֹא פָנִים וְלֹא מִקַּח שֹׁחַד, שֶׁהַכֹּל שֶׁלּוֹ. וְדַע, שֶׁהַכֹּל לְפִי הַחֶשְׁבּוֹן. וְאַל יַבְטִיחֲךָ יִצְרְךָ שֶׁהַשְּׁאוֹל בֵּית מָנוֹס לָךְ, שֶׁעַל כָּרְחֲךָ אַתָּה נוֹצָר, וְעַל כָּרְחֲךָ אַתָּה נוֹלָד, וְעַל כָּרְחֲךָ אַתָּה חַי, וְעַל כָּרְחֲךָ אַתָּה מֵת, וְעַל כָּרְחֲךָ אַתָּה עָתִיד לִתֵּן דִּין וְחֶשְׁבּוֹן לִפְנֵי מֶלֶךְ מַלְכֵי הַמְּלָכִים הַקָּדוֹשׁ בָּרוּךְ הוּא.

He used to say: All that are born are destined to die; [all] the dead are [destined] to live [again through resurrection]; the living [are destined] to be judged. To know, to make known, and to be made aware that God is God, is the Maker, is the Creator, is the one who understands [everything], the one who is the judge, who is the witness, who is the litigant, who will be the one to judge; blessed be God before whom there is no injustice, no forgetfulness, no favoritism, no taking of bribes. Know that all the [reward and punishment] is according to the [true] reckoning. Let not your evil urge lull you into complacence that the afterworld will be a place to escape for you. [In the end], willing or not, you are born; willing or not, you live; willing or not, you die; willing or not, in the future you will [present a final] reckoning and account before the supreme [one,] King of kings, The Holy One, Blessed Be He.

Destined, etc.

Life, death, and resurrection are all given to human beings; they are not chosen or defined by them. These three stages are the inescapable fate of everyone.

To know, to make known, etc.

The fact of human fate communicates to us that we are just creatures in the grip of an infinite, omnipotent Creator who knows and remembers everything about us and who will judge us justly, without distortion, favoritism, or accepting bribes.

All ... is according to the [true] reckoning

R. Elazar offers an assurance to the righteous and a warning to the wicked. The final judgment will be just; our final fate will be earned the old-fashioned way, by our own behavior.

Afterworld ... a place to escape

Death is not oblivion, and therefore it will not enable anyone to escape any punishment which he or she deserves.

Willing or not

Human fate: birth, life, and death, is a divine decree and not a personally selected menu of experiences. The circumstances of our basic makeup and our life experience are given to us. We humans have the freedom to choose how to behave and how to deal with what life hands us. Neither can anyone escape the final judgment of God, the ultimate ruler, Creator of the world and shaper of human destiny and experiences.

The bottom line of these reflections is to feel awe before God, to feel our own finitude, to live on the side of good because we are conscious that we will be held accountable for all that we do – before an all-knowing, inescapable (albeit, loving) Judge.

Chapter 5

In this chapter, the structure of the tractate shifts dramatically from a chain of succession and quotes from sages of the different generations to mishnas with teachings organized around numbers (ten, seven, four, etc.). What does this shift suggest about the purpose and organization of *Pirkei Avot*?

One could answer that this chapter extends the chain of transmission back to the very beginning of Creation. By implication, the narrative of Torah transmission is a central part of God's plan for the world. Nevertheless, the shift calls attention to possible models for Ethics of the Fathers that may have been derived from the cultural milieu. It is known that there were schools in the Hellenistic world that published anthologies of wisdom sayings attributed to specific wise men. Some of these anthologies were organized around numbers and themes associated with those numbers. Of course, organizing material around numbers makes it easier to memorize – an important advantage in a world where oral culture was still very strong. It must be remembered that R. Yehuda the Prince broke with precedent when he wrote down and published the Mishna; up until then, this set of laws and instruction was deliberately studied and transmitted only orally. It is possible that the editorial circle of *Pirkei Avot* learned from – or borrowed – the currency of such numerically organized wisdom collections in order to give the tractate instant recognition and credibility.

Some scholars have drawn the analogy to the volumes published during the renaissance of rhetoric, known in Hellenistic culture as the Age of the Second Sophistic. Especially during the second century CE, Hellenic cities flourished under the *Pax Romana*, with local elites "making peace" with the Roman domination – even as R. Yehuda the Prince's family (and he himself) accommodated to Rome and worked out a constructive *modus vivendi* in the aftermath of the catastrophic failure of the Bar Kokhba revolt.

The second century CE is marked by affirmation of antiquity and even of archaism. This approach flourished all over the empire, including in the general culture surrounding the rabbinic communities. Scholars point to Diogenes Laërtius' history of philosophy written in the beginning of the third century, just after Tractate Avot was completed. Diogenes' book and other Sophist works focus on a chain of transmission from teachers to pupils, and on the way each philosophical school grew in relation to its founder. The parallels – classicism (in *Pirkei Avot*: the Torah), archaic language (in *Pirkei Avot*: Hebrew), linguistic purism, establishing credibility by showing that these scholars were legitimate heirs of the old traditions – are striking.

One need not assume borrowing and interchange. The main point is that this type of literary model and wisdom anthology was in the air. Ethics of the Fathers could tap into the prestige and cultural status of such models to establish its own special authority. It would be natural for the patriarch, with his connections to Rome and exposure to Hellenistic culture, to adopt such literary and philosophical conventions in order to organize his own materials. Thus, in evoking the Hellenistic models around him, he gained the automatic cultural cachet for *Pirkei Avot* which such a collection bestowed.

The sages were not oblivious to Hellenistic culture. Nor did they simply resist it. They felt free to learn from it and even to borrow from it, as long as they could shape it in the image of Torah values and thereby enrich rabbinic culture.[1]

---

1. For further information, see the excellent analyses in Tropper, *Wisdom, Politics, and Historiography*, 136–172. I am indebted to the author for opening this window for us.

Mishna 1

בַּעֲשָׂרָה מַאֲמָרוֹת נִבְרָא הָעוֹלָם. וּמַה תַּלְמוּד לוֹמַר, וַהֲלֹא בְּמַאֲמָר אֶחָד יָכוֹל לְהִבָּרְאוֹת, אֶלָּא לְהִפָּרַע מִן הָרְשָׁעִים, שֶׁמְּאַבְּדִין אֶת הָעוֹלָם שֶׁנִּבְרָא בַּעֲשָׂרָה מַאֲמָרוֹת, וְלִתֵּן שָׂכָר טוֹב לַצַּדִּיקִים, שֶׁמְּקַיְּמִין אֶת הָעוֹלָם שֶׁנִּבְרָא בַּעֲשָׂרָה מַאֲמָרוֹת.

With ten sayings, the world was created [by God]. Why does the Torah tell [us] this? After all, the whole [world] could have been created with one [divine] utterance. It is to hold accountable the wicked, who destroy the world which was created with ten sayings, and to give good reward to the righteous, who sustain the world which was created with ten sayings.

Ten sayings

In the first chapter of the Book of Genesis, which is an account of Creation, God speaks ten times, giving the instructions to create the world. "Let there be light" (v. 3) is followed by nine more divine utterances, in verses 6, 9, 11, 14, 20, 24, 26, 28, and 29.

Ten

The number ten signifies complete, total, or perfect situations in the Bible. The ultimate punishment that finally broke the tyrannical Pharaoh was ten plagues. The ultimate précis of God's instructions for a good life was the Ten Commandments given at Mount Sinai. Ten sayings of Creation means that God spoke the maximum number of times to do a complete job. The image created by this metaphor is one of the infinite Almighty laboring mightily to bring Creation into being. It takes tremendous energy, substance, and organization to bring the universe into being and to sustain it. All the more so should we take seriously our every action in the world.

Wicked... righteous

The world is so complex, so exact in its perfection, that it needs a total effort by human beings to uphold, continue, and improve it. Those who destroy life and damage the world are committing terrible sins because they degrade a creation that took infinite divine power to establish. Those who uphold and improve the world are doing an eternally great thing, because they are partnering with God in sustaining creation.

Mishna 2

עֲשָׂרָה דוֹרוֹת מֵאָדָם
וְעַד נֹחַ, לְהוֹדִיעַ כַּמָּה
אֶרֶךְ אַפַּיִם לְפָנָיו, שֶׁכָּל
הַדּוֹרוֹת הָיוּ מַכְעִיסִין
וּבָאִין, עַד שֶׁהֵבִיא
עֲלֵיהֶם אֶת מֵי הַמַּבּוּל.

There were ten generations from Adam until Noah. This tells you how much patience there is before God, for [all ten] generations came and aroused anger [by their evil behavior] until God [finally] brought upon them the waters of the flood.

Ten generations

In Genesis chapter 5, the Torah lists the ten generations. In this mishna, the sages stress their symbolic and literary character. These generations spanned an enormous period of time, which was full of evil behavior designed to arouse God's anger. God held back, giving humans great leeway, before taking action to purge the world through the flood.

עֲשָׂרָה דוֹרוֹת מִנֹּחַ וְעַד
אַבְרָהָם, לְהוֹדִיעַ כַּמָּה
אֶרֶךְ אַפַּיִם לְפָנָיו, שֶׁכָּל
הַדּוֹרוֹת הָיוּ מַכְעִיסִין
וּבָאִין, עַד שֶׁבָּא
אַבְרָהָם אָבִינוּ וְקִבֵּל
שְׂכַר כֻּלָּם.

There were ten generations from Noah to Abraham. This tells you how much patience there is before God, because each of the [ten] generations came and aroused [His] anger [by their evil behavior], until our father Abraham came and received the reward that all of them [could have earned].

Ten generations

These ten generations are listed in Genesis chapter 11. The Torah's use of genealogies throughout the Book of Genesis communicates that the Jewish religion is all about the development and direction of human life in general. The emergence of Abraham's family is a breakthrough for humanity; their experiences would show the way for the rest of the world throughout the generations. In the end, "all the families of the earth will be blessed through you [Abraham]."[2] The sages again stress that the number ten signifies the extraordinary patience and self-restraint which God has shown to humanity even when it behaved wickedly. Choosing Abraham is a statement of love and patience, because God is instructing humanity through an example instead of coercing good behavior by punishing people.

Abraham ... received the reward that all of them [could have earned]

- God wanted to give reward to each generation. Instead, they acted against His will. When Abraham arrived, his merit was so great by contrast that he received the total reward that all could have earned if they had behaved properly.
- These ten generations were so evil that another catastrophic punishment was in order. Instead, Abraham did such good before the Lord that the evil was redeemed by his merit. The punishment was not inflicted, and he received the reward of all ten generations.

Noah ... Abraham

- Unlike Noah, who was righteous and was spared from the flood but who did nothing to save the rest of humanity from its fate, Abraham's merit was extended to the rest of the generation. Abraham used his standing as a righteous person before God to

2. Genesis 12:3.

try and save Sodom from catastrophe. By implication, he may have saved the whole world from a catastrophic punishment.

- Noah and the fate of his generation symbolize the divine wrath at the cumulative human evil which corrupted the earth. By Abraham's time, however, God was committed by the covenant with humanity (Noah) to never bring a cataclysmic, intimidating form of punishment to the world ever again. How then did God deal with the human behaviors which frustrated the divine purpose of creating a perfect world? He made a special, limited covenant with Abraham, Sarah, and family. They would teach their children after them "the way of the Lord to do righteousness and justice."[3] This would provide a model of covenantal living that would instruct humans to live the good life and to pace humanity to work toward the perfection of the world. Thus, the covenant with Abraham singled out God's love for Israel. At the same time, it is an act of love toward humanity. Instead of punishing the nations or coercing them to do His will, God elects to set up a model to persuade and inspire the rest of humanity, by example, to turn to the good life.

3. Ibid., 18:19.

Mishna 3

עֲשָׂרָה נִסְיוֹנוֹת נִתְנַסָּה אַבְרָהָם אָבִינוּ וְעָמַד בְּכֻלָּם, לְהוֹדִיעַ כַּמָּה חִבָּתוֹ שֶׁל אַבְרָהָם אָבִינוּ.

Our father Abraham was tested with ten trials, yet he stood up to all of them. This tells you how great was the love of our father Abraham [for God].

Ten trials

Abraham was tested to the limit of testing (ten). The Torah does not enumerate the ten trials. The Midrash does not offer a definitive list either, although it is commonly assumed that the ultimate (tenth) trial was *Akedat Yitzḥak*, the command to bind Isaac upon an altar and sacrifice him.[4]

There has been much speculation concerning what the actual ten trials were. Not counting the trials articulated in the later rabbinic Midrash (such as Abraham's being thrown into a furnace for daring to destroy idols), there are fourteen potential cases in the Torah narrative:

- to leave his homeland and go to an unknown land;
- having found and been promised the land of Canaan, to have to go out of the land and down to Egypt due to a famine;
- to face Pharaoh and his absolute monarchy and not lose his own moral way and religious orientation to God;

4. Ibid., ch. 22.

- to allow his nephew Lot (his successor?) to split from him and take up residence near Sodom, and to still believe God's promise that he would inherit the land;
- to fight the five conquering kings in order to rescue their captive, his nephew Lot (who had left him!);
- to believe God's promise that he would not be inherited by his servant Eliezer but by his own biological son, although he and Sarah were childless and too old to have children;
- to go on willingly with the covenant with God (the Covenant between the Pieces), even though he was told that his children would suffer servitude and oppression;
- to circumcise himself at the age of ninety-nine in order to enter into the covenant with God;
- to believe the promise that Sarah, in her old age, would bear his child;
- to argue with God to save Sodom rather than abandon the Sodomites to His wrathful punishment;
- to face the mockery of those who whispered that Sarah conceived shortly after being taken into the harem of King Avimelekh of Gerar;
- to listen to Sarah and send away Hagar even though Ishmael was his beloved, biological son;
- to endure the heart-wrenching, mettle-testing trial of the Binding of Isaac for three whole days;
- having no piece of land in which to bury Sarah when she died, and so being forced to buy a grave site for an astronomical sum, despite God's repeated promises that the whole land of Canaan (Israel) would belong to him.[5]

Rabbi Joseph B. Soloveitchik suggested yet one more trial, which ironically tests Abraham beyond the Binding of Isaac: to accept with equanimity that his brother Naḥor had eight sons from his wife Milca and

5. The sources for these fourteen trials are, respectively, Genesis 12:1; 12:10; 12:11–20; 13:5–17; 14:1–24; 15:1–6; 15:2–18; 17:1–14, 23–27; 17:15–21, 18:10–15; 18:17–33; ch. 20, 21:1–8; 21:9–14; 22:1–18; and 23:1–19.

four additional sons from his concubine Reuma.[6] Rabbi Soloveitchik says: Knowing that his idol-worshiping brother had twelve sons with no effort and no excruciating test of his willingness to sacrifice one of them might have been harder to endure than some of the other, more "extreme" experiences with which he was tested.

How great was the love

An alternative, but less likely, translation is: How great was [God's] love of our father Abraham.

6. Ibid., 22:20–24.

Mishna 4

עֲשָׂרָה נִסִּים נַעֲשׂוּ לַאֲבוֹתֵינוּ בְּמִצְרַיִם, וַעֲשָׂרָה עַל הַיָּם.

Ten miracles were done for our ancestors in Egypt and ten at the Red Sea.

Ten miracles

This ultimate act of miraculous intervention was done by God for the Children of Israel.

Are the sages counting the ten plagues on the Egyptians also as ten miracles done for the sake of the Israelites? Or is this a reference to a midrashic tradition that for every plague inflicted on the Egyptians there was a parallel miracle done for the Israelites? It is also possible that this is a reference to the fact that the Israelites were shielded from the plagues, e.g., only the Egyptian water turned to blood, not that of the Jews; it was pitch dark in Egyptian homes but there was light in the Israelite quarters, etc.

עֶשֶׂר מַכּוֹת הֵבִיא הַקָּדוֹשׁ בָּרוּךְ הוּא עַל הַמִּצְרִיִּים בְּמִצְרַיִם, וְעֶשֶׂר עַל הַיָּם.

Ten plagues did The Holy One, Blessed Be He, bring down on the Egyptians, and ten [more] at the [Red] Sea.

Ten plagues – The *ne plus ultra* of miraculous punishments were inflicted on the Egyptians; the first ten in Egypt to compel them to let the Israelites go, and another ten at the sea when their arrogant attempt to take them back into slavery was smashed.

עֲשָׂרָה נִסְיוֹנוֹת נִסּוּ אֲבוֹתֵינוּ אֶת הַקָּדוֹשׁ בָּרוּךְ הוּא בַּמִּדְבָּר, שֶׁנֶּאֱמַר: וַיְנַסּוּ אֹתִי זֶה עֶשֶׂר פְּעָמִים, וְלֹא שָׁמְעוּ בְּקוֹלִי:

Our ancestors tested The Holy One, Blessed Be He, with ten trials on their journey through the desert, as it says: "They tested Me ten times and did not listen to My voice."[7]

Tested

- The Israelites tested, i.e., strained God's love to the limit (ten times) by continuously responding to acts of deliverance and miraculous intervention with displays of complete lack of faith and trust.
- There were ten divine acts of special provision for the Israelites. They were followed by behaviors exhibiting lack of faith and/or questioning God's care the minute some problem or danger loomed:
  - The Israelites were liberated in the Exodus through ten astonishing plagues, yet when they faced the Red Sea and feared that the Egyptian army would capture them, they initially said: "What did you do to us, taking us out of Egypt?… Better to slave for the Egyptians than die in the desert."
  - They were miraculously saved at the Red Sea, yet three days later, when they found only bitter water at Mara, they grumbled at Moses: "What shall we drink?"
  - Having been led to the oasis at Eilim and given water without limit, they traveled in the desert of Sin. Worried about a food shortage, they immediately charged: "You took us out to this desert to starve this whole congregation to death!"
  - The Israelites were granted manna to assure them bread aplenty, and flocks of quail to provide them with unlimited meat. Moses told them not to leave any manna over for the next day but to depend on God's overflowing bounty, which would provide them with new manna every morning. Yet

7. Numbers 14:22.

  "they paid no attention to Moses," and some left manna overnight (and it became maggoty and rotten).
  - They were given a double portion of manna on Friday, yet they violated instructions and went out to gather food on Shabbat, which was forbidden.
  - In Refidim, there was no water. They threatened Moses, accusing him: "Why did you take us out of Egypt to kill us... with thirst?" Their accusations against Moses (and Aaron) showed a total lack of trust in and gratitude to God. Hence, this place was named Massa (trial) and Meriva (quarrel), for they tried God, saying: "Is God in our midst or not?"
  - At Mount Sinai (Horeb), God revealed His Divine Presence and had Moses present the Ten Commandments to the people. Yet within days, the people betrayed the covenant they had entered into and demanded of Aaron that he create a god they could see and worship. They turned to the Golden Calf with song and dance.
  - Deeper in the desert at Tav'era, the people complained bitterly, as if God had abandoned them there.
  - At Kivrot HaTaava, they turned against the manna, saying: "Our gullets are shriveled." They demanded meat and waxed sentimental about the food they ate in the good old days in Egypt.
  - Having come through the entire desert safely, standing on the border of Canaan, they panicked at the spies' report that the native population was "fierce" and too strong for them to overcome. Instead of trusting God, they cried: "Why did God bring us to this land to die by the sword?" They even turned to go back to Egypt.[8]
- God's covenantal (i.e., committed) loving-kindness outlasted the ten trials and a continuous, generation-long display of childish, fearful, and selfish behaviors. God did not reject the covenant or disown the people. He took the next generation, which

8. The sources for these ten events are, respectively, Exodus 14:12; 15:23; 16:3; 16:20; 16:22–30; 17:1–7; chs. 19, 20; 31:18, chs. 32, 33, 34:1–10; Numbers 11:1–3; 11:4–6; 13:1–33, 14:3–4.

was capable of dealing with the challenges of freedom, into the Promised Land.

- This mishna complements mishna 3, which refers to Abraham's ten trials. The point is that living up to the covenant – as with every committed love relationship – involves moments of trial and even failure. Sometimes one partner can question whether the whole relationship was worth it or whether it was a mistake. Sometimes it seems as if only the sense of commitment carries a partner through. Yet the covenant between God and Israel persisted because each partner's love turned out to be limitless. By implication, just as Abraham's ten trials prove "how great was the love of our father Abraham," so do the trials in the desert prove how great was (and still is) the love of our heavenly Father.

Mishna 5

עֲשָׂרָה נִסִּים נַעֲשׂוּ
לַאֲבוֹתֵינוּ בְּבֵית הַמִּקְדָּשׁ.
לֹא הִפִּילָה אִשָּׁה מֵרֵיחַ
בְּשַׂר הַקֹּדֶשׁ, וְלֹא הִסְרִיחַ
בְּשַׂר הַקֹּדֶשׁ מֵעוֹלָם,
וְלֹא נִרְאָה זְבוּב בְּבֵית
הַמִּטְבְּחַיִם, וְלֹא אֵרַע קֶרִי
לְכֹהֵן גָּדוֹל בְּיוֹם הַכִּפּוּרִים,
וְלֹא כִבּוּ הַגְּשָׁמִים אֵשׁ
שֶׁל עֲצֵי הַמַּעֲרָכָה, וְלֹא
נִצְּחָה הָרוּחַ אֶת עַמּוּד
הֶעָשָׁן, וְלֹא נִמְצָא פְסוּל
בָּעֹמֶר וּבִשְׁתֵּי הַלֶּחֶם
וּבְלֶחֶם הַפָּנִים, עוֹמְדִים
צְפוּפִים וּמִשְׁתַּחֲוִים רְוָחִים,
וְלֹא הִזִּיק נָחָשׁ וְעַקְרָב
בִּירוּשָׁלַיִם מֵעוֹלָם, וְלֹא
אָמַר אָדָם לַחֲבֵרוֹ: צַר לִי
הַמָּקוֹם שֶׁאָלִין בִּירוּשָׁלָיִם.

Ten miracles were done for our ancestors in the Holy Temple. No woman miscarried because of the strong smell of the sacrificial meat; the sanctified meat never decayed or stank; no fly was ever seen in the slaughterhouse; no semen ejaculation occurred to a High Priest [on] the [night] of Yom Kippur; the rains never quenched the fire of the [altar's] wood; no wind ever blew away the column of smoke [rising from the altar]; no disqualifying defect was ever found in the sheaf [Omer] and in the two loaves and in the show bread; the pilgrims stood packed together [in the Temple courtyard], yet there was ample room for them to prostrate themselves; no snake or scorpion ever did harm in Jerusalem; no one ever said to his friend, "The place is too crowded for me to sleep in Jerusalem."

Ten miracles

Natural phenomena were suspended in the Temple due to its sanctity. This sanctity, as well as the intensity of the Divine Presence in the Temple, were given direct witness by a host of unusual phenomena that were statistically unlikely but still happened.

In the Holy Temple

This mishna is saturated with nostalgia for the lost Temple, which all the superhuman efforts and blood-soaked rebellions over a century and more could not recover.

Mishna 6

עֲשָׂרָה דְבָרִים נִבְרְאוּ בְּעֶרֶב
שַׁבָּת בֵּין הַשְּׁמָשׁוֹת. וְאֵלּוּ הֵן,
פִּי הָאָרֶץ, פִּי הַבְּאֵר, פִּי הָאָתוֹן,
הַקֶּשֶׁת, וְהַמָּן, וְהַמַּטֶּה, וְהַשָּׁמִיר,
הַכְּתָב, וְהַמִּכְתָּב, וְהַלּוּחוֹת.
וְיֵשׁ אוֹמְרִים, אַף הַמַּזִּיקִין,
וּקְבוּרָתוֹ שֶׁל מֹשֶׁה, וְאֵילוֹ שֶׁל
אַבְרָהָם אָבִינוּ. וְיֵשׁ אוֹמְרִים,
אַף צְבָת בִּצְבַת עֲשׂוּיָה.

Ten phenomena were created on Friday afternoon at twilight of the week of Creation. They are: the mouth of the earth,[9] the mouth of the [Miriam's] well,[10] the mouth of the donkey,[11] the rainbow,[12] the manna,[13] the rod,[14] the *shamir*,[15] writing,[16] and the engraving pen,[17] and the tablets.[18] Some say also the destructive spirits and Moses' grave[19] and Abraham's ram,[20] and some say the tongs made with tongs.

9. Which opened up to swallow Korah and his allies. See Numbers 16:29–34.
10. Numbers 20:2; 21:16.
11. Which spoke to Balaam. See ibid., 22:28–35.
12. Which was designated as the sign of the Noahide covenant. See Genesis 9:12–17.
13. Which miraculously sustained the Israelites in the desert. See Exodus 16:11–36.
14. Used by Moses in bringing plagues on Egypt. See ibid., 4:2–5; 7:9–13, 15–17, etc.
15. See Jeremiah 17:1; Ezekiel 3:9. This is translated as the adamant stone – a substance of such hardness that it can inscribe figures on stone. In rabbinic Midrash, the *shamir* is identified as a mysterious creature able to smooth and carve stone. Hence it was used to shape the Temple sacrificial Altar, for the Torah prohibits shaping or cutting it with an iron tool; see Exodus 20:22. The sages explain this prohibition: Iron is used in weapons of war. Therefore, it may not be used in the manufacture of the Altar, which is totally dedicated to making peace (between people, between God and people, etc.).
16. Possibly, this refers to Exodus 34:1, 27–35, when Moses wrote the second set of tablets, or it is possible the mishna means that all writing is "miraculous."
17. Possibly: the divine writing. See Exodus 32:15–16.
18. Ibid.
19. Deuteronomy 34:5–6. No one knows where it is because no human dug it.
20. Genesis 22:13.

Ten phenomena

At first glance, this records the creation of ten miraculous objects, plus, some say, four additional, inexplicable phenomena. However, the deeper meaning of the mishna may be the reverse of its superficial message. The average person thinks of manna, Miriam's well (which provided water for the hundreds of thousands of Israelites on their forty-year journey through an arid desert), and other changes in nature as miraculous phenomena and that God overrode natural laws to create these items for when they would be needed. But the mishna says no. All these phenomena were created in the course of the natural creation of the cosmos. Therefore, their appearance is the expression of natural process and scientific law, not a reversal of natural law. They were built into the essence of nature, says the mishna. The miracle is in the timing, in their appearance precisely when needed. From this perspective, one need not contradict science and the laws of nature in order to believe in miracles.

This interpretation fits the general tendency of the sages to stress that nature itself and its machinations are the real miracle, and not so much the "magical" interventions which most people think of when they pray for miracles. Compare the *Modim* prayer in the *Shemoneh Esreh*: "We thank You [God]... for Your miracles which are with us daily, and for Your wonders and favors [which are with us] all the time – evening, morning, and afternoon."[21] This shift is appropriate especially in light of the divine *tzimtzum* which made God's actions less "visible" and openly interventionist – yet ever more present.[22]

Destructive spirits

These are hidden powers that hurt humans. At the time of the redaction of the Mishna, illness-causing bacteria and viruses were not visible to the naked eye, so people projected the existence of demons.

Tongs made with tongs

Since tongs are needed in order to manufacture tongs, where did the first pair of tongs come from? They must have come into being by a miracle!

---

21. Birnbaum, *Ha-Siddur Ha-Shalem,* 91.
22. See Introduction.

If we follow the naturalistic interpretation of this mishna, then the "some say" opinion is that an invention that human beings make for the first time, e.g., tongs made with tongs, is a miracle. When humans use their God-given, God-like minds to uncover possibilities in God-created nature (say, a wonder drug, the use of metals, agriculture), this is a miracle. It uncovers the blessing and support built into reality which is subtle, hidden, but nevertheless powerful testimony to the divine presence operating in the world.

Mishna 7

שִׁבְעָה דְבָרִים בְּגֹלֶם,
וְשִׁבְעָה בְּחָכָם. חָכָם
אֵינוֹ מְדַבֵּר לִפְנֵי מִי שֶׁגָּדוֹל
מִמֶּנּוּ בְּחָכְמָה, וְאֵינוֹ נִכְנָס
לְתוֹךְ דִּבְרֵי חֲבֵרוֹ, וְאֵינוֹ
נִבְהָל לְהָשִׁיב, שׁוֹאֵל
כָּעִנְיָן וּמֵשִׁיב כַּהֲלָכָה,
וְאוֹמֵר עַל רִאשׁוֹן רִאשׁוֹן
וְעַל אַחֲרוֹן אַחֲרוֹן, וְעַל
מַה שֶּׁלֹּא שָׁמַע אוֹמֵר
לֹא שָׁמַעְתִּי, וּמוֹדֶה עַל
הָאֱמֶת. וְחִלּוּפֵיהֶן בְּגֹלֶם.

There are seven characteristics found in an uncultured person and seven in a wise person. A wise person does not speak in the face of one who is greater in wisdom and age, and does not interrupt the words of his fellow, and does not rush to reply. He asks relevant questions and replies according to the point. He speaks of first items first, and of last items last. Concerning what he has not heard, he says: I have not heard. He acknowledges the truth. The opposite characteristics are found in an uncultured person.

Seven

Seven is another number signifying completeness, wholeness, and perfection in the conventional numerology of biblical and rabbinic literature.

An uncultured person . . . a wise person

Wisdom is one of the greatest virtues in a human being. When King Solomon was offered any divine gift he chose, he wisely asked for the wisdom of "a listening [understanding] heart."[23] He put this gift ahead of long life, or riches, or the total obliteration of his enemies. Therefore,

23. I Kings 3:5–9.

God granted him "a wise and discerning heart."[24] David Hadar points out that the first request in the weekday *Shemoneh Esreh* (*Amida*) prayer is to be given knowledge, understanding, and insight; in other words, wisdom. One might think, however, that a person is born with this gift – or not. Not so, says the mishna: The uncultured person lacks wisdom, but can develop into a wise person – starting with acting according to the seven behaviors of one.

Does not speak...does not interrupt

A wise person is aware of his or her limits, and thus listens to and refrains from interrupting others.

Relevant...to the point

A wise person focuses on the core issues and sticks to the topic.

He says: I have not heard. He acknowledges the truth

A wise person admits when he or she has not heard some piece of information or does not know something, and acknowledges the truth even if it turns out to be the opposing viewpoint.

In sum: Uncultured people are full of themselves. They listen little, interrupt, and do not stay on topic, because they speak just to hear themselves speak. Their arrogance prevents them from acknowledging when they have not heard a particular piece of information, or when the truth opposes their own position. But the wise person seeks to find the right outcome. This is reflected in self-restrained behavior and in openness to the other case, the other viewpoint.

24. Ibid., v. 11–12.

Mishna 8

שִׁבְעָה מִינֵי פֻרְעָנִיּוֹת בָּאִין לָעוֹלָם עַל שִׁבְעָה גּוּפֵי עֲבֵרָה. מִקְצָתָן מְעַשְּׂרִין וּמִקְצָתָן אֵינָן מְעַשְּׂרִין, רָעָב שֶׁל בַּצֹּרֶת בָּא, מִקְצָתָן רְעֵבִים וּמִקְצָתָן שְׂבֵעִים. גָּמְרוּ שֶׁלֹּא לְעַשֵּׂר, רָעָב שֶׁל מְהוּמָה וְשֶׁל בַּצֹּרֶת בָּא. וְשֶׁלֹּא לִטּוֹל אֶת הַחַלָּה, רָעָב שֶׁל כְּלָיָה בָּא.

דֶּבֶר בָּא לָעוֹלָם עַל מִיתוֹת הָאֲמוּרוֹת בַּתּוֹרָה שֶׁלֹּא נִמְסְרוּ לְבֵית דִּין, וְעַל פֵּרוֹת שְׁבִיעִית. חֶרֶב בָּאָה לָעוֹלָם עַל עִנּוּי הַדִּין, וְעַל עִוּוּת הַדִּין, וְעַל הַמּוֹרִים בַּתּוֹרָה שֶׁלֹּא כַהֲלָכָה.

חַיָּה רָעָה בָּאָה לָעוֹלָם עַל שְׁבוּעַת שָׁוְא וְעַל חִלּוּל הַשֵּׁם. גָּלוּת בָּאָה לָעוֹלָם עַל עֲבוֹדָה זָרָה, וְעַל גִּלּוּי עֲרָיוֹת, וְעַל שְׁפִיכוּת דָּמִים, וְעַל שְׁמִטַּת הָאָרֶץ.

Seven types of afflictions come upon the world due to seven categories of sin. When some give tithes and some do not tithe, then a famine due to drought comes so some people are hungry and some are full. If they decided not to tithe [at all], a famine through upheaval and drought comes [so all go hungry]. If they have decided not to set aside the [ḥalla] offering, then an all-consuming famine comes. Pestilence comes to the world because of sins punishable by death according to the Torah [that were committed] which were not brought to the court [for action]. The sword comes to the world because of the delaying of justice and perversion of justice, and on account of those who do not interpret the Torah according to halakha. Wild beasts come to the world because of [the taking of] false oaths and because of profanation of [God's] name. Exile comes to the world because of idolatry, sexual perversion, murder, and neglect of releasing the land (*Shemitta*).

Seven types of afflictions ... seven categories of sin

This mishna seeks to find a one-to-one correspondence between sins that the population in general commits and afflictions that strike the Land of Israel. The goal of the punishment is to evoke repentance and to get people to stop committing the sins. This interpretation of natural calamities is based on two principles, strongly present in rabbinic tradition, whose persuasiveness has weakened in modern culture. One is the principle of measure-for-measure, that everything that occurs in this life is providentially arranged to give people a natural consequence of their behavior, negative and positive. The other principle is that because the Land of Israel is holy, the Lord (or God operating as Lord of this land) cannot abide sins committed on it. Therefore, the Lord expels people via measure-for-measure, retaliatory punishments.

In later cultures, especially in modern civilization, the atmosphere has been less sympathetic to finding this correspondence in worldly life. Instead, some authorities have stressed the World to Come as the moral balance to the perceived imbalance in this world. Others, from Maimonides and Gersonides on, have stressed that the divinely arranged order operates within a cosmic, providential infrastructure in which actions do have effects and, sometimes, direct outcomes (*olam keminhago noheg*). Within this order, measure-for-measure does not represent miraculous or unnatural interference, but the outcomes that flow from decision-making, roads taken, and the interaction implicit in the natural order and process.

Mishna 9

בְּאַרְבָּעָה פְּרָקִים הַדֶּבֶר מִתְרַבֶּה,
בָּרְבִיעִית, וּבַשְּׁבִיעִית, וּבְמוֹצָאֵי
שְׁבִיעִית, וּבְמוֹצָאֵי הֶחָג שֶׁבְּכָל
שָׁנָה וְשָׁנָה. בָּרְבִיעִית, מִפְּנֵי מַעְשַׂר
עָנִי שֶׁבַּשְּׁלִישִׁית. בַּשְּׁבִיעִית, מִפְּנֵי
מַעְשַׂר עָנִי שֶׁבַּשִּׁשִּׁית. בְּמוֹצָאֵי
שְׁבִיעִית, מִפְּנֵי פֵּרוֹת שְׁבִיעִית.
בְּמוֹצָאֵי הֶחָג שֶׁבְּכָל שָׁנָה וְשָׁנָה,
מִפְּנֵי גֶזֶל מַתְּנוֹת עֲנִיִּים.

[There are] four seasons in which pestilence increases: in the fourth [year of the seven-year cycle]; in the seventh [year]; in the year after the seventh; and in the post-Sukkot festival days every year. In the fourth year, because of neglect of the tithe for the poor [required] in the third year; and in the seventh year, because of [neglect of] the tithe for the poor [required] in the sixth year; in the year after the seventh, because of the [improper use] of the fruits of the seventh [sabbatical] year, and in the days after the Sukkot festival each year, because of the robbing of the gifts assigned to the poor.

Four seasons

There are special good deeds during these time periods which people are tempted to neglect. Some people even steal gifts that have been commanded to be given from their intended recipients. This mishna warns that providence will retaliate for such sins, so the desire to give in to temptation should be resisted. Note in particular that harming as well as not helping the poor is the dominant reason for pestilence.

Mishna 10

אַרְבַּע מִדּוֹת בָּאָדָם. הָאוֹמֵר שֶׁלִּי שֶׁלִּי וְשֶׁלְּךָ שֶׁלָּךְ, זוֹ מִדָּה בֵּינוֹנִית, וְיֵשׁ אוֹמְרִים, זוֹ מִדַּת סְדוֹם. שֶׁלִּי שֶׁלָּךְ וְשֶׁלְּךָ שֶׁלִּי, עַם הָאָרֶץ. שֶׁלִּי שֶׁלָּךְ וְשֶׁלְּךָ שֶׁלָּךְ, חָסִיד. שֶׁלְּךָ שֶׁלִּי וְשֶׁלִּי שֶׁלִּי, רָשָׁע.

There are four types of people: One who says: What is mine is mine and what is yours is yours – this is the average character; and some say this is the quality that [characterizes] Sodom. [One who says:] Mine is yours and yours is mine is an uncultured person. [One who says:] Mine is yours and yours is yours is pious (*ḥasid*). [One who says:] Yours is mine and mine is mine is wicked.

Four types

In this mishna, people are classified according to their willingness to be generous with their property. "Mine is mine and yours is yours" is a kind of live-and-let-live philosophy. It is commonplace and involves neither restraint nor generosity. "Mine is yours and yours is mine" also reflects a type of live-and-let-live psychology, but it is undisciplined and mixes up everybody's possessions; this is the mark of an uncultivated person. "Mine is yours and yours is yours" is the view of an utterly unselfish person, a pious, saintly type who gives without asking anything in return. "Yours is mine and mine is mine" is the characteristic of a completely selfish person. This is a wicked individual in that he tries to take for himself everything from everybody.

The quality that [characterizes] Sodom

On one level, the middle-of-the-road attitude is average and acceptable. On another level, this middling approach is rooted in the psychology of "every man for himself." Many commentators see this attitude as a prescription for moral deterioration, because this approach easily turns into an unwillingness to help others even if it costs one little or nothing. The next step of moral decline is that given the habit of looking out only for oneself, the "average" person is more likely to act as an indifferent bystander in the face of evil. After all, it's every man for himself. People then allow poverty or injustice to go on and do nothing about it. On a societal basis, this philosophy can generate a society like Sodom, where no help is extended to the poor and no hospitality is offered to strangers (see Ezekiel 16:49 and the rabbinic interpretation of Sodomite society). The line between a social atmosphere of respect for individuals (which seeks to maximize their autonomy) and a self-centered, narcissistic culture is very thin.

Mishna 11

אַרְבַּע מִדּוֹת בַּדֵּעוֹת. נוֹחַ לִכְעֹס וְנוֹחַ לִרְצוֹת, יָצָא הֶפְסֵדוֹ בִּשְׂכָרוֹ. קָשֶׁה לִכְעֹס וְקָשֶׁה לִרְצוֹת, יָצָא שְׂכָרוֹ בְּהֶפְסֵדוֹ. קָשֶׁה לִכְעֹס וְנוֹחַ לִרְצוֹת, חָסִיד. נוֹחַ לִכְעֹס וְקָשֶׁה לִרְצוֹת, רָשָׁע.

There are four types of character dispositions: [One whom it is] easy to get angry and easy to pacify; his advantage is outweighed by his disadvantage. [One whom it is] hard to get angry and hard to pacify; his loss is outweighed by his advantage. [One whom it is] hard to get angry and easy to pacify is pious. [One whom it is] easy to get angry and hard to pacify is wicked.

Character dispositions

Some try to distinguish between character (as being more basic and harder to modify) and disposition (which is more malleable). However, rabbinic tradition calls on people to work at shaping and reshaping both character and disposition. Human beings have free will, and they should use it not only to make correct individual decisions but to change their general temperament and character for the better.

Types of character dispositions

R. Ilai states that three things reveal the true nature of a person: *koso* (his cup), meaning how he handles alcohol and how he behaves when he has been drinking; *kiso* (his pocket), whether he is honest in business dealings, has integrity in keeping financial commitments, and displays generosity with regard to charity and gifts; and *kaaso* (his anger): whether he is quick or slow to anger, what kind of behavior he exhibits when angry, etc.[25]

Easy to get angry and easy to pacify

It makes life more comfortable that this person can be easily pacified, but this is outweighed by the burden of his frequently being too easily aroused to anger.

Hard to get angry and hard to pacify

That this person is hard to pacify is a problem, but it is more than offset by the fact that the he rarely gets angry.

Hard to get angry and easy to pacify is pious

- This person is self-effacing and concerned for others, and this reflects a true piety.
- What gives this person such equanimity? It is likely he feels so anchored in the divine that human-generated annoyances are shrugged off.

Easy to get angry and hard to pacify is wicked

- This person must be very self-centered, and therefore is constantly angry and prickly. Apparently, he consistently blames or disrespects others. This is a wicked behavior pattern.
- These bad traits and constant anger will lead the person to do evil to others, and thus he will become wicked.
- Such high sensitivity to real or perceived slights suggests that one with this character trait is totally wrapped up in people's reactions. He must have little or no sense of trust in or relationship to God which could induce a greater degree of tranquility or patience toward others. The absence of a relationship with something greater than oneself leads to wickedness.

25. Eruvin 65b.

Mishna 12

אַרְבַּע מִדּוֹת בַּתַּלְמִידִים. מָהִיר לִשְׁמֹעַ וּמָהִיר לְאַבֵּד, יָצָא שְׂכָרוֹ בְּהֶפְסֵדוֹ. קָשֶׁה לִשְׁמֹעַ וְקָשֶׁה לְאַבֵּד, יָצָא הֶפְסֵדוֹ בִּשְׂכָרוֹ. מָהִיר לִשְׁמֹעַ וְקָשֶׁה לְאַבֵּד, זֶה חֵלֶק טוֹב. קָשֶׁה לִשְׁמֹעַ וּמָהִיר לְאַבֵּד, זֶה חֵלֶק רָע.

There are four types of disciples: Quick to learn and quick to lose it – the gain is outweighed by the loss. Slow to learn and slow to lose it – the loss is outweighed by the gain. Quick to learn and slow to lose it – this is a good portion. Slow to learn and quick to lose it – this is a bad portion.

Quick to learn and quick to lose it

In the end, little learning is left.

Slow to learn and slow to lose it

The lessons are absorbed with difficulty, but once learned, they stick – so there is profit in teaching such a student.

A good portion

- Fortunate is the teacher who draws such a student.
- Fortunate is the student who has these gifts.

A bad portion

- The teacher who draws such a poor-quality student has bad teacher's luck.
- The student who was endowed with a poor capacity for learning has drawn a bad lot in life.

Mishna 13

אַרְבַּע מִדּוֹת בְּנוֹתְנֵי צְדָקָה. הָרוֹצֶה שֶׁיִּתֵּן וְלֹא יִתְּנוּ אֲחֵרִים, עֵינוֹ רָעָה בְּשֶׁל אֲחֵרִים. יִתְּנוּ אֲחֵרִים וְהוּא לֹא יִתֵּן, עֵינוֹ רָעָה בְּשֶׁלּוֹ. יִתֵּן וְיִתְּנוּ אֲחֵרִים, חָסִיד. לֹא יִתֵּן וְלֹא יִתְּנוּ אֲחֵרִים, רָשָׁע.

There are four types of givers of *tzedaka*: One who wants to give but does not [want] others to give – his eye is evil toward others. [One who wants] others to give but does not [want] to give – his eye is evil toward his own [giving. One who wants] to give and [wants] others to give is a pious person. [One who] does not [want] to give and does not [want] others to give is wicked.

Four types of givers

- The ideal is to be generous of spirit personally and to encourage others to be generous as well.
- *Tzedaka* is righteousness; all people should engage in it.
- Giving charity should not be viewed as a competition or a zero-sum game.

Mishna 14

אַרְבַּע מִדּוֹת בְּהוֹלְכֵי בֵית הַמִּדְרָשׁ. הוֹלֵךְ וְאֵינוֹ עוֹשֶׂה, שְׂכַר הֲלִיכָה בְּיָדוֹ. עוֹשֶׂה וְאֵינוֹ הוֹלֵךְ, שְׂכַר מַעֲשֶׂה בְּיָדוֹ. הוֹלֵךְ וְעוֹשֶׂה, חָסִיד. לֹא הוֹלֵךְ וְלֹא עוֹשֶׂה, רָשָׁע.

There are four qualities in those who go to the house of Torah study: One who goes to study but does not perform [the good deeds recommended in the text – he] has the reward of [the effort] of going. One who performs [the good deeds] but does not go [much to the house of study – he] has the reward [of the good deeds]. One who goes and performs good deeds is a pious person. One who neither goes nor performs [good deeds] is wicked.

Goes to study but does not perform [the good deeds]

We might be tempted to discount such a person as a hypocrite because he studies Torah but does not act in accordance with its recommendations. Not so, says the Mishna. No good act is dismissed. The person will be rewarded for the mitzva of Torah study even though the ideal would be for him to follow through with actions that match his learning.

Performs [the good deeds] but does not go... [study]

Although we value learning Torah, neither the value nor the effect of good deeds is undermined by the failure to study it.

Goes and performs good deeds

The religious ideal is to combine Torah study with good deeds. When Torah study is the grounding and motivator of behavior, then the good deeds are likely to be of greater depth and backed by more understanding. Therefore, the person will more likely keep on performing good deeds whatever the obstacles or counter-pressures.

Neither goes nor performs [good deeds]

- The lack of both Torah study and good action bespeaks a wicked, self-centered person.
- In the absence of these two activities, a person will likely turn to bad behaviors.

Mishna 15

אַרְבַּע מִדּוֹת בְּיוֹשְׁבִים לִפְנֵי
חֲכָמִים, סְפוֹג, וּמַשְׁפֵּךְ, מְשַׁמֶּרֶת,
וְנָפָה. סְפוֹג, שֶׁהוּא סוֹפֵג אֶת
הַכֹּל. וּמַשְׁפֵּךְ, שֶׁמַּכְנִיס בְּזוֹ
וּמוֹצִיא בְזוֹ. מְשַׁמֶּרֶת, שֶׁמּוֹצִיאָה
אֶת הַיַּיִן וְקוֹלֶטֶת אֶת הַשְּׁמָרִים.
וְנָפָה, שֶׁמּוֹצִיאָה אֶת הַקֶּמַח
וְקוֹלֶטֶת אֶת הַסֹּלֶת.

There are four qualities of those who sit in front of the sages [to study]: A sponge, a funnel, a strainer, and a sieve. A sponge absorbs everything. A funnel draws in at one end and lets it out at the other. A strainer gives out the wine and holds back the dregs. A sieve lets the coarse flour pass through and collects the fine flour.

Sponge...strainer

The sponge absorbs and holds everything but keeps the material as is. The strainer improves the teaching by passing on the wine while holding back the dregs.

Funnel

The student's inability to hold on to the material means that little is retained. The teacher does not accomplish much despite his efforts.

Sieve

There are two possible interpretations of this metaphor:

- The sieve (student) passes through but does not retain the coarse flour; rather, the disciple retains the fine flour and thereby improves his rabbi's Torah.

- The sieve passes on coarse teachings and holds back the better quality. This means that what the student teaches is of lesser quality than what he received. This interpretation fits the pattern of the other mishnas comparing four types, whereby the fourth type is the worst. On the other hand, the student is studying Torah from the sages, so what he retains is of some value.

Mishna 16

כָּל אַהֲבָה שֶׁהִיא תְּלוּיָה בְדָבָר, בָּטֵל דָּבָר, בְּטֵלָה אַהֲבָה. וְשֶׁאֵינָהּ תְּלוּיָה בְדָבָר, אֵינָהּ בְּטֵלָה לְעוֹלָם. אֵיזוֹ הִיא אַהֲבָה שֶׁהִיא תְּלוּיָה בְדָבָר, זוֹ אַהֲבַת אַמְנוֹן וְתָמָר. וְשֶׁאֵינָהּ תְּלוּיָה בְדָבָר, זוֹ אַהֲבַת דָּוִד וִיהוֹנָתָן.

All love which is dependent on a specific quality [in the beloved], if that specific quality ceases to be, then the love ceases to be. Love which is not dependent on one [specific] quality [in the beloved] will never cease to be. What is [an example of] a love that is dependent on one quality? The love between Amnon and Tamar. What is [an example of] a love that is not dependent on one quality? The love between David and Jonathan.

Love which is dependent on a specific quality

Love may start with a particular attractive quality in the other: beauty, goodness, fame. As love matures, it relates to the total person beyond any one quality – even the quality that attracted the lover in the first place. If the love remains fixed on a particular quality in the beloved, it is immature. And if that particular quality is lost or loses its appeal, the love is vulnerable and liable to disappear also. In Amnon and Tamar's case, Amnon lusted for Tamar's beautiful body. Once he raped her, his lust was satisfied. Her desirability then evaporated and his love turned to hatred and rejection. In the case of David and Jonathan, however, they may well have started by being enamored of each other's youthful vitality, military prowess, leadership ability, universal admiration, or ability to be useful to the other. But the love matured to embrace the whole person.

Therefore, to Jonathan, the fact that David was about to become a fugitive unable to be of service to him – or that, over time, David's military prowess and bodily vigor were liable to fade – did not change his deep respect and love for David. And as for David, he was also eventually attached to the whole person of Jonathan, not to the crown prince celebrity, the fellow warrior, the friendly, helpful co-conspirator.

When love matures in a couple, their marriage becomes a lifetime covenantal (committed) relationship. They know full well that youthful good looks and bodily health will inevitably fade. They understand the risk that success, wealth, celebrity, and charm may all be lost. But this possible loss no longer matters because each loves the whole person, the totality of the other. Thus love will persist beyond the loss of any particular quality, beyond the successes and vicissitudes of life. (This is not to deny that people are human and that sometimes even mature love can be eroded by the wounds of daily struggles or by a loss of some magnitude, especially the loss of an important quality in the other.)

Love which is not dependent on one [specific] quality

Unconditional love also describes the relationship between God and the People of Israel when the two entered into the covenant at Mount Sinai. The prophet Jeremiah describes this as: "I [God] remember... the covenantal love of your youth, the love of your marriage vows, when you followed Me into the desert, into an unknown, trackless land."[26] Perhaps God thought of rejecting Israel when the people sinned and betrayed Him and the Torah repeatedly. But divine love was not dependent on a specific quality, not even on Israel's faithfulness and obedience. Therefore God's love overcame divine anger, and He remembered the covenant after the Destruction of the Temple. (This is proclaimed in the prophecies of Isaiah, Jeremiah, Hosea, et al.)

Similarly, over the course of history, Jewish tragedy and suffering have challenged the seriousness of the Jews' love for and commitment to God and the covenant. During the Holocaust, being a Jew was a death sentence, and the suffering inflicted on Jews could have undermined the relationship between Israel and God. It turned out that the love was truly

26. Jeremiah 2:2.

covenantal: mature, open-ended, not dependent on God's protecting or glorifying the Jewish people. This love proved to be as strong as death.[27] The Jewish people (and its Lord) renewed the covenant of Torah, the covenant of *tikkun olam*. And as this mishna testifies, the love persisted forever. The people created the State of Israel and renewed Jewish life around the world, showing the people's love for its Creator, its mission, and its dream.

27. Song of Songs 8:6.

Mishna 17

כָּל מַחֲלֹקֶת שֶׁהִיא לְשֵׁם שָׁמַיִם, סוֹפָהּ לְהִתְקַיֵּם. וְשֶׁאֵינָהּ לְשֵׁם שָׁמַיִם, אֵין סוֹפָהּ לְהִתְקַיֵּם. אֵיזוֹ הִיא מַחֲלֹקֶת שֶׁהִיא לְשֵׁם שָׁמַיִם, זוֹ מַחֲלֹקֶת הִלֵּל וְשַׁמַּאי. וְשֶׁאֵינָהּ לְשֵׁם שָׁמַיִם, זוֹ מַחֲלֹקֶת קֹרַח וְכָל עֲדָתוֹ.

Every controversy that is for the sake of Heaven, its final [outcome] will endure. And [every controversy] that is not for the sake of heaven, its final [outcome] will not endure. Which is a controversy for the sake of Heaven? This is a controversy [between] Hillel and Shammai. And which is not for the sake of Heaven? This is the controversy of Korah and his entire congregation.

Controversy...for the sake of Heaven

In most people's minds, controversy is associated with conflict (i.e., truths of questionable status), with division and disunity, and with disagreeable disagreements; hence, it must be a bad thing. Not so, says the mishna. Controversy can be good or bad, depending on how and why it is pursued. Controversy and argument can clarify issues and enrich the understanding of a truth. Done improperly, however, arguments can disturb or skew judgments and sow confusion.

For the sake of Heaven

- If the motivation for both sides is to understand what God wants.

- If the parties in disagreement are motivated by the search for truth in Torah rather than driven by ego or lust for power, or a desire to win the argument.
- If the interlocutors are seeking to advance a noble goal, or to improve the world and not to destroy or degrade it. In all these situations, different perspectives likely will enrich the conversation and lead to more nuanced or more sophisticated understanding.

Its final [outcome] will endure

- The outcome of the argument will be of enduring value.
- Both positions will be studied and will give insight over the ages, even if only the majority view will be practiced for the sake of public order.
- An alternate translation of this phrase would be: The argument itself will be validated permanently, i.e., the disagreement will be recognized as legitimate.

Warning against the tendency for controversialists to wrap their own view in the mantle of divine truth, Rabbi Israel Salanter offered the following, ironic commentary on this teaching: In any controversy, people may come to some mutual understanding and solve the matter. However, when the participants mistakenly convince themselves that they are fighting God's battle (i.e., for the sake of Heaven), then instead of coming to a common understanding through give and take they will insist that they are absolutely right, that they are upholding God's view. In such a case, they will never yield. As a result, the *controversy* will endure and continue on and on.

Not for the sake of Heaven ... will not endure

Controversies motivated by base goals and wrong personal motivations will not yield a lasting result. The parties may achieve temporary victory. However, only the word of God and "pure" arguments designed to elicit the truth can yield truths that can stand the test of time.

Hillel and Shammai

The great teachers disagreed in only a few cases. However, their schools, Beit Hillel and Beit Shammai, disagreed on hundreds of issues. At first, people thought that the disagreements reflected the fact that the students had not studied enough or analyzed deeply enough. But when the number of controversies exploded, the fear arose that the teachings would degenerate into two separate Torahs which were incompatible with each other. Yet the goal of both schools was truly to understand and teach God's will in the divine way, which was shifting from use of prophetic revelation to greater use of human judgment (rabbinic learning) to discover what God wanted. Human perspectives can be varied and more than one analysis is possible and legitimate.

The two schools came to see that the disagreements were rooted in legitimate (if contradictory) analysis. A voice from heaven confirmed that "both views are the words of the living God."[28] However, the views of Beit Hillel were upheld by the majority, and the majority view was practiced in the public arena. The Talmud also suggests that Beit Hillel won its majority by being more modest and more open to hearing their opponents' views (they even let them speak first in arguments). We continue to study both views down to this day.

Korah and his ... congregation

Korah behaved like a demagogue. He claimed that he wanted to elevate the whole congregation to equal status, but in fact sought only to seize power for himself and his family and associates. In the end he was utterly defeated, and nothing lasting or worthwhile came out of the controversy.

---

28. Eruvin 13b.

Mishna 18

כָּל הַמְזַכֶּה אֶת הָרַבִּים, אֵין חֵטְא בָּא עַל יָדוֹ. וְכָל הַמַּחֲטִיא אֶת הָרַבִּים, אֵין מַסְפִּיקִין בְּיָדוֹ לַעֲשׂוֹת תְּשׁוּבָה. מֹשֶׁה זָכָה וְזִכָּה אֶת הָרַבִּים, זְכוּת הָרַבִּים תָּלוּי בּוֹ, שֶׁנֶּאֱמַר: צִדְקַת יהוה עָשָׂה וּמִשְׁפָּטָיו עִם־יִשְׂרָאֵל: יָרָבְעָם בֶּן נְבָט, חָטָא וְהֶחֱטִיא אֶת הָרַבִּים, חֵטְא הָרַבִּים תָּלוּי בּוֹ, שֶׁנֶּאֱמַר: עַל־חַטֹּאות יָרָבְעָם אֲשֶׁר חָטָא וַאֲשֶׁר הֶחֱטִיא אֶת־יִשְׂרָאֵל:

Whoever leads the masses to virtue, no sin will come out of his work. Whoever leads the masses to sin will not be given the chance to repent. Moses was virtuous and led the masses to virtue; thus the virtue of the masses is credited to him, as it says: "He continued the righteousness of the Lord and God's judgments with Israel."[29] Jeroboam, son of Nevat, sinned and led the masses to sin, so the sins of the masses are attributed to him, as it says: "The sin of Jeroboam who sinned and who caused Israel to sin."[30]

Leads the masses to virtue

Because there are so many crosscurrents in the community and in individuals, leaders hesitate to lead. They fear that even well-intentioned policies may cause evil behaviors or bad outcomes. This mishna assures that they will be credited with the good the community does as a result of their intervention, and thus they will be upheld as good and righteous leaders. The good that a virtuous leader leaves behind is multiplied by

29. Deuteronomy 33:21.
30. 1 Kings 14:16.

the good behavior of the many he influenced, and their leader will be vindicated.

Leads the masses to sin

On the other hand, if an evil leader sets out to corrupt the masses, then all their sins are attributed to him. The evil he leaves behind will far outweigh his individual sins as well as good behaviors. In sum: The leader is responsible for the behavior of the masses for good and for bad.

Mishna 19

כָּל מִי שֶׁיֵּשׁ בּוֹ שְׁלֹשָׁה דְּבָרִים הַלָּלוּ, הוּא מִתַּלְמִידָיו שֶׁל אַבְרָהָם אָבִינוּ, וּשְׁלֹשָׁה דְּבָרִים אֲחֵרִים, הוּא מִתַּלְמִידָיו שֶׁל בִּלְעָם הָרָשָׁע. עַיִן טוֹבָה, וְרוּחַ נְמוּכָה, וְנֶפֶשׁ שְׁפָלָה, תַּלְמִידָיו שֶׁל אַבְרָהָם אָבִינוּ. עַיִן רָעָה, וְרוּחַ גְּבוֹהָה וְנֶפֶשׁ רְחָבָה, תַּלְמִידָיו שֶׁל בִּלְעָם הָרָשָׁע. מַה בֵּין תַּלְמִידָיו שֶׁל אַבְרָהָם אָבִינוּ לְתַלְמִידָיו שֶׁל בִּלְעָם הָרָשָׁע. תַּלְמִידָיו שֶׁל אַבְרָהָם אָבִינוּ אוֹכְלִין בָּעוֹלָם הַזֶּה וְנוֹחֲלִין הָעוֹלָם הַבָּא, שֶׁנֶּאֱמַר: לְהַנְחִיל אֹהֲבַי יֵשׁ וְאֹצְרֹתֵיהֶם אֲמַלֵּא: אֲבָל תַּלְמִידָיו שֶׁל בִּלְעָם הָרָשָׁע יוֹרְשִׁין גֵּיהִנָּם וְיוֹרְדִין לִבְאֵר שַׁחַת, שֶׁנֶּאֱמַר: וְאַתָּה אֱלֹהִים תּוֹרִדֵם לִבְאֵר שַׁחַת, אַנְשֵׁי דָמִים וּמִרְמָה לֹא־יֶחֱצוּ יְמֵיהֶם, וַאֲנִי אֶבְטַח־בָּךְ:

Whoever possesses these three qualities is [defined as] one of the disciples of our father Abraham. [Whoever possesses] three other qualities is [defined as] one of the disciples of the wicked Balaam. [Whoever has] a good [generous] eye, a lowly spirit, and a humble soul is [of the] disciples of our father Abraham. [Whoever has] an evil [grudging] eye, a haughty spirit, and an arrogant soul is [of the] disciples of the wicked Balaam. What is the difference [in the outcome] between the disciples of our father Abraham and the disciples of the wicked Balaam? The disciples of our father Abraham eat [the fruits of their good deeds] in this world and they inherit [a portion in] the World to Come, as it says: "I will give those that love Me to inherit substance and I will fill their treasuries."[31] The disciples of Balaam the wicked will inherit Gehenna and will go down to the pit of destruction, as it says, "But you, Lord, will lower them into a pit of destruction; those men of spilled blood and deceit will not live out half their days, but I will trust in You." [32]

31. Proverbs 8:21.

32. Psalms 55:24.

Our father Abraham ... Balaam

Like Moses, Balaam is portrayed in the Torah as a great seer with access to God. But Balaam corrupts his gifts and tries to use his godly power to curse the Israelites in return for the Moabite king Balak's remuneration. His evil nature and venal character undermine his prophetic inheritance. By contrast, Abraham refused to take a penny of the spoils when he rescued Lot (and thereby, the king of Sodom) from the hands of the five conquering kings.[33]

Three qualities ... of the disciples of ... Abraham ... of the disciples of ... Balaam

The teachings of Torah (and of Balaam the seer) are more than intellectual exercise. They attract – and shape – a certain character. Their followers are called disciples, not just students, for their whole character has been shaped in the image of their master.

A good eye, a lowly spirit, and a humble soul

A true child of Abraham is generous and giving toward fellow human beings, but is modest in taking for himself. The disciple of Abraham is humble because he genuinely respects others.

An evil eye, a haughty spirit, and an arrogant soul

The follower of Balaam is stingy in giving to others, but expansive in demanding for himself. He feels superior to others and therefore assumes an arrogant attitude toward them.

Eat [the fruits] in this world and ... inherit the World to Come

Those who subscribe to the worldview of Abraham eat the fruits of their good attitudes and good deeds in the form of a good society and a better life in this world. They also merit their portion in the World to Come. The disciples of Balaam tear the fabric of society in this world by giving little to others and demanding much for themselves. In the end, they live in a poorer, less humane society, and they forfeit their share in the World to Come.

---

33. Genesis ch. 15.

Gehenna ... the pit of destruction

In the Axial Age (ca. 800 BCE–200 BCE), the awareness of an existence, of a world beyond this mortal coil, swelled among Jews and non-Jews alike. This became a powerful force in choosing religion, a way of life, and a moral code. The concept of a pit of destruction and a Gehenna of punishment after death strengthened religion's grip on people's minds. Nevertheless, the Talmud speaks of a twelve-month Gehenna of suffering and purging of the sins of this mortal life and not of an eternity of torment and pain.

The concept of an eternal hell was considerably developed in Jewish tradition, mostly in the Middle Ages, and its unfolding reflects in part the interchange and mutual influence of Jewish civilization and the surrounding cultures and religions.

Mishna 20

יְהוּדָה בֶּן תֵּימָא אוֹמֵר: הֱוֵי עַז כַּנָּמֵר וְקַל כַּנֶּשֶׁר, רָץ כַּצְּבִי וְגִבּוֹר כָּאֲרִי, לַעֲשׂוֹת רְצוֹן אָבִיךָ שֶׁבַּשָּׁמָיִם. הוּא הָיָה אוֹמֵר: עַז פָּנִים לְגֵיהִנָּם, וּבֹשֶׁת פָּנִים לְגַן עֵדֶן. יְהִי רָצוֹן מִלְּפָנֶיךָ, יהוה אֱלֹהֵינוּ וֵאלֹהֵי אֲבוֹתֵינוּ, שֶׁיִּבָּנֶה בֵּית הַמִּקְדָּשׁ בִּמְהֵרָה בְיָמֵינוּ, וְתֵן חֶלְקֵנוּ בְּתוֹרָתֶךָ.

Yehuda b. Teima says: Be strong as a leopard and soar [in flight] as an eagle; run swiftly as a gazelle and be brave as a lion, to do the will of your Father in heaven. He would say: The brazen man [is destined] for Gehenna, and the humble person [is destined] for the Garden of Eden [Paradise]. May it be Your will, Lord our God and God of our ancestors, that the Holy Temple be rebuilt speedily in our days, and make Your Torah our portion.

HISTORICAL BACKGROUND

R. Yehuda b. Teima is referred to in the Talmud as one of the pillars of the Mishna,[34] so one can assume that he was a *Tanna*. He is reported to have been a student of R. Yehuda the Prince, which would place him between the late first and early second centuries CE. However, there is so little information on him in the Talmud that establishing his exact chronology is impossible. In the expanded commentary on *Pirkei Avot*, Yehuda b. Teima is quoted as calling for a synthesis of contradictory emotions to serve God fully: "Be a lover of Heaven [and] one who fears Heaven, one who is deeply concerned [*ḥared*; lit., shudders] and [one who is] joyful for all the commandments." [35]

34. Ḥagiga 14a.
35. *Avot DeRabbi Natan* 41.

Be strong as a leopard... run swiftly as a gazelle

On the surface, this mishna is an extended, fanciful metaphor, calling on people to exhibit the strengths associated with various animals in order to do God's will. On a deeper level, however, these various characteristics are found in very different animal natures. The fleet animals run for their lives because they are not strong in battle. Eagles soar majestically but cannot pull a plow and persist through the daily grind.

The mishna says that a person should incorporate these differing qualities – which normally are not associated with each other – and use them all in the service of God. Unlike animals, which are primarily programmed by instinct and differentiated from one another by musculature and skeletal structures, humans are polymorphous – capable of developing a wide range of emotions and behavior. There will be a chance and a time to use all these different qualities in order to fulfill God's instructions for us. There is a time to be bold and even heavy-handed in pursuing justice. There is a time to be strong and fleet. There is a time to judge and a time to forgive. God calls on humans to use all their capacities to do good and to help others.

This view is illuminated in Rabbi Israel Salanter's dictum that to be a fully religious person, one must cultivate all of his human capacities. On Yom Kippur, the tradition asks people to practice total self-denial: no food, drink, washing, or conjugal activity; on Purim, people are instructed to feast (even to get drunk) like *bon vivants*. Therefore, Rabbi Salanter concludes: To be a complete person, "one must have every human quality and its opposite."[36] There is a call to be generous toward others and tightfisted toward oneself; to be judgmental with regard to evil and forgiving in response to trespass, and so on.

Another explanation of this mishna is that each animal is programmed to exhibit the specific qualities associated with it. But R. Yehuda is urging people to develop these qualities through education and training, in order to serve God better.

---

36. R. Israel Salanter, *Or Yisrael* (Vilna: 1920; reprinted in Benei Berak, 1969), 84, col. 1.

May it be Your will

This appears to be a closing prayer rather than an aphorism. It would appear that Tractate Avot ended here at one point during its redaction, so the prayer was inserted (Meiri). Presumably, then, the remainder of the material in this chapter was added in a later stage of editing.

Mishna 21

הוּא הָיָה אוֹמֵר: בֶּן חָמֵשׁ שָׁנִים לַמִּקְרָא, בֶּן עֶשֶׂר שָׁנִים לַמִּשְׁנָה, בֶּן שְׁלֹשׁ עֶשְׂרֵה לַמִּצְוֹת, בֶּן חֲמֵשׁ עֶשְׂרֵה לַגְּמָרָא, בֶּן שְׁמוֹנֶה עֶשְׂרֵה לַחֻפָּה, בֶּן עֶשְׂרִים לִרְדֹּף, בֶּן שְׁלֹשִׁים לַכֹּחַ, בֶּן אַרְבָּעִים לַבִּינָה, בֶּן חֲמִשִּׁים לָעֵצָה, בֶּן שִׁשִּׁים לַזִּקְנָה, בֶּן שִׁבְעִים לַשֵּׂיבָה, בֶּן שְׁמוֹנִים לַגְּבוּרָה, בֶּן תִּשְׁעִים לָשׁוּחַ, בֶּן מֵאָה כְּאִלּוּ מֵת וְעָבַר וּבָטֵל מִן הָעוֹלָם.

He would say: At five years old, [time to study] Scripture; at ten years old, [time to study] Mishna; thirteen years old, [time to observe] the commandments; fifteen years old, [time to study] Talmud; eighteen years old, [time to go] to the wedding canopy; twenty years old, [time] to pursue [a livelihood]; thirty years old, [a time] of full strength; forty years old, [time to achieve] wisdom; fifty years old, [time to give] counsel; sixty years old, [time of] old age; seventy years old, [time of] ripe old age; eighty years old, [one has been given] strength to live long; at ninety years of age, [one is] bent and bowed; at one hundred years old, it is as if one is dead and has passed away and gone from the world.

At five years old…at one hundred years old

- People develop and mature, and as they grow older they enter into different stages of life.
- There are benchmarks for life. Study of Scripture should start no later than at five years old, Mishna no later than at ten years old, etc.

- One must ripen into capacity. A child will get little out of Talmud study before the age of fifteen, wisdom comes only with life experience and is rarely attained before the age of forty, etc. And note that even after attaining wisdom by the age of forty, R. Yehuda b. Teima feels that one needs another decade of life experience before being qualified to offer counsel to another person.
- There is "a season in life for everything; a time for every experience under heaven" (Eccl. 3:1). At twenty, for instance, people set out to conquer the world, but that energy and enthusiasm is tempered over the years. One is at full strength for a decade but not much more. No one can escape the debilitating effects of growing older. The price of a truly long life is frailty and ebbing vitality.

As R. Yehuda b. Teima affirms the seasonal, limited duration of life forces, the implication is that one should use his capacities for the good and to the maximum when they are in full bloom – with a sense of urgency to get the job done while each one is at its peak.

Mishna 22

בֶּן בַּג בַּג אוֹמֵר: הֲפֹךְ בָּהּ וַהֲפֵךְ בָּהּ דְּכֹלָּא בַהּ, וּבַהּ תֶּחֱזֵי, וְסִיב וּבְלֵה בַהּ, וּמִנַּהּ לָא תְזוּעַ, שֶׁאֵין לְךָ מִדָּה טוֹבָה הֵימֶנָּה.

Ben Bag Bag says: Turn it [the Torah] over and turn it over, for everything is in it; look into it, grow old and worn in it, but do not budge from it, for you have no better measure than it.

HISTORICAL BACKGROUND

Ben Bag Bag was a convert or the son of converts. In the Talmud, his name is given as Yoḥanan ben (son of) Bag Bag.[37] Some commentators explain that Ben Bag Bag is an acronym for Ben **B**en-**G**er, **B**at-**G**er, i.e., son of a male proselyte, [son of] a female proselyte. This would mean that both his parents were converts. An alternative interpretation uses *gematria*: The word "Bag" has the *gematria* of five, i.e., *heh*, the fifth Hebrew letter. The *heh* refers to the fact that Abram became Abra**h**am when he became the first Jew. In Yoḥanan's case, this means that a "bag" (i.e., the letter *heh*) was added to his name. Thus his name Bag Bag hints that like Abraham, Ben Bag Bag became a Jew.

Turn it over

- The deeper the study of Torah, the more to be found in it. Do not read the Torah superficially. True, its surface is clear and winning,

37. Kiddushin 10b.

tempting you to understand it at that level. But the deeper truth will come to you if you keep digging again and again.

- "One cannot compare [the understanding attained by] someone who studies his [chapter of Torah] one hundred times to [that attained by] one who studies his chapter 101 times."[38] There are new insights each time we learn Torah. Its inexhaustible quality reflects its infinite Source.

Everything is in it

- The Torah has infinite wisdom and "seventy faces," i.e., many facets, for each word and verse.
- Midrash and intense analysis enabled the sages to draw forth much more wisdom and insight from the Torah than appeared on the surface.
- There is hidden wisdom in the Torah. The Kabbala finds levels of spiritual insight that appear to be very far from the text. However, that is also Torah.

Grow old and worn in it

As you grow old, you will find many new and deeper ways to understand Torah, because greater life experience and wisdom equip you to see aspects of it which the callow youth will miss.

No better measure

- No better guideline.
- No better rule with which to navigate life.
- No better portion.

38. Ḥagiga 9b.

Mishna 23

בֶּן הֵא הֵא אוֹמֵר: לְפוּם צַעֲרָא אַגְרָא.

Ben Hei Hei says: According to the pain [of the effort] is the reward.

HISTORICAL BACKGROUND

Ben Hei Hei may be another name for Ben Bag Bag, since the *gematria* of "Bag" is five, *heh* (see previous mishna). Alternatively, Ben Hei Hei might be a different person but also a convert (the letter *heh* signifying a convert). He is reported as having been in dialogue with Hillel, which would place him in the first century CE.

[Effort]... reward

- No pain, no gain. Knock yourself out – study until exhaustion, go back repeatedly to analyze the text – and you will get great reward from the Torah.
- With regard to all good deeds and great accomplishments, intense effort is the key to achieving high performance or breakthrough.
- Persistence in the face of difficulty and opposition are needed in order to make major accomplishments in Torah, in good deeds, and truly in all aspects of life.

Chapter 6
Kinyan Torah

This chapter was added to the five that originally comprised *Pirkei Avot*. It constitutes the weekly study portion of Ethics of the Fathers for the sixth and final Shabbat between Passover and Shavuot. In anticipation of Shavuot, which commemorates and celebrates the Israelites' acceptance of the Torah, this chapter tells of the pleasures and rewards of Torah study, the stature and dignity it bestows on student and teacher alike, and the preciousness of the Torah to God as well as to people. Chapter 6 is popularly named *Kinyan Torah* – Acquiring Torah – and it tells how to acquire Torah knowledge (a life of sacrifice of worldly pleasures and steadfast, devoted study) and the importance of studying Torah properly (for its own sake, not for ulterior motives such as power, fame, or wealth). These teachings are not taken from the Mishna but are from the *Baraita*, Torah teachings by sages of the mishnaic period that were not incorporated into the final edition of the Mishna.

שָׁנוּ חֲכָמִים בִּלְשׁוֹן הַמִּשְׁנָה, בָּרוּךְ שֶׁבָּחַר בָּהֶם וּבְמִשְׁנָתָם.	The sages taught these teachings in the language of the Mishna. Blessed is God, who chose them and their teachings.

Teachings in the language of the Mishna

- Like the Mishna, these teachings are in Hebrew. This may be a reference to the fact that the Gemara (the expanded, rabbinic analysis and discussion based on the Mishna) is mostly in Aramaic. Aramaic was the language of the Jewish community in Babylonia and the Galilee. The intellectual-spiritual leadership of Jewry passed to the Babylonian Diaspora community from the third century CE on, as a result of the oppression and economic decline of the surviving Jewish communities in the Land of Israel. However, the Mishna was articulated and edited while the Torah-learning community was still centered in the Land of Israel, and its main teachers spoke and thought in Hebrew. The reasons for editing and publishing the Mishna in the classical language of Hebrew, rather than in the everyday Aramaic tongue, are explored above, on pages 60–61.
- A full-disclosure notice: These teachings most closely resemble the mishnaic style, but they are not part of the Mishna. As *baraitot*, they do not have the same status and authority as the first five chapters.

Teaching 1

רַבִּי מֵאִיר אוֹמֵר: כָּל הָעוֹסֵק בַּתּוֹרָה לִשְׁמָהּ, זוֹכֶה לִדְבָרִים הַרְבֵּה. וְלֹא עוֹד, אֶלָּא שֶׁכָּל הָעוֹלָם כֻּלּוֹ כְּדַאי הוּא לוֹ. נִקְרָא רֵעַ, אוֹהֵב אֶת הַמָּקוֹם, אוֹהֵב אֶת הַבְּרִיּוֹת, מְשַׂמֵּחַ אֶת הַמָּקוֹם, מְשַׂמֵּחַ אֶת הַבְּרִיּוֹת, וּמַלְבַּשְׁתּוֹ עֲנָוָה וְיִרְאָה, וּמַכְשַׁרְתּוֹ לִהְיוֹת צַדִּיק, חָסִיד, יָשָׁר, וְנֶאֱמָן, וּמְרַחַקְתּוֹ מִן הַחֵטְא, וּמְקָרַבְתּוֹ לִידֵי זְכוּת,

R. Meir says: Whoever engages in Torah study for its own sake becomes worthy of many rewards. Not only that, but the whole entire world would [be an appropriate reward] for him. He is known as friend, beloved, lover of God, lover of God's creatures [humanity], giver of joy to God, [and] giver of joy to [God's] creatures. It clothes him with humility and reverence [for God]; and it trains him to be righteous and beneficent, straight and trustworthy; it distances him from sin and brings him closer to virtue.

וְנֶהֱנִין מִמֶּנּוּ עֵצָה וְתוּשִׁיָּה, בִּינָה וּגְבוּרָה, שֶׁנֶּאֱמַר: לִי־עֵצָה וְתוּשִׁיָּה, אֲנִי בִינָה, לִי גְבוּרָה: וְנוֹתֶנֶת לוֹ מַלְכוּת וּמֶמְשָׁלָה, וְחִקּוּר דִּין, וּמְגַלִּין לוֹ רָזֵי תוֹרָה, וְנַעֲשֶׂה כְּמַעְיָן הַמִּתְגַּבֵּר וּכְנָהָר שֶׁאֵינוֹ פוֹסֵק, וְהֹוֶה צָנוּעַ, וְאֶרֶךְ רוּחַ, וּמוֹחֵל עַל עֶלְבּוֹנוֹ, וּמְגַדַּלְתּוֹ וּמְרוֹמַמְתּוֹ עַל כָּל הַמַּעֲשִׂים.

People benefit from him, receiving counsel, wisdom, discernment, [and] courage [from him], as it says: "Mine [says the Torah] are counsel and wisdom; I am discernment; mine is courage."[1] It bestows on him royalty and dominion and penetrating judgment. The secrets of Torah are revealed to him and he becomes like an overflowing spring and a river that never runs dry. He becomes modest, patient, and forgiving of insult. It makes him great and lifts him above all happenings.

1. Proverbs 8:14.

Torah study for its own sake

Despite the divinity and holiness of the Torah, it does not automatically generate a good person. If people expose themselves to the Torah's best values, they will become the best of people (as per the continuation of this mishna). But to be affected properly, people have to study Torah for its own sake and internalize it. "Torah for its own sake" is defined in one place in the Talmud as a Torah of loving-kindness.[2] If one comes up with a Torah which is without this, it means that he has studied Torah improperly (that is, not for its own sake).[3] In another place the Talmud defines study for its own sake as study motivated solely by love of God, in fulfillment of the verse: "To love the Lord your God, to listen to His voice, to cling to Him."[4] Being motivated solely by love means that one approaches Torah study selflessly, without impure motives or being driven by the wrong emotions or goals.

If one studies Torah to achieve power, celebrity, or social acceptance, or if he relates to others with hostility, he will likely use the Torah improperly. Such a person can internalize the wrong values and distort Torah teachings. Thus, a person who seeks power may narrowly focus on the Torah's command to establish a king,[5] ignoring the critique of royalty elsewhere in Scripture.[6] A bigot or xenophobe can focus on the Torah's exclusion of Moabites from the Israelite camp[7] or its rejection of the seven nations of Canaan,[8] adopting an anti-gentile, anti-outsider worldview.

A loving person will absorb the message of "Love your neighbor as yourself";[9] a person willing to be trained in loving others will internalize the words of Psalms: "God is good to all [because] His compassion [interpreted as "mother love"] is over all His creatures."[10] An angry

2. Sukka 49b.
3. Yoma 72b; Berakhot 17a.
4. Deuteronomy 30:20.
5. Ibid., 17:15.
6. Ibid., 23:16–20; I Samuel 8:5–6, 7–8, 11–20.
7. Deuteronomy 23:4.
8. Exodus 23:27–33; Deuteronomy 12:28–31.
9. Leviticus 19:18.
10. Psalms 145:9.

person with a need to feel superior can translate "your neighbor" as only those with identical values (a minimal group) and reject all others, citing the verse: "And your [God's] haters, I will hate,"[11] and applying it to anyone who differs in observance or interpretation – not to mention one who is lax in keeping the mitzvot.

As mentioned in the Author's Preface, Rabbi Israel Salanter stated that the Torah's goal is "to create a *mentsch*." However, he warned that unless an individual's instincts are controlled and his emotions directed properly, he can block the Torah's beneficial influence and even distort Torah into a weapon of abuse or hostility toward others. Rabbi Salanter would say that so great is the human capacity to distort that "there are those [religious Jews] who are extremely careful and meticulous in performing petty religious acts, but neglect the central, core practices." He used to say: "A person can be seen as a Torah genius; righteous, pious, holy, and pure, and at that very moment, he is a denier, evildoer, murderer, thief, and robber," and "Someone racing to fulfill a mitzva can destroy the whole world on his way." The Talmud summarized this issue by saying: "If he is worthy [open to the goodness of the Torah's instructions], it (Torah) is a healing medicine for him; if he is unworthy [uses Torah improperly], it becomes a poison for him."[12]

Note: There is an opposing view in the Talmud, where Rav Yehuda says in the name of Rav: "A person should always [engage in Torah study and mitzvot] even if not for its own sake, for out of such self-interest he will come [to Torah study and the performance of mitzvot] for its own sake."[13]

Friend

He is trained to be a good friend by the model of Abraham standing by his nephew Lot,[14] by such commandments as "Love your neighbor,"

11. Ibid., 139:21.
12. Yoma 72b.
13. Pesaḥim 50b.
14. Genesis ch. 14.

"Correct your friend,"[15] "When your kinsman is falling into poverty... uphold him,"[16] and the admonition: "A friend is devoted at all times."[17]

Beloved

The Torah trains him to be loving, as in "Love your neighbor as yourself."[18]

Lover of God

The Torah teaches: "You shall love the Lord your God with all your heart, with all your soul, and with all your capacities."[19]

Lover of God's creatures

In imitation of God, "His compassion [mother love] is over all His creatures."[20]

Humility

Seeing the greatness of God and the importance of putting others' needs first, and in imitation of Moses, "who was the most humble of all human beings on the face of the earth."[21]

Reverence [for God]

"You shall revere the Lord Your God."[22]

Righteous

"To walk in the way of God, to do righteousness and justice."[23]

15. Leviticus 19:18, 17.
16. Ibid., 25:35.
17. Proverbs 12:17.
18. Leviticus 19:18.
19. Deuteronomy 6:4.
20. Psalms 145:9.
21. Numbers 12:3.
22. Deuteronomy 6:13.
23. Genesis 18:19.

Beneficent

In imitation of God, who "is beneficent in all actions."[24] An alternative translation is "saintly" or "pious in all actions," as it says: "Bring to Me My pious ones."[25]

Straight and trustworthy

In imitation of God: "God looks to the straight";[26] "The word of God is straight and all God's actions are faithful and trustworthy."[27]

24. Psalms 145:17.
25. Ibid., 50:5.
26. Ibid., 11:7.
27. Ibid., 33:4.

Teaching 2

אָמַר רַבִּי יְהוֹשֻׁעַ בֶּן לֵוִי: בְּכָל יוֹם וָיוֹם, בַּת קוֹל יוֹצֵאת מֵהַר חוֹרֵב וּמַכְרֶזֶת וְאוֹמֶרֶת, אוֹי לָהֶם לַבְּרִיּוֹת מֵעֶלְבּוֹנָהּ שֶׁל תּוֹרָה, שֶׁכָּל מִי שֶׁאֵינוֹ עוֹסֵק בַּתּוֹרָה נִקְרָא נָזוּף, שֶׁנֶּאֱמַר: נֶזֶם זָהָב בְּאַף חֲזִיר, אִשָּׁה יָפָה וְסָרַת טָעַם: וְאוֹמֵר: וְהַלֻּחֹת מַעֲשֵׂה אֱלֹהִים הֵמָּה, וְהַמִּכְתָּב מִכְתַּב אֱלֹהִים הוּא, חָרוּת עַל־הַלֻּחֹת: אַל תִּקְרָא חָרוּת אֶלָּא חֵרוּת, שֶׁאֵין לְךָ בֶּן חוֹרִין אֶלָּא מִי שֶׁעוֹסֵק בְּתַלְמוּד תּוֹרָה. וְכָל מִי שֶׁעוֹסֵק בְּתַלְמוּד תּוֹרָה, הֲרֵי זֶה מִתְעַלֶּה, שֶׁנֶּאֱמַר: וּמִמַּתָּנָה נַחֲלִיאֵל, וּמִנַּחֲלִיאֵל בָּמוֹת:

R. Yehoshua b. Levi said: Every single day, a heavenly voice goes forth from Mount Horeb [Sinai] and proclaims and says: "Woe to humanity for their disregard of the Torah," for whoever does not occupy himself with Torah is considered rebuked, as it says: "As a gold ring in a pig's snout, so is a beautiful woman without common sense."[28] And it says: "The tablets were God's handiwork, and their writing was God's writing, inscribed [*ḥarut*] on the tablets."[29] Do not read the word as [*ḥarut*] "inscribed," but as [*ḥerut*] "freedom," for no one is truly free except if he engages in Torah study. And whoever engages in Torah study elevates himself, as it says: "From Mattana [gift of Torah] to Naḥaliel ['God is my inheritance'], and from Naḥaliel to Bamot [the heights]."[30]

28. Proverbs 11:22.

29. Exodus 32:16.

30. Numbers 22:19.

HISTORICAL BACKGROUND

R. Yehoshua b. Levi is a member of the first generation of *Amora'im*, the formulators of the Gemara after the close of the Mishna (first half of the third century CE). The inclusion of his teaching reflects the fact that this sixth chapter was added after Rabbi's lifetime. R. Yehoshua lived in and led the Jewish community of Lod, which was one of the main centers of Jewish life at the time. He represented the Jewish community in missions to the local Roman rulers and to Rome. R. Yehoshua specialized in Aggada (lore, narrative, tradition, theological reflection) as opposed to halakha (laws and observances). His piety and goodness became so legendary that the common people insisted that he was a wonder-worker. Among the stories told about him were that the prophet Elijah came and studied Torah with him, and that he entered Paradise alive.

Whoever does not occupy himself with Torah is ... rebuked ... as a gold ring in a pig's snout

This is another midrashic play on words. In Hebrew, a nose ring is *nezem* and a nose or snout is *af*. Combine them, and it sounds like *nazuf*, rebuked or condemned. A person who fails to study Torah is like a beautiful woman who lacks common sense. The juxtaposition of external beauty and impressiveness to inner emptiness, or even filth, is upsetting and evokes revulsion.

Do not read the word as *ḥarut*, but as *ḥerut*

- God is the liberator and Torah is the Emancipation Proclamation. Henceforth, no human being can be enslaved: "For they are My servants ... they shall not be sold into a slave purchase."[31]
- God has implanted freedom and liberty in the teachings and instructions of the Torah.

31. Leviticus 25:42.

- "Obedience to God is resistance to tyranny." One who internalizes the reality of God and reverence for the divine fears no man[32] and obeys no tyrant.
- If you internalize reverence for God and the wisdom of the Torah, then all human conventional wisdom and social etiquette fade into irrelevance. Then you are truly free in thought and actions, as they are not distorted or imposed by social expectations or political correctness, but reflect genuine perceptions and conclusions based on evidence and substance.

Elevates

If you allow Torah to shape you, you will be ennobled and raised to a higher human and moral plane.

Mattana … Naḥaliel … Bamot

These were way stations in the Jews' desert trek.[33] In the Midrash, the sages make a play on words with these names. Mattana is a gift. The gift of Torah leads to Naḥaliel, "God is my inheritance," and from there to Bamot, the heights.

32. Deuteronomy 1:17.
33. Numbers 21:19.

Teaching 3

הַלּוֹמֵד מֵחֲבֵרוֹ פֶּֽרֶק אֶחָד, אוֹ הֲלָכָה אַחַת, אוֹ פָּסוּק אֶחָד, אוֹ דִּבּוּר אֶחָד, אוֹ אֲפִלּוּ אוֹת אַחַת, צָרִיךְ לִנְהָג בּוֹ כָּבוֹד. שֶׁכֵּן מָצִֽינוּ בְּדָוִד מֶֽלֶךְ יִשְׂרָאֵל, שֶׁלֹּא לָמַד מֵאֲחִיתֹֽפֶל אֶלָּא שְׁנֵי דְבָרִים בִּלְבָד, קְרָאוֹ רַבּוֹ אַלּוּפוֹ וּמְיֻדָּעוֹ, שֶׁנֶּאֱמַר: וְאַתָּה אֱנוֹשׁ כְּעֶרְכִּי, אַלּוּפִי וּמְיֻדָּעִי: וַהֲלֹא דְבָרִים קַל וָחֹֽמֶר. וּמַה דָּוִד מֶֽלֶךְ יִשְׂרָאֵל, שֶׁלֹּא לָמַד מֵאֲחִיתֹֽפֶל אֶלָּא שְׁנֵי דְבָרִים בִּלְבָד, קְרָאוֹ רַבּוֹ אַלּוּפוֹ וּמְיֻדָּעוֹ, הַלּוֹמֵד מֵחֲבֵרוֹ פֶּֽרֶק אֶחָד, אוֹ הֲלָכָה אַחַת, אוֹ פָּסוּק אֶחָד, אוֹ דִּבּוּר אֶחָד, אוֹ אֲפִלּוּ אוֹת אַחַת, עַל אַחַת כַּמָּה וְכַמָּה שֶׁצָּרִיךְ לִנְהָג בּוֹ כָּבוֹד. וְאֵין כָּבוֹד אֶלָּא תוֹרָה, שֶׁנֶּאֱמַר: כָּבוֹד חֲכָמִים יִנְחָֽלוּ: וּתְמִימִים יִנְחֲלוּ־טוֹב: וְאֵין טוֹב אֶלָּא תוֹרָה, שֶׁנֶּאֱמַר: כִּי לֶֽקַח טוֹב נָתַֽתִּי לָכֶם, תּוֹרָתִי אַל־תַּעֲזֹֽבוּ:

One who learns a single chapter, or one halakha, or one verse, or one saying, or even one letter [of Torah] from a friend must show honor to [the teacher]. Thus we found with David, king of Israel, that he learned only two teachings from Ahitophel, yet called him his master, his teacher, his [covenant] friend, as it says: "But it is you, a human being, my equal, my teacher, my [covenant] friend."[34] And do not these words present an argument from minor to major? If David, king of Israel, who learned only two teachings from Ahitophel yet called him master, teacher, friend, then one who learns one chapter, or one halakha, or one verse, or one saying, or even one letter from a friend, how much more so must he show honor to [the teacher]! And honor can mean only Torah, as it says: "The sages inherit honor";[35] and "the perfect shall inherit good."[36] And good can mean only Torah, as it says: "For I give you good teaching; do not forsake My Torah."[37]

34. Psalms 55:14.

35. Proverbs 3:35.

36. Ibid., 28:10.

37. Ibid., 4:2.

A single chapter or…one letter

The Torah is infinite. If someone teaches you one fraction of infinity, the gift is unlimited. You should honor the teacher for giving such a great gift.

Ahitophel

Ahitophel is described as the king's counselor.[38] He went with Absalom when the latter led the people in a revolt against King David, his father. The king and a group of followers barely escaped Jerusalem alive. Ahitophel advised Absalom to strike swiftly, to pursue and wipe out the fleeing David. However, Absalom listened to the advice of Hushai the Archite, who told him to hold back and first gather a vast army before attacking. Hushai was secretly in league with David; the delay gave the king a chance to rest and rally his troops and go on to win the battle. Once his advice was rejected, Ahitophel saw the handwriting on the wall. He went home and committed suicide lest a victorious David punish him for backing Absalom.

Learned only two teachings from Ahitophel

The Midrash suggests that following Uzza's death while transporting the Ark of the Tablets,[39] Ahitophel taught David that the Ark must be carried only by special people and on their shoulders, not on a cart as Uzza had done.[40] The second teaching came when David sought to calm the raging waters which were under the Temple's foundation stone. Ahitophel taught that it was permissible to write God's Ineffable Name down and insert it into the maelstrom in order to calm the flood, even though the divine name would be erased (which is normally prohibited).[41] Ahitophel pointed out that God's name can be written and erased to remove suspicion of the allegedly adulterous wife.[42] If God's name can be erased to bring peace between one man and wife, then all the more

38. II Samuel ch. 17.
39. See ibid., 6:2–10.
40. See Numbers 4:4–14.
41. See Deuteronomy 12:3–4.
42. See Numbers 5:14–24.

so it can be erased to stop the raging waters and save the lives of countless numbers of God's creations.

Show honor to [the teacher]

This is a serious matter, as the Talmud ranks the honor due a teacher on a level with the honor due a parent (which is one of the Ten Commandments). Indeed, if there is a teacher of Torah who has been the primary shaper of one's outlook and character, then the teacher's honor comes before that of his parents. This priority is laid down because even though the parent has given the "infinite" gift of physical existence in this world, the teacher has given a greater gift: quality of life, the spiritual physiognomy, the character and values which shape the disciple's life (and bring him into the World to Come). Honor can express itself in serving the one honored, standing up to show him respect, etc.

Teaching 4

כָּךְ הִיא דַּרְכָּהּ שֶׁל תּוֹרָה. פַּת בַּמֶּלַח תֹּאכֵל, וּמַיִם בַּמְּשׂוּרָה תִּשְׁתֶּה, וְעַל הָאָרֶץ תִּישַׁן, וְחַיֵּי צַעַר תִּחְיֶה, וּבַתּוֹרָה אַתָּה עָמֵל. אִם אַתָּה עוֹשֶׂה כֵּן, אַשְׁרֶיךָ וְטוֹב לָךְ, אַשְׁרֶיךָ בָּעוֹלָם הַזֶּה, וְטוֹב לָךְ לָעוֹלָם הַבָּא.

This is the way of Torah [study]: You eat a loaf of [bread] with salt, and you drink a measured amount of water, and you sleep on the ground, and you live a life of hardship. But you keep on laboring in the Torah. If you do this you shall be happy and well-off:[43] "[You shall be] happy in this world, and well-off in the World to Come."[44]

The way of Torah

Torah is not the way to affluence and luxuries. Torah scholarship is not an easy life. In order to devote yourself to it, you may have to live on bread and water, sleep on a hard floor, and give up the pleasures of affluence. But here comes the paradox: You will find this straitened life to be joyous and filled with meaning. The lesson is that meaning is a greater, more persistent source of happiness than pursuing pleasure and exciting experiences.

Happy and well-off

The sacrifice is worth it. The Torah bestows happiness, purpose, and satisfaction with life in this world, and bliss in the World to Come.

43. Psalms 128:2.
44. Berakhot 8a.

Teaching 5

אַל תְּבַקֵּשׁ גְּדֻלָּה לְעַצְמְךָ, וְאַל
תַּחְמֹד כָּבוֹד. יוֹתֵר מִלִּמּוּדְךָ
עֲשֵׂה. וְאַל תִּתְאַוֶּה לְשֻׁלְחָנָם
שֶׁל מְלָכִים, שֶׁשֻּׁלְחָנְךָ גָּדוֹל
מִשֻּׁלְחָנָם, וְכִתְרְךָ גָּדוֹל
מִכִּתְרָם. וְנֶאֱמָן הוּא בַּעַל
מְלַאכְתְּךָ, שֶׁיְּשַׁלֶּם לְךָ שְׂכַר
פְּעֻלָּתֶךָ.

[If you are a Torah scholar,] do not seek importance for yourself. Do not covet honor; let your [good deeds] exceed your learning; do not lust for [a place at] the royal table, for your table is greater than the kings' table and your crown is greater than theirs. And your employer is trustworthy to pay the wages of your labor.

Do not seek importance … honor

There is a danger of becoming intoxicated with the importance of Torah learning and thereby seeking honor, recognition, rule over others, etc. This subverts the positive effect of Torah study for its own sake.

Your table is greater

Greatness is not measured by the amount of power, fame, or wealth achieved. Greatness is spiritual and moral. Thus a life of Torah learning is greater than the life of a king.

Your crown is greater

- The crown of Torah is greater than the crown of royalty or the priesthood.
- In the secular world, people want to associate with celebrity (which a king amply possesses). The Torah scholar must learn

to see the world *sub specie aeternitatus*. From the divine perspective, eternity, scholarship, good deeds, and piety are the truly important entities.

- One should strive to associate and eat with Torah scholars, not with wielders of power in this world. The Talmud states that when it comes to redeeming a captive, a Torah scholar takes precedence over a king. It explains the rationale as follows: If we lose a Torah scholar, no one can replace his unique wisdom. However, if we lose a king, all of Israel are worthy (and capable) of being king![45] The Talmud also rates a scholar who is of illegitimate ancestry ahead of a High Priest, if the latter is an ignoramus.

Your employer is trustworthy

It may appear that kings and wealthy people have received the rewards of importance, honor, and power. However, we can trust God to give the ultimate, promised rewards, which are beyond wealth and power. They are fulfillment and a high quality of life in this mortal world and in the World to Come. "It [the Torah] is a tree of life for those who take hold of it, and all its supporters are happy."[46]

45. Horayot 13a.
46. Proverbs 3:18.

Teaching 6

גְּדוֹלָה תוֹרָה יוֹתֵר מִן הַכְּהֻנָּה וּמִן הַמַּלְכוּת. שֶׁהַמַּלְכוּת נִקְנֵית בִּשְׁלֹשִׁים מַעֲלוֹת, וְהַכְּהֻנָּה בְּעֶשְׂרִים וְאַרְבַּע, וְהַתּוֹרָה נִקְנֵית בְּאַרְבָּעִים וּשְׁמוֹנָה דְבָרִים. וְאֵלּוּ הֵן, בְּתַלְמוּד, בִּשְׁמִיעַת הָאֹזֶן, בַּעֲרִיכַת שְׂפָתַיִם, בְּבִינַת הַלֵּב, בְּאֵימָה, בְּיִרְאָה, בַּעֲנָוָה, בְּשִׂמְחָה, בְּטָהֳרָה, בְּשִׁמּוּשׁ חֲכָמִים, בְּדִקְדּוּק חֲבֵרִים, בְּפִלְפּוּל הַתַּלְמִידִים, בְּיִשּׁוּב, בְּמִקְרָא, בְּמִשְׁנָה, בְּמִעוּט סְחוֹרָה, בְּמִעוּט דֶּרֶךְ אֶרֶץ, בְּמִעוּט תַּעֲנוּג, בְּמִעוּט שֵׁנָה, בְּמִעוּט שִׂיחָה, בְּמִעוּט שְׂחוֹק, בְּאֶרֶךְ אַפַּיִם, בְּלֵב טוֹב, בֶּאֱמוּנַת חֲכָמִים, בְּקַבָּלַת הַיִּסּוּרִין, הַמַּכִּיר אֶת מְקוֹמוֹ, וְהַשָּׂמֵחַ בְּחֶלְקוֹ, וְהָעוֹשֶׂה סְיָג לִדְבָרָיו, וְאֵינוֹ מַחֲזִיק טוֹבָה לְעַצְמוֹ, אָהוּב, אוֹהֵב אֶת הַמָּקוֹם, אוֹהֵב אֶת הַבְּרִיּוֹת, אוֹהֵב אֶת הַצְּדָקוֹת, אוֹהֵב אֶת הַמֵּישָׁרִים, אוֹהֵב אֶת הַתּוֹכָחוֹת, וּמִתְרַחֵק מִן הַכָּבוֹד, וְלֹא מֵגִיס לִבּוֹ בְּתַלְמוּדוֹ, וְאֵינוֹ שָׂמֵחַ בְּהוֹרָאָה, נוֹשֵׂא בְעֹל עִם חֲבֵרוֹ, וּמַכְרִיעוֹ לְכַף זְכוּת,

Torah is greater than priesthood or kingship, for kingship is acquired through thirty virtues and the priesthood through twenty-four. But the Torah is acquired through forty-eight [such qualities]. And these are the [forty-eight virtues]: study; listening [well]; speaking [thoughtfully]; a discerning heart; awe; reverence; modesty; joy; purity; apprenticing with sages; associating with colleagues; analyzing back and forth with students; carefully weighing [passages] of Scripture; and Mishna; engaging in a minimum of business, worldly pursuits, pleasures, sleep, social conversation, and entertainment; patience; good heartedness; trust in sages; taking suffering in stride; being one who knows his place; who is content with his lot; who limits his words; who claims no credit for himself; [being] beloved; loving God; loving humanity; loving righteousness;

וְהַמְכַוֵּן אֶת שְׁמוּעָתוֹ, וְהָאוֹמֵר דָּבָר וּמַעֲמִידוֹ עַל הָאֱמֶת, וּמַעֲמִידוֹ עַל הַשָּׁלוֹם, וּמִתְיַשֵּׁב לִבּוֹ בְּתַלְמוּדוֹ, שׁוֹאֵל וּמֵשִׁיב, שׁוֹמֵעַ וּמוֹסִיף, הַלּוֹמֵד עַל מְנָת לְלַמֵּד, וְהַלּוֹמֵד עַל מְנָת לַעֲשׂוֹת, הַמַּחְכִּים אֶת רַבּוֹ, בְּשֵׁם אוֹמְרוֹ. הָא לָמַדְתָּ, כָּל הָאוֹמֵר דָּבָר בְּשֵׁם אוֹמְרוֹ, מֵבִיא גְאֻלָּה לָעוֹלָם, שֶׁנֶּאֱמַר: וַתֹּאמֶר אֶסְתֵּר לַמֶּלֶךְ בְּשֵׁם מָרְדֳּכָי:

loving justice; loving correction; [being one] who distances himself from honor; who does not swell with pride in his learning; who does not give legal decisions light-headedly; [being one] who shares burdens with his friend and gives him the benefit of the doubt; who [seeks to place] him [on the path to] the truth; [who] seeks to place him [on the path to] peace; who [helps] him concentrate on his study; being one who asks and answers; who listens and adds [wisdom; who] learns with the intention of teaching [others; who] learns with the intention of practicing [what he learns]; who makes his teacher wiser; [who] is precise in stating what he has heard [and understood]; and who, in repeating Torah [insights], credits the one who said it originally. Thus you have learned: Whoever repeats a statement in the name of the one who said it brings deliverance to the world, as it says: "And Esther told the king [about the plot] in the name of Mordekhai."[47]

Torah is acquired through forty-eight [virtues]

To attain greatness as a king or priest requires many qualities that will assure wise judgment, fair-minded administration of justice, and avoidance of the temptations of power and status. However, greatness in Torah requires the attainment of even more positive character traits: intellectual, spiritual, emotional, moral. To acquire many of these traits requires help from friends, colleagues, students, and others. Becoming suffused with Torah requires modesty, openness to others, and willingness to learn. Since Torah covers all of human life and experience, the more modest, open, and willing to learn that a person is, the more wisdom he will bring to the Torah and the more he will get out of studying it.

---

47. Esther 2:22.

Credits the one who said it originally

- Giving credit achieves more than following the rules of scholarship or avoiding plagiarism. By giving credit to the others, their greatness and contribution may be recognized and rewarded. In the Purim story, Esther credited Mordekhai with uncovering the plot to kill King Aḥashverosh, although as a newcomer to the court she could have raised her status by taking all the credit for herself. When the king was sleepless one night and they read him the palace chronicles, he realized that Mordekhai had never been rewarded properly. This led to the reversal of Haman's plot and the salvation of the Jews from annihilation. (See also 3:8, above.)
- Someone who studies Torah for its own sake will gladly acknowledge another person as the source of a teaching, as the goal of Torah study is not self-aggrandizement or being recognized as a scholar.
- In the Talmud, thousands of statements are made by Rav A in the name of Rav B in the name of Rav C, etc.

Teaching 7

גְּדוֹלָה תוֹרָה, שֶׁהִיא נוֹתֶנֶת חַיִּים לְעוֹשֶׂיהָ בָּעוֹלָם הַזֶּה וּבָעוֹלָם הַבָּא, שֶׁנֶּאֱמַר: כִּי־חַיִּים הֵם לְמֹצְאֵיהֶם, וּלְכָל־בְּשָׂרוֹ מַרְפֵּא: וְאוֹמֵר: רִפְאוּת תְּהִי לְשָׁרֶּךָ, וְשִׁקּוּי לְעַצְמוֹתֶיךָ: וְאוֹמֵר: עֵץ־חַיִּים הִיא לַמַּחֲזִיקִים בָּהּ, וְתֹמְכֶיהָ מְאֻשָּׁר: וְאוֹמֵר: כִּי לִוְיַת חֵן הֵם לְרֹאשֶׁךָ, וַעֲנָקִים לְגַרְגְּרֹתֶךָ: וְאוֹמֵר: תִּתֵּן לְרֹאשְׁךָ לִוְיַת־חֵן, עֲטֶרֶת תִּפְאֶרֶת תְּמַגְּנֶךָּ: וְאוֹמֵר: כִּי־בִי יִרְבּוּ יָמֶיךָ, וְיוֹסִיפוּ לְךָ שְׁנוֹת חַיִּים: וְאוֹמֵר: אֹרֶךְ יָמִים בִּימִינָהּ, בִּשְׂמֹאולָהּ עֹשֶׁר וְכָבוֹד: וְאוֹמֵר: כִּי אֹרֶךְ יָמִים וּשְׁנוֹת חַיִּים וְשָׁלוֹם יוֹסִיפוּ לָךְ:

Great is Torah, for it gives life to those who practice its [mandates], in this world and in the World to Come, as it says: "For [the instructions of wisdom] are life to those that discover them and healing to all their body;"[48] and it says: "It will be a cure for your body and a tonic for your bones;"[49] and it says: "It [Torah] is a tree of life for those who take hold of it, and all its supporters are happy;"[50] and it says: "For they [Torah instructions] are a graceful wreath around your head and a necklace around your throat;"[51] and it says: "By Me your days shall be multiplied and they will add years of life to you";[52] and it says: "Long life is in its right hand, and in its left hand are riches and honor;"[53] and it says: "[The words of Torah] will give length of days and years of life and peace to you."[54]

48. Ibid., 4:22.
49. Ibid., 3:8.
50. Ibid., v. 18.
51. Ibid., 1:9.
52. Ibid., 9:11.
53. Ibid., 3:16.
54. Ibid., v. 2.

Gives life

The Torah is all about life: It commands human beings to create and nurture life. Its vision is of filling the world with life,[55] and then honoring the dignity of and upholding the quality of life. Living by the Torah, then, is a pledge to give life the highest priority and an attempt to live life to the fullest. "The saving of a life overrides the commandments of the entire Torah: 'And you shall live by them'[56] and not die by them."[57] "Holiness means the holiness of earthly, here-and-now life.... Holiness does not wink at us from... beyond... but appears in our actual, very real lives.... An individual does not become holy through mystical adherence to the absolute... but rather through his whole biological life, through his animal actions."[58] In turn, the Torah's prescriptions guide the individual to richer life experiences, including love, relationships, humane and peaceful interaction with others, and being part of a harmonious society.

The Torah's way of life bestows the blessing of a longer life. Maimonides writes: "The general object of Torah law is twofold: the well-being of the soul and the well-being of the body." According to Maimonides, the well-being of the body is established by a proper management of human relations. This includes having all one's material needs and wants supplied. Furthermore, he continues, this is possible only in a society where good mutual relations are established by "removing injustice and creating the noblest feelings." He summarizes: "'And the Lord commanded us to do all these statutes... for our good always, that God might preserve us alive to this day.'[59] I explain the words 'for our good always' to mean that we may come into the world 'that is all good and eternal' [i.e., the World to Come], and the words 'that God might preserve us alive to this day' I explain as referring to... our body."[60] In short, living the Torah's way leads literally to a longer, healthier life – a reward not based on miraculous, divine intervention but on the effects of these behaviors on the individual's body and on society.

55. See Genesis 1:22, 24, 28.
56. Leviticus 18:5.
57. Yoma 85b.
58. Soloveitchik, *Halakhic Man*, 33, 34, 46.
59. Deuteronomy 6:24.
60. Moses Maimonides, *Guide for the Perplexed*, trans. M. Friedländer (London: Routledge & Kegan Paul, 1904), III:27 (129–131).

Teaching 8

רַבִּי שִׁמְעוֹן בֶּן יְהוּדָה מִשּׁוּם רַבִּי שִׁמְעוֹן בֶּן יוֹחַאי אוֹמֵר: הַנּוֹי, וְהַכֹּחַ, וְהָעֹשֶׁר, וְהַכָּבוֹד, וְהַחָכְמָה, וְהַזִּקְנָה, וְהַשֵּׂיבָה, וְהַבָּנִים, נָאֶה לַצַּדִּיקִים וְנָאֶה לָעוֹלָם, שֶׁנֶּאֱמַר: עֲטֶרֶת תִּפְאֶרֶת שֵׂיבָה, בְּדֶרֶךְ צְדָקָה תִּמָּצֵא: וְאוֹמֵר: עֲטֶרֶת חֲכָמִים עָשְׁרָם: וְאוֹמֵר: עֲטֶרֶת זְקֵנִים בְּנֵי בָנִים, וְתִפְאֶרֶת בָּנִים אֲבוֹתָם: וְאוֹמֵר: תִּפְאֶרֶת בַּחוּרִים כֹּחָם, וַהֲדַר זְקֵנִים שֵׂיבָה: וְאוֹמֵר: וְחָפְרָה הַלְּבָנָה וּבוֹשָׁה הַחַמָּה, כִּי־מָלַךְ יהוה צְבָאוֹת בְּהַר צִיּוֹן וּבִירוּשָׁלַםִ, וְנֶגֶד זְקֵנָיו כָּבוֹד:

R. Shimon b. Yehuda, in the name of R. Shimon b. Yoḥai, says: Beauty, and strength, and riches, and honor, and wisdom and old age, and gray hair, and children all beautify the righteous and beautify the world, as it says: "Grey hair is a crown of glory; it is found on the path of righteousness;"[61] and it says: "The glory of young men is their strength, and the majesty of the elders is their grey hair;"[62] and it says: "The crown of elders are children's children and the glory of children is their parents;"[63] and it says: "Then the moon shall be abashed and the sun be ashamed, for the Lord of hosts shall reign on Mount Zion and in Jerusalem, and the glory [of God's presence] shall be revealed before the elders."[64]

רַבִּי שִׁמְעוֹן בֶּן מְנַסְיָא אוֹמֵר: אֵלּוּ שֶׁבַע מִדּוֹת שֶׁמָּנוּ חֲכָמִים לַצַּדִּיקִים, כֻּלָּם נִתְקַיְּמוּ בְּרַבִּי וּבְבָנָיו.

R. Shimon b. Menasya says: These seven qualities which the sages measured out for the righteous were all fulfilled in Rabbi and his children.

61. Proverbs 16:31.
62. Ibid., 20:29.
63. Ibid., 17:6.
64. Isaiah 24:23.

HISTORICAL BACKGROUND

R. Shimon b. Yehuda was a *Tanna* of the fifth generation (end of the second century CE) and a close disciple of R. Shimon b. Yoḥai. In the Talmud, he speaks many more times in the name of his teacher R. Shimon b. Yoḥai than in his own name.

In the Jerusalem Talmud, this teaching is attributed to R. Shimon b. Menasya, who makes the editorial comment that concludes this teaching in our edition. R. Shimon b. Menasya was one of the last generation of sages of the Mishna. He was a contemporary of R. Shimon b. Yehuda and a devotee of R. Yehuda the Prince. He was also a close colleague of R. Yosei b. HaMeshulam. Together they formed and led a circle of learning and piety which became known as the *Eida Kedosha* ("holy community"). Participants spent one-third of the day in prayer, one-third in Torah study, and one-third in work. In another version, they spent the winter months learning Torah and the summer months in work.

R. Shimon b. Menasya is particularly known for his explanation of why the Shabbat commandments are overridden to save an individual's life. He cites the verse: "'Observe the Sabbath, for it is holy for you.' This means that the Sabbath is given for you [so your interest comes first] and you are not given to the Sabbath [so its observance would have priority over your physical well-being]."[65]

Beauty...old age...children

Like the previous teaching, this *baraita* tell us that the rewards of living by and studying Torah will come in this mortal life and not just in the World to Come. This promise of earthly reward (honor, riches) and long life (grey hair, children) is in tension with two other trends expressed in the first chapter of Ethics of the Fathers. First, there is the affirmation that the righteous (and all of Israel) are promised an eternally good life and will receive their just rewards in the next form of existence, i.e., spiritual existence in the World to Come. Given the experience of the sufferings of the innocent and the triumphs of the wicked in this world, the *baraita*'s affirmation is at once courageous and problematic.

65. Yoma 85b.

Secondly, there is a strong theme in talmudic literature – undoubtedly enhanced and made credible by the dualism of body and spirit endemic to Hellenistic culture – that pleasures of the body are unimportant because they are at best fleeting and marginal. At worst, they turn into indulgences and become the enemies of righteous living. They undermine self-discipline and weaken the capacity for dedicated Torah study and for moral and spiritual excellence. (See the fourth teaching in this chapter, where it states that asceticism and self-denial are the way of the Torah.) By this logic, the human body is ephemeral, and not a dependable foundation for proper religious living. Therefore, in the words of Proverbs 31:30: "Grace is deceptive and beauty is illusory. It is for her fear of the Lord that a woman is to be praised."

But our *baraita* suggests that a beautiful body is also a value. R. Shimon proclaims that worldly honor for the righteous and a vital, respected old age for the religious are desirable. Seeing the rewards of the righteous in this life adds to the feeling that "God is in His heaven and all is right with the world."

Beautify the righteous

These gifts, when given to wicked or inappropriate people, make them more unworthy. Thus, good looks will increase the hauteur of vain people. Riches given to an unworthy person may corrupt him or turn him arrogant, etc. However, when given to a righteous person, strength and wisdom will be used to elevate the lives of others. Riches will be applied to *tzedaka*, to helping others, and to improving society.

As it says

The repeated citations of verses from the Book of Proverbs in this *baraita* and the preceding one reflect the affinity of wisdom instructions in the Bible with the wisdom aphorisms collected in *Pirkei Avot*. In contrast to the emphasis on law and specific observances in much of the Talmud, these chapters stress the virtues needed to be a religious Jew and a *talmid ḥakham* (sage). They also report the wisdom of life found in the sages and their teachings. Ideally of course, halakha and virtue go hand in hand. Good character traits and wisdom express themselves in halakhic behavior; in turn, the commandments offer detailed guides and training to become a righteous human being.

Teaching 9

אָמַר רַבִּי יוֹסֵי בֶּן קִסְמָא: פַּעַם אַחַת הָיִיתִי מְהַלֵּךְ בַּדֶּרֶךְ, וּפָגַע בִּי אָדָם אֶחָד, וְנָתַן לִי שָׁלוֹם וְהֶחֱזַרְתִּי לוֹ שָׁלוֹם. אָמַר לִי, רַבִּי, מֵאֵיזֶה מָקוֹם אָתָּה. אָמַרְתִּי לוֹ, מֵעִיר גְּדוֹלָה שֶׁל חֲכָמִים וְשֶׁל סוֹפְרִים אָנִי. אָמַר לִי, רַבִּי, רְצוֹנְךָ שֶׁתָּדוּר עִמָּנוּ בִּמְקוֹמֵנוּ, וַאֲנִי אֶתֵּן לָךְ אֶלֶף אֲלָפִים דִּינְרֵי זָהָב וַאֲבָנִים טוֹבוֹת וּמַרְגָּלִיּוֹת. אָמַרְתִּי לוֹ, אִם אַתָּה נוֹתֵן לִי כָּל כֶּסֶף וְזָהָב וַאֲבָנִים טוֹבוֹת וּמַרְגָּלִיּוֹת שֶׁבָּעוֹלָם, אֵינִי דָר אֶלָּא בִּמְקוֹם תּוֹרָה, וְכֵן כָּתוּב בְּסֵפֶר תְּהִלִּים עַל יְדֵי דָוִד מֶלֶךְ יִשְׂרָאֵל: טוֹב־לִי תוֹרַת־פִּיךָ מֵאַלְפֵי זָהָב וָכָסֶף: וְלֹא עוֹד, אֶלָּא שֶׁבִּשְׁעַת פְּטִירָתוֹ שֶׁל אָדָם, אֵין מְלַוִּין לוֹ לְאָדָם לֹא כֶּסֶף וְלֹא זָהָב וְלֹא אֲבָנִים טוֹבוֹת וּמַרְגָּלִיּוֹת, אֶלָּא תּוֹרָה וּמַעֲשִׂים טוֹבִים בִּלְבָד, שֶׁנֶּאֱמַר: בְּהִתְהַלֶּכְךָ תַּנְחֶה אֹתָךְ, בְּשָׁכְבְּךָ תִּשְׁמֹר

R. Yosei b. Kisma says: Once I was walking on the road when a man met me and greeted me, and I returned his greeting. He said to me: Rabbi, where do you come from? I said to him: I come from a great city [full] of wise men and scribes. He said to me: Rabbi, if you will [agree to] live with us in our place, I will give you a thousand thousands of golden dinars and precious stones and pearls. I said to him: If you were giving me all the silver and gold and precious stones and pearls in the world, I still would live only in a place of Torah. And so it is written in the Book of Psalms written by King David: "The Torah of Your mouth is better to me than thousands [in] gold and silver."[66] Furthermore, in the hour of a person's passing away, neither silver nor gold nor precious stones and pearls will accompany the person, but [only] Torah and good deeds, as it says: "When you walk,

66. Psalms 119:72.

עָלֶיךָ, וַהֲקִיצוֹתָ הִיא תְשִׂיחֶךָ: בְּהִתְהַלֶּכְךָ
תַּנְחֶה אֹתָךְ, בָּעוֹלָם הַזֶּה. בְּשָׁכְבְּךָ
תִּשְׁמֹר עָלֶיךָ, בַּקֶּבֶר. וַהֲקִיצוֹתָ הִיא
תְשִׂיחֶךָ, לָעוֹלָם הַבָּא. וְאוֹמֵר: לִי הַכֶּסֶף
וְלִי הַזָּהָב, נְאֻם יהוה צְבָאוֹת:

it [Torah] will lead you; when you lie down, it will guard you; and when you awaken, it will [talk with] you."[67] "When you walk it will lead you" – in this world; "when you lie down it will watch over you" – in the grave; "when you awaken it will talk with you" – in the World to Come. And it says: "The silver is Mine, and the gold is Mine, says the Lord of hosts."[68]

HISTORICAL BACKGROUND

R. Yosei b. Kisma (second century CE) was a member of the third generation of *Tanna'im*, a contemporary of R. Ḥanania b. Teradyon. Unlike R. Ḥanania, however, he lived and died on good terms with the Romans. R. Ḥanania was martyred by the Romans. They wrapped him in a Torah scroll and burned him alive. R. Yosei repeatedly warned him that this would be his fate because of his open defiance of the Romans.

R. Yosei died a natural death. According to the Talmud, great figures of Rome attended his funeral. Given the generation in which he lived, the "great city" from which R. Yosei came may well have been Yavneh, the center of rabbinic study and community in the aftermath of the Destruction of the Temple.

R. Yosei's overall points are:

- Torah is more precious than all the wealth in the world.
- In order to study and grow in Torah learning, one should live in a community full of scholars, who create a dynamic environment for learning and growth.

---

67. Proverbs 6:22.
68. Haggai 2:8.

Teaching 10

חֲמִשָּׁה קִנְיָנִים קָנָה הַקָּדוֹשׁ בָּרוּךְ הוּא בְּעוֹלָמוֹ. וְאֵלּוּ הֵן, תּוֹרָה קִנְיָן אֶחָד, שָׁמַיִם וָאָרֶץ קִנְיָן אֶחָד, אַבְרָהָם קִנְיָן אֶחָד, יִשְׂרָאֵל קִנְיָן אֶחָד, בֵּית הַמִּקְדָּשׁ קִנְיָן אֶחָד. תּוֹרָה מִנַּיִן, דִּכְתִיב: יהוה קָנָנִי רֵאשִׁית דַּרְכּוֹ, קֶדֶם מִפְעָלָיו מֵאָז: שָׁמַיִם וָאָרֶץ מִנַּיִן, דִּכְתִיב: כֹּה אָמַר יהוה הַשָּׁמַיִם כִּסְאִי וְהָאָרֶץ הֲדֹם רַגְלָי, אֵי־זֶה בַיִת אֲשֶׁר תִּבְנוּ־לִי, וְאֵי־זֶה מָקוֹם מְנוּחָתִי: וְאוֹמֵר: מָה־רַבּוּ מַעֲשֶׂיךָ יהוה, כֻּלָּם בְּחָכְמָה עָשִׂיתָ, מָלְאָה הָאָרֶץ קִנְיָנֶךָ:

The Holy One, Blessed Be He, acquired five possessions in His world, and they are: Torah, one possession; heaven and earth, one possession; Abraham, one possession; Israel, one possession; the Holy Temple, one possession. How do we know that Torah [is a divine possession]? It is written: "The Lord possessed me at the beginning of His way, the first of His works of old."[69] How do we know that heaven and earth [are divine possessions]? It is written: "Thus says the Lord: The heaven is My throne and the earth is My footstool. What kind of house could you build for Me? And what place could be My resting place?"[70] And it says: "How many are Your works, O Lord! You made all with wisdom. The earth is filled with Your possessions."[71] How do we know Abraham [is a divine possession]?

---

69. Proverbs 8:22.
70. Isaiah 66:1.
71. Psalms 104:24.

אַבְרָהָם מִנַּיִן, דִּכְתִיב: וַיְבָרְכֵהוּ וַיֹּאמַר, בָּרוּךְ אַבְרָם לְאֵל עֶלְיוֹן, קֹנֵה שָׁמַיִם וָאָרֶץ: יִשְׂרָאֵל מִנַּיִן, דִּכְתִיב: עַד־יַעֲבֹר עַמְּךָ יהוה, עַד־יַעֲבֹר עַם־זוּ קָנִיתָ: וְאוֹמֵר: לִקְדוֹשִׁים אֲשֶׁר־בָּאָרֶץ הֵמָּה, וְאַדִּירֵי כָּל־חֶפְצִי־בָם: בֵּית הַמִּקְדָּשׁ מִנַּיִן, דִּכְתִיב: מָכוֹן לְשִׁבְתְּךָ פָּעַלְתָּ יהוה, מִקְּדָשׁ אֲדֹנָי כּוֹנְנוּ יָדֶיךָ: וְאוֹמֵר: וַיְבִיאֵם אֶל־גְּבוּל קָדְשׁוֹ, הַר־זֶה קָנְתָה יְמִינוֹ:

It is written: "And he [King Melchizedek] blessed him and said, 'Blessed be Abraham to El Elyon [God the most high], the possessor of heaven and earth.'"[72] How do we know [that] Israel [is a divine possession]? As it is written: "Until Your people passes over, O Lord, until the people which You have possessed passes over."[73] And it says: "As to the holy ones that are in the land, and the mighty ones, all My desire is for them."[74] How do we know that the Holy Temple [is a divine possession]? It is written: "You have made a place for Your presence, O Lord, a Sanctuary [the Holy Temple] which Your hands have prepared;"[75] and it says: "He brought them to His holy realm, this mountain which His right hand possessed."[76]

The Holy One... acquired five possessions

At first glance, this is just a list of five elements which Judaism holds sacred and for which one can find a verse stating that God possessed them. However, a deeper message can be discerned. God is the Creator of the whole universe and all that is in it; therefore, He is connected to all. However, the sages teach that there are five phenomena in which God has a special presence and is "intertwined" almost tangibly. One is Torah, which represents God's revelation and the divine blueprint for the goal and direction of the universe. This text plays off the tradition, articulated again in kabbalistic literature, that the Torah is literally the blueprint by which God fashioned the universe. Another phenomenon is heaven and earth, which represent the eternal, divine realm and the

72. Genesis 14:19.
73. Exodus 15:16.
74. Psalms 16:3.
75. Exodus 15:17.
76. Psalms 78:54.

mortal, human realm which God holds in tandem and in unity with a special feeling of attachment.

The third phenomenon is Abraham. God loves all humanity ("His compassion [mother love] is over all His creatures"[77]). Still, surely God feels a special connection to Abraham, the one who "discovered" God and brought Him and His way of righteousness and justice[78] to the attention of his family and then to all of humanity. The fourth phenomenon is God's special feeling for the People of Israel, who bear witness to humankind and proclaim God's presence and will to the earth's inhabitants.[79] Indeed, Israel's devotion through millennia of struggle and suffering must have won a special place in the divine heart, or, as suggested in the language of this teaching, God has become attached to and invested in the People of Israel.

Finally, there is the Holy Temple. Although it was destroyed by the time this teaching was edited and published, the conviction that the Divine Presence never left that place remained strong. Moreover, the Temple represents a microcosm of perfection; a place of divine immediacy, of peace and the absence of death. The Temple is a place of sound bodies, exemplified in the priests (and in the animals that are sacrificed), who give a glimpse of the healed, whole human (and animal) bodies that will be universal in messianic times.

77. Ibid., 145:9. See also the prayer *Barukh SheAmar* in the morning service.

78. Genesis 18:19.

79. Isaiah 43:10, 44:8.

Teaching 11

כָּל מַה שֶׁבָּרָא הַקָּדוֹשׁ בָּרוּךְ הוּא בְּעוֹלָמוֹ, לֹא בְרָאוֹ אֶלָּא לִכְבוֹדוֹ, שֶׁנֶּאֱמַר: כֹּל הַנִּקְרָא בִשְׁמִי וְלִכְבוֹדִי בְּרָאתִיו, יְצַרְתִּיו אַף־עֲשִׂיתִיו: וְאוֹמֵר: יהוה יִמְלֹךְ לְעֹלָם וָעֶד:

All that The Holy One, Blessed Be He, created in this world, He created for His glory. As it says: "All that is linked to My name, whom I have created, shaped, and made for My glory;"[80] and it says: "The Lord shall reign for ever and ever."[81]

All that the Holy One... created in this world, He created for His glory

The cosmos is so vast that one should not define it from the human perspective or judge it by the criterion of whether it meets human needs.[82] Instead, one should view it with reverence, as infinitely awesome and wondrous. Yet the universe is an image (or a pale reflection) of the Infinite One who created it. This implies that human beings should work and tend to this wonder, not use it up or abuse it. It follows, then, that human beings are renters, not owners; dwellers, not masters of the land – nor are they the sole masters of their possessions and their lives.

Torah is meant to be a virtual representation (or representative) of the cosmic vastness and its eternal illumination. Therefore, this last

80. Ibid., 43:7.

81. Exodus 15:18.

82. See Job chs. 38–41.

chapter ends with a celebration of the divine greatness and infinity. The Lord will reign for ever and ever. Long after this universe has contracted and been swallowed up in eternal darkness, void, and silence, the cosmic Maker will reign and likely preside over the creation and decay of further universes.[83] But in the moment that humans grasp the process and the Maker, they are one with infinity and eternity.

83. Genesis Rabba 3:7; Ecclesiastes Rabba 3:14.

Postscript

רַבִּי חֲנַנְיָא בֶּן עֲקַשְׁיָא אוֹמֵר: רָצָה הַקָּדוֹשׁ בָּרוּךְ הוּא לְזַכּוֹת אֶת יִשְׂרָאֵל, לְפִיכָךְ הִרְבָּה לָהֶם תּוֹרָה וּמִצְוֹת. שֶׁנֶּאֱמַר: יהוה חָפֵץ לְמַעַן צִדְקוֹ, יַגְדִּיל תּוֹרָה וְיַאְדִּיר:

R. Ḥanania b. Akashia says: The Holy One, Blessed Be He, wanted to vindicate Israel. Therefore, He gave them Torah and mitzvot in great abundance, as it says: "The Lord wanted His [servant's] vindication. Therefore, God will magnify and glorify Torah."[84]

HISTORICAL BACKGROUND

Very little is known about R. Ḥanania b. Akashia. He was probably a member of the fourth generation of *Tanna'im* (second century CE). This is one of two statements given in his name in the Talmud.

R. Ḥanania

This saying is actually the final passage of Tractate Makkot. However, it was added editorially to be said at the end of the recitation of every chapter of Tractate Avot, as they were read chapter by chapter over the Sabbaths of the spring and summer. This recitation assured and reassured the ordinary people who studied the Torah, as they may have been inspired by its insights and then become concerned that they were guilty of neglecting it by not studying all the time. R. Ḥanania gives assurance: Whatever one studies and does increases his merits. God (and God's

84. Isaiah 52:21.

human partners) shaped the Torah to be constantly adding merit and insight to the lives of all who connect to it.

Vindicate Israel

There is so much Torah to learn and so many mitzvot to do that one may become discouraged or overwhelmed. Paul argued that the law was oppressive because people inevitably felt guilt at not living up to it. R. Ḥanania says: On the contrary, the Torah with all its commandments should be viewed as an inexhaustible supply of wisdom, instruction for a good life, and opportunities to do good. The more one does, the more pleasure. God expresses love in preparing so many good deeds and thoughts for the Israelites to savor, to explore, and to do.

Sages Index

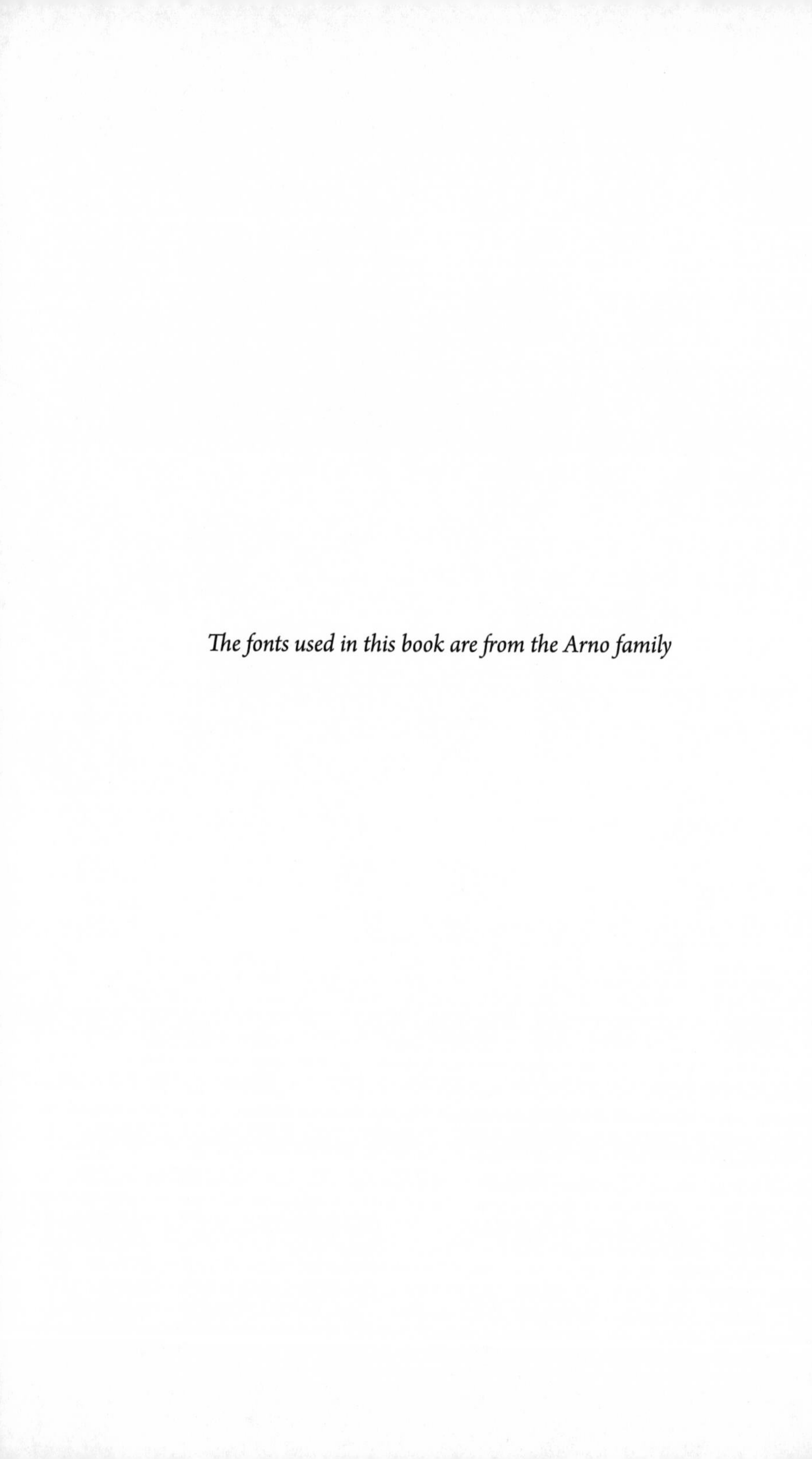

The fonts used in this book are from the Arno family

Maggid Books
The best of contemporary Jewish thought from
Koren Publishers Jerusalem Ltd.